ON THE TRAIL OF THE JACOBITES

ON THE TRAIL OF THE JACOBITES

JACOBITES

Ian and Kathleen Whyte

London and New York

First published 1990
by Routledge 11 New Fetter Lane, London EC4P 4EE
29 West 35th Street, New York, NY 10001

© 1990 Ian and Kathleen Whyte
Typset in 11½/12 pt Garamond Autologic by Times Graphics Singapore
Printed in Great Britain by T.J. Press, Padstow Cornwall

British Library Cataloguing in Publication Data
Whyte, I. D. (Ian D.)
  On the trail of the Jacobites.
  1. Great Britain. Political events, 1714-1837
  I. Title II. Whyte, Kathleen
  941.07
  ISBN 0 415 03334 9

Library of Congress Cataloging in Publication Data
Whyte, Ian (Ian D.)
  On the trail of the Jacobites/Ian and Kathleen Whyte.
  p.   cm.
  Includes bibliographic references.
  ISBN 0 415 03334 9
  1. Jacobites.   2. Scotland – History – 18th century.   3. Great Britain –
  History – 18th century.   I. Whyte, Kathleen A.   II. Title.
  DA813.W49 1990
  941.07–dc20   89-10931

For Donald Charles Reid Hutchings
and
Mary Hutchings

CONTENTS

ILLUSTRATIONS

MAPS

ACKNOWLEDGEMENTS

We would like to express our thanks to Mr Nick Adrianou of the Geography Department at Lancaster University for drawing the maps, and to the Inter-Library Loan Office in the University Library for their help. We are grateful to the National Trust for Scotland for supplying the illustrations credited to them. All the other photographs are our own.

INTRODUCTION
WHO WERE THE JACOBITES?

The Jacobites were the supporters of the exiled Stuart dynasty in the late seventeenth and eighteenth centuries. They were so called from Jacobus, the Latin version of the name James held by the first two 'kings over the water'. The Jacobite period opens with the flight into exile of James II of England and VII of Scotland in the 'Glorious Revolution' of 1688. The end of effective Jacobite hopes came in 1746 with the victory of the Duke of Cumberland over Prince Charles Edward Stuart at the battle of Culloden, the last major military conflict on British soil. Despite this Jacobite dreams persisted for another forty years or so, as did government action to curb their activities. Nevertheless, the real core of the Jacobite era lasted only for about sixty years. The birth, in 1688, of James Francis Edward Stuart (James III to his supporters, the Old Pretender to his opponents), helped to precipitate the Revolution which sent his father into exile. James lived right through the Jacobite era to die in 1766 when all serious hopes of a Stuart restoration had long gone. The lives of other prominent Jacobites spanned the period in a similar way. The redoubtable Gordon of Glenbucket fought at Killiecrankie in 1689 as a boy and was active in the rising of 1745 as an old man. Although the heart of the Jacobite period occupied only a single lifespan the story is an involved, fascinating, and often exciting one.

Many different types of people supported the Jacobite cause, and for a variety of reasons. Support within Britain waxed and waned over time. At certain periods it was more broadly based and at others less so. When the reigning monarch was particularly unpopular and there was widespread dissatisfaction with the government, almost anyone who was disenchanted with the status quo was a potential Jacobite. This was the case in England in the period of Whig domination from 1715 until after 1745 when the Tories were out of power. Many Tories turned to Jacobitism as a means of staging a comeback. They were, however, insufficiently well organized to pose a real threat to the Hanoverian government. At this level Jacobitism was as much a social as a political force. Tory squires would gather in convivial groups to grouse about the Whig government. Drinking toasts to 'the King over the water' gave their complaints some focus and added a spice of daring. Workmen and apprentices rioting over wage levels or lack of employment might shout Jacobite slogans to emphasize their discontent. Such people were part of the Jacobite story but their role was rarely an active one. It was this groundswell of potential but passive and uncertain support which Jacobite activists in Britain and on the Continent continually overestimated in their schemes to restore the exiled Stuarts. There was a much smaller core of committed Jacobites who saw monarchy and the line of inheritance as something God-given and considered that the Stuarts were thus the rightful rulers of Britain regardless of their personal qualities. Religion also played a part; Catholics throughout Britain wished to have a monarch of their religion and considered that they might have a good deal to gain from the restoration of a Roman Catholic monarch. James II had been a zealous convert to Catholicism and his efforts to promote his new religion were one of the principal reasons for the Revolution of 1688.

In Scotland support for the Jacobites was partly linked to nationalism; remember that the Stuarts were originally a Scottish dynasty. At certain times discontent with heavy-handed English interference in Scottish affairs broadened Jacobite support north of the Border. This was particularly true following the parliamentary and economic union of England and Scotland in 1707. Scotland was largely forced into the Union with the connivance of many leading Scottish politicians but without the support of a large proportion of the population. Scotland's loss of independence, and the barefaced political manipulation that produced it, combined with the fact that the economic disadvantages of Union were immediately apparent and the advantages much more nebulous and long term, greatly increased Jacobite support in Scotland.

Throughout Britain certain individuals and groups were particularly prone to have Jacobite leanings, sometimes for political reasons, sometimes on religious grounds. Politicians who had been ousted from power or felt that their services had not been sufficiently rewarded were tempted to engage in secret correspondence with the court in exile. Some of the most dissatisfied of them found a refuge there. Many people who were concerned about the religious settlement which followed the Revolution of 1688 also had Jacobite leanings. Scottish episcopalians who saw their established church ruthlessly overthrown and replaced by presbyterianism were one such body.

There were also some innately conservative groups in British society which may have adhered to the Stuarts as a reaction against change. Some of the clans of the Scottish Highlands fell into this category. The Highland clans are strongly linked with support for the exiled Stuarts in popular tradition. The Scottish Highlands were a focus of Jacobite activity partly because this was the only area in Britain where, due to the survival of an outdated social system, bodies of fighting men could be easily mobilized. It must be emphasized, however, that only a small proportion of the Highland clans actively supported the Stuarts and that many of the major chiefs and magnates consistently supported William of Orange and the House of Hanover.

JACOBITE MYTH AND REALITY

The Jacobites' cause was lost long ago but their memory remains fresh. Popular history has romanticized them. Their story has attracted misunderstandings, over-simplification and much partisan writing, often in the Jacobites' favour. Figures like 'Bonnie Prince Charlie' are often presented as characters of heroic stature while their opponents are portrayed either as dull, colourless, and incompetent or as brutal bullies.

This bias is partly due to the success of the Jacobites' own publicity machine from the eighteenth century until modern times. They produced many rousing, chauvinistic songs, some contemporary and others, like the Skye Boat Song, retrospective. These, with their black-and-white values, have entered the modern folk song repertoire and help to perpetuate the romantic myth of the lost cause. It is easy to forget that the winners of political struggles do not need self-glorifying songs to console themselves with!

The biased approach to Jacobite history is also due to surviving historical sources which tend to glorify one side and defame the other. Even the titles given to certain people predispose you towards one side or the other. Leaving aside 'Bonnie Prince Charlie', does one refer to Charles Edward Stuart as the Prince or the Pretender? Much of the crucial source material for Jacobite history consists of individual memoirs and eye-witness accounts which are heavily slanted. One might think that the task would be simplified by sticking to ascertainable facts rather than interpretations and motives. Alas no! As we shall see, the course of events in major battles like Sheriffmuir in 1715 and even the actual location of the battlefield are in doubt because surviving accounts contradict each other or are vague and imprecise. Establishing what happened is often not much easier than deciding why it happened. As Professor Youngson has shown in his intriguing book *The Prince and the Pretender*, it is possible to write two totally different accounts of the 1745 rebellion favouring the opposing sides by the selective yet legitimate use of different sources.

If popular tradition has glorified the Jacobites, more serious historians have often treated them less sympathetically. The 'Whig' tradition of British history which views the Revolution of 1688 as the origin of Britain's later achievements still has plenty of exponents. This anti-Jacobite school is exemplified by Lord Macaulay's famous *History of England* which still remains the most stylishly readable history of the Revolution of 1688 and the early phases of the Jacobite movement. Macaulay's prose is matchless and his character assassinations are splendid even when he is being demonstrably unfair to the people concerned!

A good many romantic tales have been written – and doubtless will continue to be written – about the Jacobites. The literature on this topic is enormous and many themes are heavily overworked. Innumerable biographies of Charles Edward Stuart have been written yet more keep appearing. One historian suggested that a law be passed imposing dire penalties on any new writers who ventured into this field! Indeed, so cliché-ridden is the topic that it takes a brave historian to risk his reputation by publishing in this area. Even responsible organizations like the National Trust for Scotland, in the exhibitions at some of their visitor centres, can fall victim to the rosy romantic glow of the Jacobite myth. Given this it is hardly surprising that misunderstandings and half-truths about this period in our history abound. For example, the Jacobites are often considered as a purely Scottish phenomenon, a view encouraged by the Scots themselves as one of their great folk myths. Seen in these nationalistic terms Jacobite versus Hanoverian becomes Scots versus English. It is often forgotten that there were Scots on both sides at Culloden!

It is true that a good deal of the action did occur in Scotland. However, it should always be remembered that this was largely a response to activities not merely south of the Border but throughout Europe. The Jacobite court in exile was the centre of a web of intrigue. European powers, notably France, often cynically exploited the Jacobites as pawns in their games of power politics. It should be remembered that the Jacobite movement was created by events which started in England — the overthrow of James II in 1688. Thereafter Jacobite history depended upon what happened at Westminster no matter where the action took place; in England and Ireland as well as Scotland, and in countries ranging from Spain to Russia.

THE JACOBITE TRAIL

The Jacobite period is a comparatively recent one in British history. Many of the places associated with it have not changed greatly since then. It is possible to imagine them as they must have been at the time and to visualize the events which took place there, something which is often impossible for earlier times. Despite this, most books about the Jacobites fail to highlight the background against which the events occurred. This is a pity as a visit to many of the places concerned can bring the period and its people vividly to life. An aim of this book is to try and show what these places were and what you can see there today. Our intention is, literally, to follow the trail of the Jacobites. We shall do this not in a region-by-region guidebook but by a chronological narrative which focuses on places, people, and events as the story develops.

While the trail will include famous sites like battlefields it will also lead to less familiar places with Jacobite associations ranging from castles to caves, mansions to military roads, towns to tombstones. In following the trail of the

Jacobites it is also necessary to consider how successive English, Scottish, and, from 1707, British governments responded to them for they too followed the trail of the Jacobites and their activities have also left their mark on the British landscape. Our trail then will also include features like the forts and military roads which were built to counter the Jacobite threat.

Romance apart, even sober historians will admit that the story of the Jacobites is an exciting one. Yet it has often been garbled and misrepresented. We have tried to produce an unbiased account but despite the research which has been undertaken on the Jacobites there is still considerable uncertainty about what actually happened in many instances and, even more, about the personal motivations involved. In following the trail of the Jacobites we have concentrated on places and events within Britain. These can only be fully understood when set within the context of political developments throughout Europe. Space does not permit us to discuss in detail the European political situation which influenced events in this country. Nor can we follow every byway of the Jacobite trail and we have had to be selective in our coverage. Writing about the Jacobites has tended to concentrate on events with the most romantic appeal, in particular the rebellion of 1745. We have tried to be more balanced in our treatment giving equal consideration to events and places associated with the earlier Jacobite risings.

1

REVOLUTION AND REBELLION, 1688-9

THE PATH TO REVOLUTION

The Glorious Revolution of 1688 is one of the strangest events in British history. On November 5th 1688 William of Orange landed at Torbay with an army of 15,000, the best organized and most successful invasion force since the Norman Conquest. He had come partly in response to invitations from leading members of the English nobility. He believed that dissatisfaction with the authoritarian and arbitrary rule of James II was so widespread — in Scotland as well as England — that a political coup was possible. He was right: a month later, after his attempts to bring William's army to battle had ended in mass desertion and personal humiliation, James fled into exile.

The Stuarts had been hereditary monarchs of Scotland since 1371. Their line had been durable but in many ways unfortunate. Robert II and Robert III were timid and ineffectual. James I and James III were murdered. James II was killed by a bursting cannon and James IV died in battle at Flodden. James V died young and his daughter, the feckless Mary, Queen of Scots, went to the scaffold. James VI, shrewd and canny, worked hard to be made heir to Elizabeth I of England. In 1603 he travelled triumphantly southwards to take the English throne. The seeds of conflict between monarch and Parliament were already sown in England when James died in 1625, but it was his son Charles I whose inflexibility and intransigence precipitated rebellion in both kingdoms, and led to his execution. After the upheavals of civil war and Cromwell's Protectorate the restoration of his son Charles II to the thrones of England and Scotland in 1660 was generally welcomed. Charles was determined not to 'go on his travels' again and by a combination of charm, astuteness, cynicism, and deviousness he successfully survived various clashes with Parliament.

On the death of Charles in 1685 his younger brother James inherited a monarchy which, superficially, seemed more stable than it had been for generations. Yet within three years he had so undermined the confidence of his subjects that some of the most powerful of them were openly inviting William of Orange to invade. This was partly the result of James' authoritarian approach to government which caused him to ride roughshod over established rights and procedures of decision making so that many people feared that he was trying to emulate Louis XIV and establish himself as an absolute monarch.

There was also the problem of his religion. Many Protestants had reconciled themselves to James' Catholicism. Had he left well alone this area of conflict might have died down. Unfortunately James, an enthusiastic convert himself, wanted to spread the Catholic faith widely and rapidly through English society. Many people thought that he was trying to bring back Catholicism as the established religion and oust the reformed church. Whether or not this was true his efforts to improve the position of English Catholics certainly gave that impression. To do this quickly required him to take measures of dubious legality which caused increasing alarm among the population. While his marriage to his second wife, the Catholic Mary of Modena, was childless and his heir was Mary, the eldest daughter of his first, Protestant wife, many people were prepared to wait and see whether matters improved. However, the birth of a son in June 1688 seemed to assure a Catholic dynasty and helped to precipitate revolution.

James' daughter Mary had married William of Orange who was himself a nephew of the King. He was a staunch Protestant engaged in a perennial struggle against the expansionist policies of Louis XIV of France. If James had manifest faults William comes over as even less likeable. Undersized, weak, and unhealthy, his face pitted by smallpox, William was plagued by ill health. Despite this he was determined and hard-working though contemporaries found him morose, reserved, and serious. His cause, his life's work, was opposing French expansion in Europe. As time was to show he had little real feeling for his adopted country, England, and even less for Scotland. In 1688 he may have been genuinely concerned about affairs in England but his real interest was to the wider issues of European politics. A Catholic-directed England would make a potential ally for France. He took a remarkable gamble in assembling a fleet of several hundred vessels and attempting to invade England in November, denuding the Low Countries of troops and leaving them vulnerable to a French attack. The gamble paid off though. He landed at Torbay on November 5th and began to move towards London. After a hesitant start support for him grew rapidly. James ordered his larger professional army westwards to meet William. There was serious disaffection among James' senior officers, however, many of them resenting the way in which Catholics had been given preference in the army by James. From the royal camp at Salisbury men began slipping away to join William.

In his younger days James had acquired a considerable reputation as a soldier in the service of France. Later, after his brother's restoration, he had successfully commanded the English fleet against the Dutch. Now, however, he was vacillating and irresolute. Strong leadership and positive action might still have saved the situation. His army was, on paper, more than a match for

William's and even a minor reverse would have threatened the Prince of Orange's position. However, James failed to take any effective action and it has been suggested that he suffered a nervous breakdown.

James abandoned his disintegrating army and returned to London. Two weeks later he fled. His first attempt to escape abroad was a dismal failure when his boat was intercepted by fishermen who took him for a Jesuit and roughly manhandled him. James' escape would have suited William very well but now it looked as if he would have to start negotiating. However, William managed to scare James into a second flight; after a few uneasy days in London he sailed to France and perpetual exile. Had he stayed he would probably have been able to retain his throne through some sort of compromise with William.

James received a bad press from both contemporaries and later historians. He remains an enigmatic character in many ways and was not the sort of person with whom it is easy to sympathize. Perhaps he had been overshadowed by his elder brother for too long. As a young man he was a notorious womanizer with a reputation at least as bad as that of Charles. Pig-headed obstinacy and arrogance were prominent features of his behaviour during his brief reign. Certainly he did not possess Charles II's engaging charm nor his flexibility with regard to politics. Instead he stuck rigidly to his principles, a distinctive Stuart trait. Unfortunately, he had no grasp of politics and was unable to appreciate the impression which his authoritarian actions made on other people and felt that as King he did not have to answer for his actions to anyone. He was also singularly bad at judging people and had surrounded himself with advisors who alienated much potential support, a characteristic which came out in his son and grandson.

'BONNIE' DUNDEE

If events in England had moved with bewildering rapidity during the winter of 1688-9 the situation in Scotland was even stranger. Scotland was still an independent nation, though since 1603, when the crowns of England and Scotland had been united, Scotland had become ever more closely linked to her southern neighbour. When William's invasion was imminent James made the mistake of ordering the Scottish army south, thereby depriving the Scottish Privy Council of effective support. After William had established himself in London most members of the Council hurried south hoping to ingratiate themselves, leaving Scotland virtually without any government.

Among the waverers, the men who changed sides, and those who were hostile to James, one man stood out for his unswerving loyalty and his eagerness to take positive action. John Graham of Claverhouse, Viscount Dundee, was a professional soldier who had never had the opportunity to demonstrate his full military talents. As a young man he served as a junior officer in the French army at a time when Charles II had allied himself with France. His fellow officers had included John Churchill, later Duke of Marlborough, and Hugh Mackay of Scourie, who was to be his opponent in the first Jacobite campaign.

Claverhouse later served under William of Orange in the Low Countries. His subsequent steadfast loyalty to James and his refusal to go over to William may have stemmed in part from a personal dislike of the Prince of Orange. One story is that he saved the Prince's life on the battlefield and that William, having promised him promotion, subsequently passed him over, causing Dundee to resign in disgust. From 1678 he was back in Scotland with a commission as a cavalry officer operating against the rebellious ultra-Protestant Covenanters in the south west. His duties were more those of a policeman than a soldier and there was little opportunity to gain military distinction. It was hard, dangerous, sometimes dirty work which earned him the title 'Bloody Clavers' from his opponents. Nevertheless, he carried out his duties meticulously and made himself extremely useful to the government.

Claverhouse became a close friend of James, who furthered his career. On the eve of William's invasion he was made a brigadier commanding the cavalry of the Scottish army which James ordered south to England. A week after William landed James created him Viscount Dundee. When James' army at Salisbury began to disintegrate with most of its officers deserting to William's camp, Dundee stayed loyal, vainly urging James to fight, to negotiate with William, or to retreat to Scotland and carry on the struggle from there. After James fled to France, Dundee, having refused to serve William, returned to Scotland with about sixty troopers, the loyal remnants of his former regiment. Dundee was just over forty years old; small, slim, dark haired, and handsome, he was something of a dandy, the 'Bonnie Dundee' of Scott's poem. A typical career soldier, he was ambitious but uncomplicated, though more politically astute than many. He had charisma and his integrity was widely respected. He seems to have modelled himself on his famous ancestor the Marquis of Montrose who had upheld Charles I's cause in Scotland forty years earlier. The immediate future of the Jacobite cause in Scotland depended on Dundee.

THE CONVENTION IN EDINBURGH

As William had not yet been crowned King of Scotland he could not summon a parliament but various nobles urged him to call a Convention of Estates — an unofficial parliament — to decide on what action was to be taken. The Convention opened in Edinburgh in March 1689. At this time Edinburgh had a substantial population; around 50,000 if the suburbs and the port of Leith were included. Despite this it was one of the smallest, most tightly-packed cities in Europe. The medieval burgh had been established on a gently sloping ridge running down from the steep rock on which the Castle stood. To north and south the ridge fell away steeply into deep valleys. The one to the north, occupied today by Princes Street Gardens and Waverley Station, had been dammed to form the Nor' Loch, an effective defence and well-used rubbish tip. Because of the awkward topography, the continuing need for defence, and difficulties in acquiring additional land to build on, Edinburgh had grown upwards rather than outwards.

Most of the inhabitants still lived within the Flodden Wall, a line of defence estabished in the sixteenth century following the disastrous Scottish defeat of 1513. Within these limits the two- and three-storey timber-framed houses of the fifteenth century had been replaced by tall stone tenements some of which, built into the steep slope behind the church of St Giles and Parliament House, reached ten or twelve storeys in height. The lower part of the ridge running down from the Castle was occupied by the separate burgh of the Canongate whose main street continued the line of Edinburgh's High Street to the gates of Holyrood Palace. The Canongate was effectively a suburb, less densely built up than Edinburgh itself, where many noblemen had their town houses.

Since December the Duke of Gordon, governor of Edinburgh Castle, had placed the fortress on a war footing, in support of King James. The Convention met in Parliament House behind St Giles. The Scottish Parliament had only been properly accommodated since 1639 when Parliament House was built on the site of the former St Giles churchyard. The irregular but picturesque seventeenth-century facade of the building was replaced by the present stiff classical front in the early nineteenth century. Inside, however, the hall in which the Convention met, with its finely carved and gilded seventeenth-century hammer-beam roof, is little changed and now forms part of the Scottish central courts. The Convention was not yet fully opposed to James but he had no control over it. Both he and William sent letters to canvas support. William's letter was conciliatory and vague in its promises, offending nobody. The one from James was arrogant and dictatorial, coldly demanding his subjects' allegience. It dismayed his supporters and alienated many waverers.

Because of the small size of the city it was easy for an aggressive mob or a small, disciplined force to threaten not only the burgh authorities but also Parliament and the Privy Council. Dundee, with his troop of cavalry, might have been able to influence the Convention had not the city been swamped by an influx of Protestant extremists, Covenanters from the west of Scotland, to whose anti-Stuart opinions was added a fierce hatred of Dundee, who had been so prominent in curbing their activities in the previous few years. Word was brought to Dundee of a plot to assassinate him. He was not the sort of man to be unduly worried: he had been a marked man for years. However, it gave him a convenient pretext for withdrawing from the Convention without making an outright declaration of opposition to William.

On the 19th of March Dundee and his small troop of horsemen left the city by Leith Wynd and rode westwards along what is now Princes Street. It is not clear whether, at this stage, he intended to raise a rebellion in Scotland. He had implied to the Convention that he might go to Ireland to join James' army there. Another possibility, which failed for lack of support, was to establish a rival Jacobite Convention at Stirling. When he came opposite Edinburgh Castle he left his men and scrambled up the cliff face to a postern gate where he spoke with the Duke of Gordon. He may have urged Gordon to leave the Castle in charge of his second-in-command and join him. Had Gordon gone to his estates in the North East and mobilized his tenants Dundee might soon have had the nucleus of an army but Gordon decided that his duty was to stay at his appointed post and hold out for as long as possible.

THE SIEGE OF EDINBURGH CASTLE

As soon as Dundee left the city a blockade of the Castle was started. Gordon's original garrison of about 120 contained many who favoured William. Having thrown out those men most likely to be disaffected, he had less than 80 left to defend the fortress. Edinburgh Castle in 1689 was a less impressive complex of buildings than today. The tall barrack and hospital blocks which dominate Princes Street and the view from the west were built in the eighteenth and nineteenth centuries. The main defences were concentrated on the eastern side, facing the approach from the city, and the rest of the rock, which was extremely hard to scale, was defended by a simple curtain wall. The Covenanters in the city were mobilized and they began to throw up rudimentary siegeworks around the Castle. Gordon refrained from firing on them as they dug their amateurish trenches because his supply of ammunition was limited, and because he wanted to avoid unnecessary bloodshed.

Ten days later General Hugh Mackay landed at Leith with 1,100 regular troops of the Scots Brigade from Holland and the siege began in earnest. Mackay, who had come to England with William, had been appointed his commander-in-chief in Scotland. His portrait suggests a genial, good-natured, bluff man. His own memoirs show him as a competent but not outstanding soldier who rapidly became disenchanted with trying to do a difficult job in the face of a perennial shortage of money and complicated political manoeuvrings within the ranks of William's supporters. A deeply religious man, he detested cynical self-seeking politicians who were concerned only with personal advancement.

His first task was to inject some vigour into the siege operations. He had a trench and rampart dug around the base of the Castle to prevent sympathizers from communicating with the garrison. Then he set up batteries of artillery near where Register House now stands at the east end of Princes Street, in the grounds of Heriot's Hospital to the south, and west of the Castle in the old tower of Coates. Gordon bombarded these positions and caused some casualties. The eastern side of the Castle Rock, sloping towards the town, was the only place where the attackers could make an assault but every time Mackay's men started to dig trenches and throw up ramparts Gordon threatened to bombard the city. Instead Mackay drained the Nor' Loch to try and interfere with the Castle's water supply.

The bombardment intensified and soon most of the buildings in the Castle were roofless ruins. Part of the curtain wall collapsed but at a point where the cliff was too steep to allow an assault. The garrison, safe in the deep cellars, suffered hardly any casualties. Time hung heavily on their hands though and they sent a message to the besiegers asking for packs of playing cards to be sent in! Rather churlishly, the request was refused. The condition of the garrison worsened as food ran out and the water supply began to fail. A providential snowfall late in May provided additional fresh water but by the end of the month the besiegers had begun to push their trenches right to the foot of the Half Moon Battery. The defenders kept them under fire as far as their limited supply of powder and ammunition allowed; one contemporary claimed that the besiegers suffered around 500 casualties during the siege. The state of the garrison had become desperate, however, and on June 14th, after lengthy negotiations, Gordon agreed to surrender.

DUNDEE RAISES THE STANDARD

Meanwhile, Dundee had gone north to his castle at Dudhope, which now stands within a small park a short distance from the centre of Dundee. Dudhope was a substantial courtyard mansion, built around 1600 when the need for defence was gradually giving way to more spacious and elegant designs. Two sides of the house still survive, with corner towers and a gateway, and are currently being restored. Dundee also owned the picturesque old tower house of Claypotts nearby and another tower, the family home, at Glen Ogilvie, a short distance south of Glamis. Along with Dudhope went the hereditary office of Constable of Dundee, an office which gave Claverhouse considerable influence in the burgh and his local power increased further in 1688 when James appointed him provost of the town.

On the 27th of March messengers from the Convention arrived at Dudhope requiring Dundee to lay down his arms and return to Edinburgh. Dundee's reply, full of outraged innocence, was designed to buy time but he realized that he could not remain undisturbed for long. Already he had been in touch with some of the Highland chiefs who were prepared to support James. They lived principally in Lochaber, a district centred on the head of Loch Linnhe where the town of Fort William stands today. The confederation of loyal chiefs was led by Ewan Cameron of Lochiel.

1 Dudhope Castle, where Viscount Dundee planned the first Jacobite rising.

Lochiel, then in his early sixties, was one of the most respected clan leaders. We know more about him than most of his contemporaries because of a biography written by his grandson. To say that he was a staunch lifelong supporter of the Stuarts is too simplistic because the interests of Clan Cameron always came first with him. Nevertheless his record of service to the Crown was impressive. Too young to join the Marquis of Montrose in his whirlwind military campaign in support of Charles I in the mid 1640s, Lochiel nevertheless played a prominent part in the Earl of Glencairn's rising against Cromwell a decade later. He had received little formal education but to his contemporaries he was the epitome of a Highland chieftain. He combined the talents of a skilled leader in war and a canny negotiator in peace with personal courage and skill with arms.

His biographer, in a particularly vivid passage, describes how, during Cromwell's occupation of Scotland, Lochiel and a party of his men attacked a larger force of soldiers from the garrison at Inverlochy (now Fort William). The fight broke up into a series of single combats, broadswords against clubbed muskets, and Lochiel found himself grappling with an English officer who was his match for strength and skill. Neither man could gain an advantage until Lochiel bit out the throat of his opponent. After the Restoration he appeared at court but received little tangible recognition for his services to the Crown. It was only in 1682 that James knighted this 'king of thieves' as he jokingly called him.

8

2 A view of Dundee in the late seventeenth century. Dundee Law, on which the Jacobite standard was raised, is the hill on the far right.

During the winter of 1688-9 Lochiel had been planning a rising and he had arranged a rendezvous in May for the chiefs who were still loyal to James. Dundee also had hopes of finding support in the north east where the influence of the Catholic Gordons was strong. In mid-April he raised James' standard on Dundee Law, a conical hill dominating both Dudhope and the town but now within the built-up area, a brisk walk from the city centre. Today the hill is crowned with a monument to two later, grimmer wars than the one Dundee was starting. He chose this spot for unfurling the standard for purely practical reasons; it was immediately above Dudhope and from it the flag could be clearly seen by the inhabitants of the town. With hindsight, however, the choice was a symbolic one. From the summit of the Law Dundee could look southward beyond the town and the Tay estuary to the Lowlands, an area which was to generate little support for the Jacobite cause in this or late rebellions. Northwards, however, his gaze must have been drawn across the low Sidlaw Hills to the long dark line of mountains marking the Highlands, the area which was to provide him with both a refuge and an army. The Convention sent a party of dragoons commanded by Sir Thomas Livingstone to capture him. Dundee was warned of their approach and, instead of surprising him at Dudhope or Glen Ogilvie, they missed him by a day. The Highland war had begun.

THE HIGHLANDS IN THE LATE SEVENTEENTH CENTURY

Before following Dundee to the Highlands it is worth pausing to consider what this region and its people were like at the end of the seventeenth century. In early medieval Scotland there had been no divide between Highland and Lowland society. However, the retreat of Gaelic language and culture under the impact of influences from the south created a growing gulf between the two areas. Highland society became inward-looking and conservative while the more progressive Lowlands looked outward to England and the Continent. The Highland/Lowland divide was probably at its greatest in the early seventeenth century but in the late seventeenth and early eighteenth centuries Highlanders and Lowlanders still viewed each other with mutual suspicion, mistrust, and contempt.

It is a truism to say that Highland society was based on the clan system but despite all that has been written about the Highland clans we know remarkably little about how they functioned. Since traditional Irish society had been almost obliterated by English plantations and land grabbing from Elizabeth I's time onwards, the Highlands sheltered the last Celtic society to retain its ancient tribal structure. Notionally clans were bodies of people related by blood and descended from a common ancestor. They possessed a surname deriving from that ancestor and inhabited a specific clan territory. Clans were ruled in an authoritarian but patriarchal way by their chiefs and the various branches of the chief's family provided a kind of middle or gentry class.

The clan system was not, however, as simple as this picture of a static, archaic society suggests. Anglo-Norman feudalism had penetrated parts of the Highlands, particularly the south and east, providing an alternative social and landholding system which could operate independently of clanship, reinforce it, or work against it. Thus some families like the Dukes of Atholl, ruled as feudal barons without being the head of a clan. Some purely feudal families, like the Gordons in the North East, used kinship and family ties in a similar way to clanship to increase their power. Other magnates used clanship and feudalism together in a formidable combination, like the Dukes of Argyll who were also chiefs of Clan Campbell. Some chiefs, like Lochiel and MacDonald of Keppoch, occupied lands to which they had no strict feudal title. In the later seventeenth century this kind of situation led to some of the most bitter disputes within the Highlands.

Although it seemed alien and barbaric to outsiders, Highland society was not unchanging. The clan system was in a state of constant flux as individual clans built up their power by acquiring territory at the expense of other clans. Sometimes a clan became too large and unwieldy, disintegrating in a welter of feuding from which new clans emerged to start the cycle once more. In the fifteenth century the MacDonalds had built up an empire, the Lordship of the Isles, which was at times, effectively, a separate kingdom. Their power had been broken by James IV in 1493 and the fragmentation of the MacDonalds into a number of separate branches gave other clans the opportunity to expand. In the seventeenth century the most notable of these were the Campbells in the south west who extended their territory at the expense of the MacDonalds, Macleans, and other clans.

Superimposed on this continuous cycle were longer-term changes as Highland society gradually came into more frequent contact with the outside world and the Scottish government tried to exert growing control over the area. In the sixteenth century the Highlands had been an area where the King's writ rarely ran with any certainty but which, apart from suppressing the occasional foray into the Lowlands, could be left mainly to its own devices. The civil wars of the mid-seventeenth century, particularly the campaigns of the Marquis of Montrose, had shown that a Highland army could influence national politics. The later seventeenth century was marked by growing contact between the Highlands and the outside world. Chiefs were frequently educated abroad. At home they might live in a style which had changed little from the Celtic Iron Age but elsewhere they moved as landed magnates in a world of educated and wealthy courtiers.

To sustain this new lifestyle they needed money but their lands were managed to maximize the numbers of fighting men on them rather than to produce cash. Rents were paid by the clansmen in kind, in hospitality, and particularly in military service. Indeed, clans were in many ways para-military organizations, with every able-bodied man expected to bear arms when needed. To turn from this to the commercial exploitation of a Highland estate was a major break with tradition. The Dukes of Argyll, more closely in touch with the Lowlands than many clan leaders, were among the first to start re-organizing the tenure of their farms to increase their cash income. Other landowners profited by the growing trade in cattle to the Lowlands and to England. Even Ewan Cameron of Lochiel, seemingly an archetypical clan chief, was engaged during the 1670s in developing an iron works near his home at Achnacarry, fuelled by charcoal from his forests.

These changes underlay many of the strains which are evident in Highland society at this time. While the chiefs strove for grander lifestyles the life of the ordinary clansman remained a hard one. The environment of the Highlands was harsh and the inhabitants struggled with simple agricultural techniques to raise crops of oats and barley on the limited areas of better soils in the glens. Lacking adequate winter fodder, their livestock were small and skinny. Poverty and malnutrition were endemic and periodically large-scale famine struck the region. Poverty reinforced the military character of clan society as cattle raiding was often easier than cattle raising; but this in turn reinforced poverty.

In addition, government involvement in the area was increasing. In the sixteenth and early seventeenth centuries Scottish monarchs, acknowledging that they had no direct control over much of the area, devolved their power to influential families like the Campbells in Argyll, the Gordons in the north east, and the Earls of Seaforth in the north, making them the King's lieutenants in their localities. The Cromwellian occupation of the Highlands in the 1650s had shown, however, that this region need not be a no-go area. A superficial study of the records of the Scottish Privy Council in the later seventeenth century might suggest that crime and violence in the Highlands was reaching epidemic proportions. This is probably misleading. Indeed, there are signs that the level of violence was actually decreasing. The fact that the Privy Council recorded it in such detail merely indicates that they were making greater efforts to control it. Highland landowners were becoming more used to pursuing their enemies with writs than with weapons, to the considerable profit of Edinburgh lawyers and the increasing insolvency of their clients.

DUNDEE'S CAMPAIGN

Dundee's campaign got off to a poor start. There was remarkably little support in Scotland for James, particularly among the nobility the greatest of whom could have raised several thousand men. James had alienated most of the magnates who held the real power and most of them, if they did not actively support William, sat on the fence to see how his regime would turn out. A year later, when it became clear that William was going to raise taxes, increase the standing army to make war on France, and let the Presbyterian extremists abolish the Episcopalian church in Scotland, support for James was to rally. However, when Dundee started his rebellion enthusiasm for James was at its lowest ebb. Dundee had to conduct a campaign with smaller forces than those raised by the Jacobites in 1715 and 1745. His main support was to come from the Highlands but the winter of 1688-9 had been long and severe. It was not feasible to mobilize the clans before May and there was a serious shortage of provisions in Lochaber. Dundee decided to try and recruit support from less hard-pressed areas before moving into the Highlands.

The first phase of the campaign was a curious game of hide and seek, through north eastern Scotland as Dundee, with his small, highly mobile band of horsemen, kept ahead of Mackay and tried to drum up support. Initially Mackay left Livingstone and his dragoons to guard the town of Dundee and set off in pursuit with 200 infantry and 300 horsemen, all he could spare from the siege of Edinburgh Castle. He hoped to crush the rebellion before it could gather momentum and only expected to be away for a couple of weeks. He tried to enlist the help of landowners in the north east who were sympathetic to William. The Laird of Grant was to raise men to watch the crossings of the Spey. The Earl of Mar was to guard the Grampians and the Marquis of Atholl was to seal the passes westward into Perthshire. Mackay hoped by these means to trap Dundee somewhere in the north east. Unfortunately his 'allies' all let him down and there was nothing to impede Dundee's small force which turned the campaign into a prolonged chase.

Dundee marched north then, hearing that the dragoons at Dundee were ready to come over to him, he doubled back to try and link up with them. Realizing that Mackay was approaching, however, he returned northwards. Mackay wore out his men trying to catch his opponent and came close on only a couple of occasions. He did manage to keep his opponent on the move and Dundee gained few recruits in the north east, the heartland of the Catholic Gordons. Sympathetic landowners would join him only if James landed in Scotland with a substantial army. Dundee began to realize that his main hope rested with the Highland clans with whom he was in regular contact.

Moving through Aberdeenshire and Moray, Dundee rode towards Inverness to be confronted with a classic example of the problems of using Highland troops. Coll MacDonald of Keppoch, with a mongrel force of 800 clansmen, was also advancing on Inverness, ostensibly to escourt Dundee to the rendezvous in Lochaber. However, the area around Inverness was Mackintosh country and Keppoch had old scores to settle with them. Having plundered the countryside he threatened to burn Inverness if the town's

3 Edinburgh Castle and the city seen from the north soon after the siege of 1689.

magistrates failed to buy him off. He had once been imprisoned there and evidently had a grudge against the townspeople!

Dundee was forced to intervene, giving Keppoch a dressing down for bringing discredit on King James' cause and giving his personal guarantee to the baillies of Inverness that the money would be repaid when King James was restored. He tried to persuade Keppoch to join him in a surprise attack on Mackay at Elgin. Mackay had heard that Keppoch had joined Dundee but despite this he pressed on with his small force hoping to bring them to battle. Keppoch had, however, come to plunder not to fight and only wanted to return home with his booty.

Dundee had little option but to go by Loch Ness into the heart of the Highlands where Mackay would not follow. He still hoped that the dragoons at Dundee would join him and once more he moved south at a pace which would have done credit to his hero, Montrose. At Dundee the dragoon commander prepared to make a sortie as an excuse for joining the Jacobites but was stopped by a suspicious officer who supported William. The gates of the town remained shut against the former provost! He returned to the Highlands and the rendezvous with the chiefs at Dalcomera, probably the place now known as Mucomir at the outfall of Loch Lochy, from where it was easy to move into either Badenoch or Atholl. He now had a small, mobile clan army with which he could take the offensive.

Hearing that reinforcements for Mackay, who was waiting in Inverness, were being sent through Atholl to Speyside Dundee moved quickly and got there first. Colonel Ramsay, commanding the reinforcements, was delayed in leaving Edinburgh by an invasion scare. The French fleet was reported to have been sighted in the Firth of Forth but it turned out to be only some Dutch fishing boats! By the time he reached the Tay valley, Ramsay found the inhabitants of Atholl so threatening that he lost his nerve and retreated. Mackay later complained that the lack of reinforcements at this crucial stage in the campaign prevented him from bringing Dundee to battle before his army had grown.

Mackay had garrisoned the castle at Ruthven, near modern Kingussie, and left it in the command of John Forbes of Culloden, a family that was to figure prominently as opponents of the Jacobites in later years. As Mackay did not arrive to relieve him, Forbes surrendered and Keppoch burnt the castle, the first but not the last occasion when a fortress on this site was destroyed by the Jacobites.

Mackay, with less than 1,000 men, marched up Speyside hoping to meet Ramsay. Discovering that his reinforcements were no longer coming and that Dundee now had a stronger force than his own, he fell back hurriedly, chased by the Highlanders down the Spey, through Glenlivet and into the Lowlands. Here he hoped to catch Dundee in an exposed position where his clansmen would be vulnerable to Mackay's cavalry. Then reinforcements for Mackay

4 Some of the ancient pinewoods on Speyside through which Dundee chased Mackay's army and back through which Dundee was, in turn, pursued.

arrived through the Lowlands from the south and the position was reversed, with Dundee in retreat and a more confident Mackay on his heels. Mackay was surprised at Dundee's failure to act more decisively and to either attack him or intercept the reinforcements. Despite his claim that most of the inhabitants north of the Tay were potentially hostile to William they do not seem to have been sufficiently enthusiastic about King James to have reported Mackay's movements to the Jacobite leader.

Dundee appears to have contracted dysentery at this stage of the campaign and he drew back into Lochaber to recover, dismissing most of the clansmen who had supported him because he had insufficient provisions to maintain them for long. Mackay, belatedly joined by Ramsay, followed him back to

Ruthven and then broke off the pursuit, retiring to Inverness and garrisoning it before marching south for Edinburgh. He evidently believed that he had got the rebellion well under control and that Dundee's army would soon disintegrate.

STALEMATE

The opening moves of the first Jacobite rebellion had achieved little beyond a lot of marching and counter-marching. Nevertheless, whether due to Mackay's activities or to a general lack of interest, most people north of the Tay had stayed at home and Dundee had not been able to recruit an army large enough to achieve anything useful. Lochiel's biographer claims that Dundee, in chasing Mackay around the Highlands, often with inferior forces, was the talk of Scotland. So fast moving was he that Mackay sometimes found Dundee attacking his outposts when he had supposed his army to be miles away. Nevertheless, Mackay had done well to keep up the pressure on his elusive foe, marching his men, sometimes through rugged terrain, over distances which were far greater than was normal in conventional warfare.

Mackay himself was a Highlander, a younger son of the laird of Scourie in Sutherland, but he had spent most of his career as a soldier abroad. After thirty years away Scotland was almost a foreign country to him. He had little sympathy with, or understanding of, the Highlanders and their fighting methods though he admired their bravery. This attitude was to cost him dearly. Dundee considered trying to fashion his Highlanders into regular soldiers fighting in proper regiments and using conventional tactics. He was dissuaded by Lochiel and the other chiefs who argued that their men would fight better in their traditional loosely-disciplined manner.

Throughout the campaign Dundee had been expecting reinforcements from Ireland where James was campaigning against William's army. James seems to have been over-optimistic about the success of Dundee's rebellion. He had originally promised to send three regiments under the command of his illegitimate son the Duke of Berwick, a young but brilliant soldier. Unfortunately, he decided to wait until the siege of Londonderry was over before sending them. By the time the city was relieved by William's men James' army was so weakened and demoralized that he could not spare the reinforcements. All Dundee got was an officer named Colonel Cannon, who turned out to be a dubious asset, and 300 dragoons without their horses, raw Irish recruits who were brave enough but completely untrained. A Highland bard who fought alongside them at Killiecrankie was to compare their charge in the battle to a cattle stampede!

The only way to subdue the Highlands, Mackay thought, was by permanent garrisons. He favoured re-establishing the fort which had been built in Cromwell's time at Inverlochy (now Fort William) in the heart of Lochaber, the most ungovernable part of the Highlands. The obvious way to send an expedition to this area was by sea but with the expense of William's campaign in Ireland funds were not available. Mackay wasted the rest of the summer trying to badger the government into providing the resources he needed. In the end there was not enough time left to mount an expedition to Lochaber before winter set in and Mackay was only granted resources for a more limited campaign.

He was preparing for this when he heard disturbing news from Atholl. The Marquis of Atholl, after sitting on the fence, had eventually come down in favour of William. To avoid having to do anything positive he used illness as an excuse for removing himself to Bath. He left his eldest son, Lord Murray, in charge of the estates with instructions to help Mackay. Most of the Atholl tenants, however, were pro-Jacobite and the Marquis' baillie, Patrick Stewart of Ballechin, took matters into his own hands by seizing Blair Castle for King James. This was a blow to Mackay because a strong garrison at Blair could dominate the routes into Lochaber which he planned to use. Moreover, if the Atholl men joined Dundee it would not only greatly increase his army but encourage other chiefs and landowners, as yet uncommitted, to support him. When Dundee heard that Ballechin had taken the castle he also reacted immediately. He gathered what forces he could and hurried eastwards towards Atholl sending messages to the chiefs who supported him to raise their men and follow as quickly as possible.

2

THE HIGHLAND WAR, 1689-91

THE BRAES OF KILLIECRANKIE

The campaign turned into a race to reach Blair Castle. As well as being the centre of the extensive Atholl estates, Blair commanded the main route from the Tay valley to Speyside and Inverness, and to Deeside via Glen Tilt. It was to figure prominently again in the 1745 rebellion. The castle which you can visit today is a complex and composite building. At its core is a thirteenth-century tower. At a later date a second tower was built and the space between filled in with a rectangular block containing the great hall. Extensive alterations were made by the second Duke of Atholl in the mid-eighteenth century when most of the towers and parapets were removed to give Blair the appearance of a Georgian country mansion. In Victorian times, when Romanticism and the cult of the picturesque were fashionable, the turrets and crow-stepped gables were restored! Despite these later changes Blair Castle gives a very good impression of the power of a major landowning family in Scotland during the period of the Jacobite rebellions.

Mackay marched from Dunkeld at around midday on the 27th of July 1689. At Pitlochry he was met by Lord Murray who had left a few men to guard the entrance to the pass of Killiecrankie, the narrow gorge nearly two kilometres long between Pitlochry and Blair through which the River Garry tumbles and roars. Travelling up the valley today the gorge does not seem a formidable obstacle but the modern road runs high above the pass: the original route was through the bottom of the gorge itself, close to the river. Mackay does not seem to have realized that Dundee was already at Blair otherwise he might have thought twice about trying to push through a defile which, at its narrowest, would only allow his men to pass three abreast. It was an ideal spot for an ambush. Dundee, however, did not expect Mackay to arrive so quickly and when word reached him at Blair that Mackay's army was already in the pass he had to make a quick decision.

Dundee had various options open to him. One was to delay battle until reinforcements arrived. Several large contingents of clansmen were expected within a day or two. This course was favoured by his Lowland officers as

Mackay's army was twice the size of Dundee's. However, he had the ability, unusual in a Lowlander and a conventional soldier, to understand the Highlanders' mentality. He realized that their pride demanded an immediate attack and that if he delayed his men might lose enthusiasm and disperse. To attack Mackay immediately was the characteristically impetuous reaction of Lochiel and the other chiefs. Dundee's own choice was a minor tactical masterpiece. An attack on Mackay's men in the narrow pass could only be a guerilla-style ambush. It might persuade Mackay to retreat but would not give Dundee the decisive victory he needed. In any case there might not even be time for this as Mackay's advance guard was already starting to emerge from the defile.

Instead, Dundee let Mackay's army come through the gorge and form up on the level ground beside the river above the pass. He then sent a small party down the valley from Blair. As intended, Mackay took this to be the Jacobite advance guard and positioned his men to meet a frontal attack. Meanwhile Dundee led his army by the circuitous route shown on Map 1. He suddenly emerged on the steep hillside of Creag Eallaich above the right wing of Mackay's army. Mackay had to wheel his forces round quickly to meet this new threat. He marched them up the steep slope above the river flats on to more gently sloping ground above. This put him in the awkward position of facing uphill with his opponents above him and the river a barrier at his back. The name of the battle sometimes leads visitors to believe that it was fought in the pass of Killiecrankie itself. This impression is reinforced by the location in the gorge of the National Trust for Scotland's information centre, which contains an interesting exhibition about the battle. In fact the armies clashed over a kilometre from the north end of the gorge on more open ground.

Mackay had some 4,000 men, around half of whom were experienced troops, the remainder being recent recruits. His veteran regiments from the Scots Brigade in Holland had arrived in Scotland badly under strength and had been increased by drafting in untrained men. He also had some cavalry and dragoons, which the Jacobites badly lacked, though he probably regretted leaving six troops of horsemen in the Lowlands to follow on behind. Highlanders were wary of fighting men on horseback and his missing dragoons would have been particularly welcome. Dundee had no more than 2,000 men but the tactical advantage clearly lay with him.

THE HIGHLAND CHARGE

It was early evening when Mackay drew up his forces for battle. For two hours Dundee held his men together without attacking. This breathing space gave them a chance to rest after their dash from Blair while he may also have hoped to tempt Mackay into some rash move uphill against him. Mackay's men, having marched over sixteen miles in their heavy knee-length red coats,

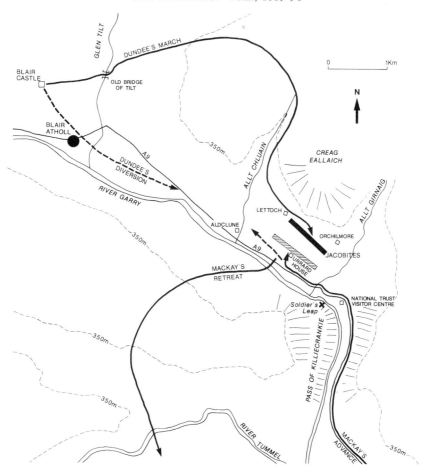

Map 1 Killiecrankie: the setting.

burdened by their cumbersome muskets and long pikes, were also tired. Mackay had brought three small leather cannons which he had intended to use against Blair Castle. To try and tempt the Highlanders downhill prematurely he opened fire with them. The travelling carriages on which they were mounted proved to be too flimsy and they broke after the first few shots. Mackay also had his men fire their muskets at the Highlanders, rolling volleys platoon by platoon which hid his line in thick smoke. This caused some casualties but the range was too great for the effects to be serious. The clansmen tried some probing shots too, their marksmen aiming at Mackay as he moved around preparing his men for battle. The Highlanders attempted to demoralize their adversaries, probably successfully, with wild war cries.

21

Few of Mackay's men had experienced warfare of this kind and it is doubtful if the general's speech, emphasizing that if they ran they would be cut down and slaughtered, improved their morale.

Instead of forming a proper line of battle, Dundee kept his clansmen in solid groups under each chief. He arranged them in two divisions, facing Mackay's left and right, with a gap in the centre in which he stationed himself and his force of about fifty horsemen. He was probably worried that if he concentrated his small army on Mackay's centre he might find himself enveloped by the troops on either flank. On the right, facing Mackay's regular regiments, he placed the bulk of his forces, about 1,400 men, including the MacDonalds of Clanranald and Glengarry, the Macleans, and the Irish troops. On his left he positioned the Camerons, and the MacDonalds of Sleat, around 550 men, facing some 2,300 Lowland and English recruits. Lochiel evidently did not consider the odds against him unreasonable!

Mackay was worried that he might be outflanked to his right and cut off from the pass. To prevent this he strung his men out in an extended three-deep line without reserves. An area of boggy ground interrupted communications between his left and right wings. He placed his horsemen in the centre, ready to sally out and take the clansmen in the flank as they charged, or to counter Dundee's cavalry. Against regular troops Mackay would have been in a stronger position, as his formation maximized the firepower of his men. Unfortunately a single thin line was the worst possible defence against the distinctive form of attack which he was now to face, the Highland charge.

The Highland charge was a traditional Celtic style of attack modified to suit contemporary warfare and weapons. Julius Caesar would have recognized its basic features from his campaigns against the Gauls: the headlong downhill charge, and the tendency to fight as individual swordsmen or in small clan groups rather than in larger disciplined units. The Highland charge had been elaborated in the 1640s under the Marquis of Montrose whose lieutenant, Alastair McColla, was probably responsible for updating it. McColla had taught his Highlanders to advance at a run, casting off their plaids for greater freedom of movement. These were large rectangles of coarsely-patterned woollen cloth which could be belted up to form both a kilt and a covering for the upper part of the body. During the charge the Highlanders threw themselves flat when fired on to minimize casualties. When they were within close musket shot they stopped, let off a single volley, then dropped their firearms and charged on through the powder smoke with their swords.

The muskets used by many of the Highlanders in the late seventeenth century were flintlocks, at least as good as those issued to the army, and at their best they were good marksmen. Their swords were far superior to anything the regular troops carried. The Highlanders no longer wielded the claymore or 'great sword', a fearsome two-handed medieval weapon. Instead

22

they used the single-handed broadsword with a dirk or dagger in their other hand and a round, leather-covered shield or targe on their arm. The broadsword, often mistakenly called a claymore, was double edged, some three feet long, with a basket hilt; a formidable weapon.

Because of the lack of discipline among the Highlanders this type of charge was a make-or-break affair. Once its impetus was checked it was almost impossible to rally the clansmen. Much of the effectiveness of the charge at Killiecrankie and in other Jacobite battles came from its use against inexperienced soldiers or regular troops accustomed to the slow set-piece manoeuvres of Continental battlefields. Conventional armies were poorly equipped to counter a wave of charging swordsmen. In fact they had been better off earlier in the seventeenth century when there was still a substantial proportion of pikemen, with helmets and half-armour, in each regiment. The pikemen were designed to protect the musketeers while they went through their slow routine of loading and firing. By this date, however, numbers of pikemen in infantry regiments had been greatly reduced.

Troops facing a Highland charge had time for little more than a single volley of musket fire whose effectiveness was liable to be impaired by the outlandish sight — and sound — of the rapidly approaching enemy. There was no time to reload before the clansmen were on them. Some of Mackay's men were still using obsolescent matchlock muskets, fired by a burning slow match, which took an age to load. Others had more modern and efficient flintlocks but in inexperienced hands they took almost a minute to load. In that time a Highlander rushing downhill could cover a lot of ground!

Bayonets were a recent innovation and those issued to Mackay's men were plug bayonets which were pushed into the barrel of the musket. The weapon could not be fired with the bayonet in place. It was as a result of the poor performance of this type of bayonet at Killiecrankie that an improved version, offset from the muzzle of the musket and attached to the outside of the barrel, was developed, something for which Mackay himself claimed the credit.

THE AVALANCHE OF STEEL

With difficulty Dundee held his men back until sunset. When the evening sun was no longer in their eyes he gave the order to charge. The Highlanders ran down the slope, a distance of perhaps 300 yards for those on the left, a little more for the men on the right, firing their muskets as they came. When they were within 100 paces Mackay's infantry opened fire. It is not clear, even from Mackay's own description of the battle, how many volleys his men managed to fire. One near-contemporary account suggests that his right wing at least managed to discharge more than one round. Given the time it took to reload even a flintlock musket this is optimistic but just about possible. The effect of this musketry was far from negligible. Most of the Jacobite casualties were inflicted at this stage before the Highlanders got to close quarters with the government troops.

Despite heavy losses in the initial charge their momentum carried the Highlanders on until they crashed into Mackay's infantry who were frantically trying to push their bayonets into the barrels of their muskets. The compact clumps of clansmen broke the thin red line into fragments. Mackay's right wing, which outnumbered their immediate opponents by nearly four to one, held for a few moments but then broke in disorder. The regiments on Mackay's left seem to have run without firing. Had they stood their ground the Jacobite losses would have been even greater. Mackay's horsemen, ordered forward to attack the clansmen, fired a few shots, wheeled, then rode back out of range. Within ten minutes the battle became a rout as Mackay's men, trapped by the River Garry at their backs, struggled to cross it or to escape back through the pass. At one of the narrower points of the gorge, below the National Trust for Scotland centre, a spot is still known as the 'Soldier's Leap': tradition has it that one of Mackay's men, fleeing from a pursuing Highlander, made a desperate jump across the river here to reach safety.

Mackay rounded up the remnants of Leven's and Hastings' regiments, some 400 men, and led them from the battlefield. Rather than retreat through the pass with all the inhabitants of Atholl out to attack and plunder stragglers, Mackay headed westward over the hills to more friendly country. Under cover of darkness they reached Castle Menzies, whose laird was a government supporter. Mackay's men were panicky and ready to scatter at the first alarm and it was all that he and his officers could do to keep them together. Next day he pushed on to Castle Drummond and the day after they arrived safe at Stirling. News of the defeat had already reached Edinburgh and the more gloomy members of the Scottish Privy Council, who believed that Mackay was dead, considered that all of Scotland north of the Tay was lost. They expected Dundee to march on Stirling and Edinburgh immediately.

It was later estimated that Mackay's army had suffered around 1,200 casualties in the battle and at least as many in the pursuit. About 500 were taken prisoner and Mackay reached Stirling with only a fifth of his original force. Viewing the battlefield the following morning even the victors were shocked at the effectiveness of their tactics and the terrible wounds made by their broadswords. The battle is sometimes described as a walk-over for the Jacobites; once the clans had shattered Mackay's thin line, it was. However, the musket fire of Mackay's troops had caused heavy casualties: at least 700, a third of the Jacobite force, or as many as 900 according to some estimates. The Jacobite left had suffered most heavily and the Camerons had lost half of their number. As the chiefs and their lieutenants had charged at the head of their men there was an unduly high proportion of officers among the

5 The 'Soldier's Leap' in the gorge at Killiecrankie. (Courtesy National Trust for Scotland)

casualties. Had Mackay's soldiers, particularly on the left, stood firm the outcome might have been different. It was a warning that the Highland charge, though formidable, was by no means invincible.

Nevertheless, the Jacobite victory was complete. Except that Dundee was dead. Before the battle Lochiel, the other chiefs, and his Lowland officers, had urged him not to endanger himself by leading the charge in person. He had replied that the Highlanders could only be led by example and that he had to prove himself to them, on this occasion at least. He led his horsemen against Mackay's cavalry but in the confusion of the battle it is not quite clear what happened next. One account claims that, with a small group of his followers, he became separated from the main body of horsemen. Raising himself in his stirrups and waving his hat above his head to try and rally

25

them, he was hit by a musket ball which penetrated his breastplate under his arm. Accounts also vary regarding whether he died on the battlefield or lived for a few hours. The former seems most likely. A letter announcing the victory survives, purporting to have been written by Dundee after the battle, but there are grounds for believing it to be a forgery. His body was taken to the old parish church at Blair and was buried there. A breastplate with a hole in it, supposedly his, is preserved at Blair Castle.

When William heard the news he shrewdly observed that he had nothing more to fear from the Highlands. The rebellion had died with Dundee. He was right: all the advantages of the victory were lost with the death of the one man with the force of personality to keep the clans together.

Because there are few contemporary descriptions of the battle there is some doubt about the precise position of the two armies. Different writers have placed them in various locations across the slopes between the modern village of Killiecrankie and the hamlet of Aldclune. Mackay's own memoirs contain details of the topography of the battlefield and Map 2 has been drawn from his description. It is probable that when he emerged from the pass he formed up his army on the flat ground beside the Garry north west of Killiecrankie village. He then turned his army through ninety degrees and marched up the steep slope bordering the flood plain on to the more level ground above Urrard House. Dundee's line was probably spread out across the slope roughly between the modern farms of Lettoch and Orchilmore. The Ordnance Survey mark the battlefield in an area that was probably closer to the left wing of Mackay's forces than the centre of the two armies.

The display at the National Trust for Scotland visitor centre in the gorge provides a good introduction for a visit to the actual site of the battle. The battlefield has been altered by the building of stone-walled enclosures and the planting of trees but it is still fairly open and it is not difficult to visualize the events of 1689. At that time the ground was probably more open than today, part farmland part moorland. If you walk up the farm track which leaves the old A9 road at grid reference 902636 the gradient eases off a little after the first climb from the river and you are on the sloping plateau where Mackay drew up his army. Looking up you can get a good idea of the slope down which the Highlanders charged. In a field south of Urrard House, close to the railway line, is Claverhouse's Stone, said to mark the place where Dundee was shot. It is a good way behind where Mackay is thought to have drawn up his troops and it is difficult to believe that his men were pushed back quite so far in the few minutes between the initial charge and Dundee's fall.

THE ATTACK ON DUNKELD

If Mackay failed dismally at Killiecrankie, his competence was more apparent in the aftermath of defeat. He concentrated his remaining forces at Stirling and immediately took the offensive once more. He pushed forward to Perth

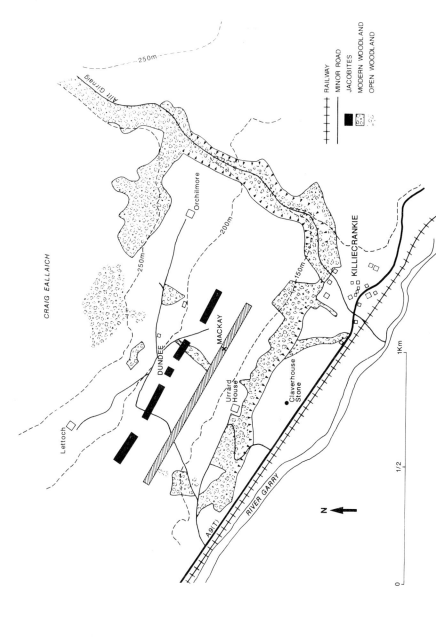

CRAIG EALLAICH

Allt Girnaig

250m

200m

250m

250m

Orchilmore

Lettoch

DUNDEE

MACKAY

Urrard House

Claverhouse Stone

150m

KILLIECRANKIE

RIVER GARRY

A9(T)

N

RAILWAY
MINOR ROAD
JACOBITES
MODERN WOODLAND
OPEN WOODLAND

0   1/2   1Km

Map 2 Killiecrankie: the battle, based on Mackay's description.

in time to cut off and disperse a party of Atholl men who had descended on the town seeking provisions. His positive action contrasted with the lacklustre performance of Dundee's successor.

Brigadier-General Cannon was a conventional soldier who lacked Dundee's drive or the personality to unite and control the clans. Within a few days of the battle reinforcements swelled the Jacobite army to around 5,000. A rapid advance towards Stirling and Edinburgh might have given them control of most of Scotland. Instead, Cannon turned eastwards through Strathmore and into Aberdeenshire to support the limited numbers of Jacobites who were in arms there. Mackay, with a small force of cavalry, followed him northwards, leaving enough infantry behind to guard access to the Lowlands. The clan chiefs soon became tired of Cannon's aimless progress and began to leave the army. Cannon needed to do something decisive before his army dispersed entirely and, hearing that forces were gathering in the lower Tay valley, he turned south again.

Mackay's officers at Perth had been contemplating an advance into Atholl to recapture Blair Castle. As part of their preparations they sent Angus' regiment, the Cameronians, forward to Dunkeld. Dunkeld was a small town beside the Tay, overlooked on all sides by hills. It was one of the market centres on the fringe of the Lowlands where Highlanders brought down their livestock to exchange for grain. It only had two or three hundred inhabitants in 1689 and is not much bigger today. But despite its small size Dunkeld was a place of some importance. Before the Reformation it had been the centre of a diocese, with a fine cathedral constructed between the fourteenth and sixteenth centuries. After the Reformation the cathedral had fallen into ruin but part of it was still used as the parish church. It was surrounded by the substantial stone houses which had accommodated the cathedral's clergy. A few years before the Revolution the Marquis of Atholl had commissioned the Scottish architect Sir William Bruce to design a mansion, Dunkeld House, which stood off the main street to the north of the cathedral. A view of Dunkeld at the end of the seventeenth century shows the cathedral and Dunkeld House dominating the skyline of the little town.

The Cameronians numbered only about 700-800 as there had been many desertions from the regiment. Those who remained, poorly equipped and without uniforms, contained a hard core of ultra-Presbyterian fanatics recruited from the Douglas estates in Clydesdale. They were almost on the point of mutiny though, grumbling that they had been moved forward into a dangerous position to get them out of the way. This may have been true; their religious extremism made the Cameronians a liability when they were quartered anywhere outside their home area. Other regiments might rape and pillage: the Cameronians preferred to assault the local clergy if their brand of religion was unacceptable! They even objected that some of their officers had

6 Dunkeld in the late seventeenth century; the little town is dominated by the cathedral and Dunkeld House, the main holding points during the siege.

been appointed not for the soundness of their religious doctrines but simply for their military experience.

They also complained that their young colonel had diverted funds for provisions and clothing for his own use. Whether this was true was never proved but nobody doubted William Cleland's bravery. Mackay described him as 'a sensible, resolute man though not much of a soldier'. This last comment may have been professional pique for Cleland had been prominent in the skirmish at Drumclog in 1679 when a gathering of armed Covenanters had routed a patrol of government dragoons commanded by John Graham of Claverhouse, later Viscount Dundee! Cleland may well have had misgivings about being sent forward without proper support but he ordered his men to dig in and fortify the town, most of whose inhabitants had, not surprisingly, fled.

The arrival of the Cameronians in Dunkeld prompted Jacobite supporters in Atholl to gather a body of men together. They marched on Dunkeld and began skirmishing with its defenders. It was with difficulty that Cleland persuaded his men to stay. Then Cannon arrived with the main Jacobite army. The Cameronians, short of ammunition, stripped the lead off the roof of Dunkeld House and melted it down to make musket balls. Their position, heavily outnumbered, was a bad one. It would have been even worse if the Jacobites had possessed proper artillery for they could have bombarded the town from the surrounding hills or used the guns at close range to smash the barricades. The three light cannon which had been captured at Killiecrankie were of little use.

The Jacobites surrounded the town and at 7 am Cannon began the attack from all sides, pushing Cleland's outposts back towards the main defences. The Highlanders advanced in their usual fashion; a single musket volley and then forward with their swords. This time, unlike Killiecrankie, they were facing a dour, dogged, and bloody-minded enemy who would give no quarter, and who had the advantage of fighting from behind prepared positions. The fight raged through the little town as the Highlanders, with heavy losses, forced the Cameronians back house by house. Cleland's men had no bayonets so they fought with pikes and clubbed muskets against the Highland broadswords while marksmen on both sides sniped from behind the cover of the houses.

After an hour or so the defenders had retreated to the centre of the town, holding only the cathedral, a few buildings around it, and Dunkeld House. Cleland was killed by a musket ball and his major was mortally wounded. As they retreated the Cameronians set fire to the houses they abandoned to deter the attackers and the Highlanders did the same to dislodge the snipers. Soon Dunkeld was in flames. After four hours of fighting the surviving Lowlanders were preparing for a desperate last stand inside Dunkeld House. The Jacobite attack had started to lose momentum though for the Highlanders did not care for this kind of fighting and many of them refused to continue. The

Cameronians seized the opportunity to repair their defences and braced themselves for a renewed assault. They were heartened by the arrival of a party of dragoons and this persuaded Cannon to give up the attack. Unlike Dundee he had commanded from the rear; a more enterprising general might have inspired his men to greater efforts or altered his plan of attack to suit changing circumstances, but Cannon had none of these qualities.

The modern layout of Dunkeld has not changed greatly from 1689 but the building of Telford's bridge over the Tay in 1809 has turned the busy route running north from it into the main street. The original axis of the town was at right angles to this, parallel with the river, and is now a quiet side street opening into a market place flanked by attractive houses which have been restored by the National Trust for Scotland. Most of these houses date from the end of the seventeenth century and were built to replace those burnt in the Jacobite attack. Beyond the market place and the tourist shops, the cathedral stands beside the river surrounded by lawns. Although the nave is ruined, the choir is still in use as a church and the chapter house is the burial place of the Atholl family. Dunkeld House has since been demolished and it is difficult to visualize, in this peaceful setting, the bitter struggle which took place here 300 years ago.

7 Some of the houses in Dunkeld built to replace those destroyed during the attack on the town. (Courtesy National Trust for Scotland)

THE HAUGHS OF CROMDALE

After the Jacobites' failure at Dunkeld morale was low. As it was harvest time, most of the clansmen dispersed and returned home to harvest their corn. Mackay advanced to Blair Castle and garrisoned it with 500 men. Cannon lay low in the Highlands consoling himself by drinking large quantities of his hosts' whisky. A good deal of small-scale raiding continued within the Highlands against clan chiefs and landowners who had not supported the Jacobites. Two raids in October 1689 had a bearing on future events in Glencoe. A detachment of the Jacobite army, including some of the Glencoe MacDonalds, burnt the Earl of Breadalbane's castle at Achallader, on the edge of Rannoch Moor. Later that month another raid was made on Glen Lyon. The installation of a small government garrison there at the Castle of Meggernie gave the Jacobites a pretext for the raid in which most of the inhabitants' livestock and moveables were carried off. Robert Campbell, laird of Glenlyon, already heavily in debt, was totally ruined.

The following spring Mackay began to prepare his expedition to Lochaber to establish a fort which would, he hoped, subdue the Lochaber clans which were the mainstay of Jacobite support in the Highlands. The Jacobite position in Ireland was improving as the English army, badly organized and supplied, was devastated by disease. There were hopes that James would be able to send substantial reinforcements to Scotland. Instead the Highlanders got Major-General Thomas Buchan, another unexceptional and uninspiring professional soldier. Yet again James had let his Scottish supporters down.

Mackay would have preferred to transport by sea the troops needed to build and garrison the new fort. The main advantage of Inverlochy was that it could be supplied by water. However, shortage of funds and the demands of the campaigns in Ireland and France prevented this so that Mackay was forced to march overland. Meanwhile Buchan was, with difficulty, raising a fresh army. Most Lowland Jacobites were reluctant to commit themselves until the Duke of Berwick landed with a substantial army. In the Highlands, shortage of food due to bad weather and the disruption caused by the previous year's fighting made it hard for Buchan and Cannon to raise and maintain more than a few hundred men at a time. With perhaps 1,500 men Buchan moved down the Spey valley trying to drum up further support. Sir Thomas Livingstone was garrisoning Inverness with a substantial force but Buchan does not seem to have been concerned by their proximity.

The Jacobites halted at Cromdale on the flat ground or 'haughs' beside the Spey. Here, the river sweeps round in a great curve. The modern hamlet of Cromdale, which stands beside the A95, has migrated nearly a kilometre from its original site beside the church in the bend of the river. The Jacobite camp was widely spread out with the main body of the army between the modern hamlet and the old castle of Lethendry. The remainder of the force was further north and closer to the river around Dallachapple. Scattering his

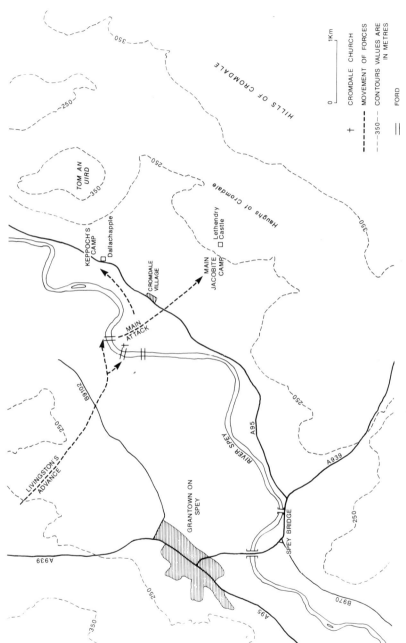

Map 3 The Haughs of Cromdale.

small army over such a wide area was a mistake that Buchan was later to regret.

MacDonald of Keppoch thought the camp too exposed and led his men to a site beyond Dallachapple at the foot of a steep hill, Tom an Uird, which rose straight from the river and offered a handy retreat if an attack were made. Buchan and Cannon considered the possibility of an attack from the west, across the river, but their preparations were inadequate. There were three fords across the Spey at Cromdale; at the church, and a short way up, and downstream. Small detachments of men were left to watch them and outposts were placed between the fords and the main camp. This was all very well if the Jacobites were attacked by infantry, but Buchan and Cannon seem to have overlooked the possibility that cavalry could cross the river and overwhelm the guards who, without any horses, would not have time to warn the main camp.

Livingstone, informed of the Jacobites' move down the Spey, marched from Inverness with a mixed force of infantry and cavalry. He came through the hills north of Grantown during the night without a clear idea of where the Jacobites had camped. He pushed on further than he had intended due to the lack of a suitable place to stop. It was only when he reached the tower of Ballachastel, scarcely a couple of miles from Buchan's camp, that he learned of their position. His men and horses were weary after their long march but at a brief council of war at 2 am all his officers favoured a surprise attack.

Livingstone realized that attacking with his fast-moving cavalry alone would give the element of surprise that he needed. Sending a small party as a diversion to harass the outpost by the ford at Cromdale Church, his horsemen crossed unopposed at the lower ford and swept on towards the main camp. Surprise was complete. There was no time for the clansmen to rouse themselves and form up before the horsemen were on them. Cromdale was not a battle; simply a rout. Those who could sought safety among the mist-covered slopes of the Hills of Cromdale to the south. Keppoch's choice of camp was vindicated for he led his men up the hill of Tom an Uird to safety without loss. Some 300-400 of the Jacobites were killed and over 100 captured. Although both Buchan and Cannon escaped, their army was dispersed. Cromdale was not the end of the first Jacobite campaign, but it was a decisive turning point, wrecking plans for that season's campaigning and undermining the chiefs' confidence in their commanders.

OUTPOSTS IN THE ISLES

Although much of the government's attention was focused on Lochaber, several of the clans in the Western Isles were also openly supporting James. In these remote areas they could defy the government almost with impunity.

If mainland castles like MacDonald of Glengarry's stronghold of Invergarry were difficult for William's forces to reach, those of the islands were almost inaccessible.

The Stewarts of Appin, on the mainland south of Glencoe, had regained from the Campbells their old fortress of Castle Stalker. Set picturesquely on a small island the tall sixteenth-century tower contrasts dramatically with the low, horizontal lines of the surrounding rocks. It has been restored in modern times and traces of the barmkin, or defensive wall, which originally enclosed it can also be seen.

The Macleans on the island of Mull had even stronger fortresses. The most important of these, at Duart, still the residence of the chief of the Macleans, was a small curtain-wall castle dating from the thirteenth century. At a later date a massive tower house had been added outside the limits of the medieval castle wall, and partly built into it. The tower stood at the edge of cliffs falling steeply to a rugged foreshore and had a well cut in solid rock. In the sixteenth and seventeenth centuries more spacious ranges of buildings were added within the courtyard encircled by the medieval curtain wall. Although the cliffs defended it on the seaward side, the landward approach was a gentle one and here a rock-cut ditch provided additional protection. Duart's position was a commanding one for it overlooked the Sound of Mull, as well as the approach up Loch Linnhe to Fort William. It had been taken by the Campbells in 1674 but the Macleans had later seized it back and it now formed the lynchpin of their defences around Mull.

If Duart was a tough nut to crack Cairnburgh Castle was even worse. Cairnburgh must be the most unusual and certainly the most remote Jacobite site in Britain. To reach it you need to have your own boat or else hire one from Oban, but if you are cruising in the waters around Mull it is a fascinating place to visit. Several kilometres west of Mull, and north west of Staffa with its famous Fingal's Cave, are a scatter of uninhabited rocky outcrops and reefs known as the Treshnish Islands. In good weather they are clearly visible, looking remote and mysterious, from the western shores of Mull. The most prominent island is the most southerly: Bac Mor, otherwise known as the Dutchman's Cap from its distinctive silhouette. At the northern end of the cluster are two small islands, Cairn na Burgh Mor and Cairn na Burgh Beg, surrounded by tide-washed rocks. These prevent large vessels from approaching closely and a landing can only be made, in calm conditions, from the narrow channel between the two islands. Even this can be tricky as there is a strong current there at certain states of the tide. Although the islands are well off the beaten track today they had tremendous strategic importance during the first Jacobite campaign as they commanded the main shipping route through the Western Isles.

Like the Dutchman's Cap on a smaller scale both islands have the same basic shape. From a low rocky foreshore a ring of basalt crags rises for up to

100 feet. These cliffs were once part of an ancient, much higher shoreline and they encircle small plateaus. On Cairn na Burgh Mor the plateau is cut in two by a huge gully and the larger part, some three and a half acres, was turned into a fortress by the Macleans of Duart simply by building rough stone walls to defend the few places where the cliffs were easily scaled. Cairnburgh Castle was the ultimate natural fortress. It could not be attacked from the sea for the cliffs were impervious to bombardment. It was extremely difficult to put a landing party on shore and, once there, they were faced with a wall of cliffs whose few weak points were well protected.

On top of the island only the remains of two roofless buildings are visible today. One is a fifteenth-century chapel and the other a two-storey barrack block dating from the late seventeenth or eighteenth century. If you are able to land on the island you will find a flight of rock-cut steps leading up through a cleft in the cliffs on the east side to a hidden gateway with the remains of a guardhouse at the top. The neighbouring island was also fortified as an annex of the main castle. Only a strong naval squadron could have made any impact on Cairnburgh and William was not prepared to spare the vessels required for an effective attack on it.

These remote sites held out against the government with impunity: Duart and Cairnburgh were not given up by Maclean of Duart until the summer of 1692. The strength of their positions, and the difficulty of trying to assault them, gave the Macleans a useful bargaining point in their negotiations for surrender. Their very existence emphasized how tenuous was government control in this area.

THE BUILDING OF FORT WILLIAM

Mackay marched into Lochaber with about 4,000 men. After Killiecrankie he was wary of being ambushed, and he took a roundabout route through the Angus glens to Braemar, Speyside, and Glen Spean before reaching Lochaber safely. Supplies had been brought to Inverlochy by government vessels and in two weeks of hectic work his men rebuilt the fort on the site Cromwell's men had used, renaming it Fort William. The strategic significance of Fort William is still evident today. All routes in the West Highlands seem to meet here and the site has grown into the largest settlement and traffic bottleneck north of Oban. Fort William is not an attractive town, although the setting by Loch Linnhe, overlooked by Ben Nevis, is magnificent. However, it preserves something of the atmosphere of an outpost in an alien environment which it certainly was in Jacobite times. The fort commanded the southern end of the Great Glen, the huge trench, excavated along a major geological fault, which runs south west from Inverness and cuts the Highlands in two. From it valleys radiated into the territories of the most troublesome of the

Lochaber clans including the Camerons, and the MacDonalds of Glengarry, Keppoch, and Glencoe.

The site of Mackay's fort should not be confused with that of old Inverlochy Castle which stands on the south shore of the River Lochy two kilometres from the centre of the town, or with the more recent Inverlochy Castle, a Victorian country house on the road to Spean Bridge. The fort was located opposite the modern pier, where the railway and bus stations and a car park now stand. The site was originally wet and boggy, overlooked by higher ground and with a poor water supply. If Mackay had not been in such a hurry he might have opted for a more suitable place but using the crumbling ramparts of Cromwell's old fort allowed him to finish the job quickly. The fort which Mackay built was only of earth and timber, defended by a dozen cannon requisitioned from his supply vessels. It was subsequently rebuilt more permanently and successfully withstood attacks during the 1715 and 1745 rebellions. After it went out of use as a military base it was acquired in 1855 by the West Highland Railway company who accommodated their navvies in the barracks and later demolished it. The only surviving part of the fort, the governor's room, was preserved and rebuilt in the West Highland Museum at Fort William where it can still be seen.

It can easily be imagined that Fort William was not a popular posting! The troops left to garrison it seem to have been continually on the verge of mutiny. This was partly because William's niggardly government left them perennially short of pay and supplies. The force of 1,200 which Mackay left behind him was reduced by a quarter within a few weeks by desertions. The fort was left in charge of Colonel John Hill. Hill had commanded the original fort in Cromwell's day and had been brought back out of retirement because he had been so successful then at dealing with the local chiefs. He had a better understanding of them and was more sympathetic to their way of life than most regular army officers.

The fiasco at Cromdale had not completely put paid to Buchan and Cannon's activities but with no prospect of reinforcements from Ireland, the Jacobites were reduced to small-scale, uncoordinated raiding. The Highlanders had not been defeated but the war had virtually fizzled out.

3

THE MASSACRE OF GLENCOE, 1692

THE VALLEY OF GLENCOE

If ever a valley deserved to be the scene of a massacre it is Glencoe. It has such a dark, brooding atmosphere that if violent events had not occurred there someone would surely have had to invent them! The Massacre of Glencoe is a popular myth of Scottish folk history like Bannockburn, Flodden, and Culloden. Many people, Scots included, believe that it was merely the result of a clan feud between the MacDonalds of Glencoe and the Campbells. The landlord of the Clachaig Hotel, near which stands the sign commemorating the supposed site of the massacre, used to keep this legend alive by refusing to serve drinks to anyone whom he knew to bear the surname Campbell! However, if the events of early 1692 had been solely due to clan hostility the affair would hardly be remembered today. The real story was far more complicated, sordid, and tragic.

The Glencoe MacDonalds were the smallest branch of the great Clan Donald. Normally they could raise only about 100 fighting men and the total population of Glencoe cannot have been more than 500 or so. The chiefs of Glencoe didn't live in a castle; merely an undefended house, larger and better furnished than any other in the glen but still primitive to a Lowland laird or an English gentleman. Nevertheless, despite the small size of the clan the MacDonalds of Glencoe had a reputation for raiding and cattle stealing out of all proportion to their numbers and their chief, MacIain, was an influential figure among the Lochaber clans. MacIain was in his middle sixties, still strong and active, well over six feet tall, the red hair of his youth turned to white. Although his lifestyle was primitive and his appearance barbaric, although to most people outside the Highlands and many within them he was a mere brigand, MacIain was not uneducated. As a young man he had been sent to France to broaden his experience. At home, however, he ruled as absolute monarch over his people and their valley.

The best introduction to Glencoe's history, geology, and wildlife is to visit the National Trust for Scotland visitor centre on the main road opposite the

38

Clachaig Hotel. The bookshop there stocks a number of accounts of the massacre, some more reliable than others. Afterwards it is worth climbing the rocky hill, Tom a Ghrianain or Signal Rock, which rises behind the Clachaig. Today its slopes are covered with forest but the summit is open. It provides the best viewpoint over the area where the massacre took place. It may well have been used as a lookout post in the past but the story that a bonfire was lit on the summit by Argyll's soldiers to signal the start of the massacre is probably untrue.

Glencoe's scenery is among the most impressive in the Highlands. From the head of the glen, where three streams meet and drop down to the level floor, scoured out by vanished glaciers, the view is dramatic. Three rocky ridges, the 'Three Sisters', dominate the valley. The nearest of them, the Gear Aonach, seems almost to overhang. The lower part of valley, for 3km or so from the sea at Loch Leven, is more open and fertile. The bulk of the population lived here in the past, scattered in small townships. Some, like Achnacon and Inverrigan, have vanished entirely. Others survive as single farms. Large stone-walled enclosures have replaced the small scattered plots of arable land on which oats and bere (a hardy form of barley) were grown. Today the lower part of the glen is sparsely settled and it is hard to visualize it as the home of several hundred people. MacIain's own house was at Carnoch, close to the sea. This was his winter residence; he also had a summer home, more simply built, whose foundations can still be seen high in Glen Leac na Muidhe, a side valley which joins the main glen opposite the Clachaig.

Even the lower part of the glen is enclosed by steep slopes but above the Clachaig it narrows between some of the most impressive peaks in Scotland. To the north the valley is dominated by the curving wall of the Aonach Eagach, the 'notched ridge', whose jagged crest, in places a knife-edge, is graded as a rock climb. The south side of the glen is more broken with a series of short, steep, tributary valleys separated by rocky ridges whose blunt ends tower above the valley. The ridges run back to the high peak of Bidean nam Bian, hidden from the valley. On calm days the mountains are mirrored in the waters of Loch Achtriochtan. A short distance up the valley from here is a farm of the same name. In 1692 this was the highest settlement in the glen.

The head of the glen, dominated by the rocky buttresses of Buchaille Etive Mor, the great shepherd of Etive, opens out on to Rannoch Moor. The moor is one of the bleakest places in the Central Highlands, a huge triangular waste of loch and peat which in 1692 formed a kind of no-man's land between Glencoe and the Campbell territories to the south. On the western side of Rannoch Moor the inhabitants of Glencoe had their shielings where they brought their cattle in summer to graze the high pastures. Like most Highlanders they depended mainly on livestock, especially cattle, for there was little arable land in Glencoe. However, cattle raiding could be more profitable than cattle raising. A side valley to the south of the glen, the Coire Gabhail, is known to modern climbers as the Hidden Valley. It has a level

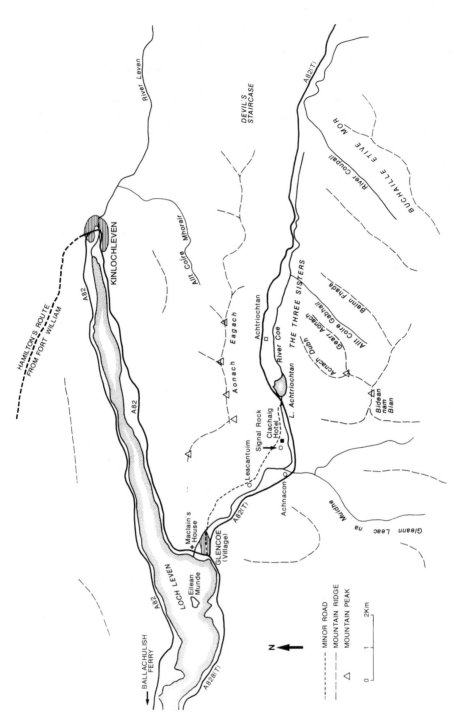

Map 4 The massacre of Glencoe.

section in its upper reaches, blocked off from the main valley by a huge rockfall. It was here, according to tradition, that stolen cattle were corralled by MacIain's people out of sight of prying eyes.

In summer, heavy with heat haze, the glen can be a peaceful place but more often the peaks are dark and threatening or hidden by swirling cloud, the black rocks slashed by white torrents and waterfalls. In winter conditions on the summits can be arctic. The glen could easily be turned into a trap as there were no easy passes southwards into Appin and Glen Etive or to the north.

The sign near the Clachaig commemorating the site of the massacre is misleading: it took place throughout the lower part of the glen, not at a particular spot. Nevertheless, the sign's location has prompted at least one American company making a film of the massacre to build their set, complete with wooden and cardboard cottages, in the middle of the area of bog between the sign and the river, a place where no one in their right minds would have chosen to live!

AN UNEASY TRUCE

After the rout at Cromdale the Jacobite campaign in the Highlands collapsed but a state of war still existed. The clans that had supported Dundee lacked the leadership and the resources to renew the conflict but were ready to rise again if James, or a suitable commander, should land with troops, provisions, and money. Meanwhile they carried on a good deal of small-scale raiding — just to keep their hand in! William, and his officials in London and Edinburgh, were running out of patience. The campaign against the French in the Low Countries was going badly and the continuing rebellion in Scotland was tying up valuable regiments. William wanted a quick end to the Highland war. Realizing that a major expedition to subdue the clans would be expensive, with success far from certain, he tried to negotiate with the chiefs for their peaceful submission.

This proved difficult for they considered themselves bound to continue fighting by the promises they had given to James. To encourage them to submit financial incentives were offered. The scheme involved giving them money to buy out the feudal superiorities over their lands so that they would hold their lands directly from the Crown rather than as vassals of the house of Argyll or other magnates. The existence of these conflicting superiorities was considered by many as one of the major sources of friction within the Highlands. The plan had originally been put forward by George Mackenzie, Viscount Tarbat, but the scheme was adopted and pushed by the Earl of Breadalbane who persuaded Queen Mary and then King William to give him a commission to negotiate with the chiefs.

Breadalbane, 'Grey John', was a Campbell and a slippery customer. Mackay called him 'one of the chiefest and cunningest fomenters of trouble (in Scotland)'. He wanted high political office but he also had ambitions to elevate his family to the leadership of Clan Campbell. He had already sent a report to William on the military strength of the Highlanders, suggesting that they should be recruited into the British army on a regular basis. He had grandiose plans for a 4,000-strong militia with himself (who else) in command, receiving a general's pay. The proposals were quietly shelved, partly because William's advisors distrusted Grey John, suspecting that any forces which he raised might be used as readily against the Crown as for it. It was an age of double dealing and Breadalbane, like many contemporaries, supported William but kept in touch with the Jacobites: just in case.

Breadalbane's military ambitions were never realized but they are strikingly commemorated in the landscape today. He had a house at Finlarig, beside Loch Tay, but his main stronghold was Kilchurn Castle, on a promontory sticking into Loch Awe in the shadow of Ben Cruachan. In Grey John's day the site was an island for the level of the loch has been lowered since then. The site is impressive, particularly when the dark waters of Loch Awe are calm and the mountains above are covered with snow. Commanding the routes through the gloomy pass of Brander to the west coast, south towards Inveraray and east towards Loch Lomond, the castle was already formidable. A five-storey tower house had been built in the fifteenth century with an attached barmkin or curtain wall protecting other buildings inside. Grey John improved and extended it by adding two four-storey barrack blocks which could accommodate some 200 men, the nucleus of his planned army. Seen from across the waters of Loch Awe these barracks with their large rectangular windows contrast with the blank walls of the earlier tower, pierced only with small openings. The modifications to Kilchurn were one of the last major schemes of private castle-building in Britain. It is a measure of how set Breadalbane was on his plan for a private army that he was prepared to risk having his fortress taken over as a government garrison by improving it in this way.

Although Breadalbane was distrusted by William's supporters and by the Jacobites, at least he was a Highlander and could speak to the chiefs in a language which they understood. His task was to persuade them to accept a ceasefire and take an oath of allegiance to William without compromising their honour. Offering money to buy out the superiorities rather than as a direct bribe was one means of doing this. After a preliminary meeting with some of the Jacobite chiefs at Kilchurn they all gathered in late June 1691 around his castle at Achallader, on the southern edge of Rannoch Moor.

Unlike Kilchurn, Achallader was merely a small tower house, a Campbell outpost on the edge of an area which was notorious as a refuge for thieves and robbers. It was, however, a convenient meeting place. It had been built by one of the Campbell lairds of Glenorchy in the sixteenth century to protect his lands and as a hunting lodge. At one stage, after Killiecrankie, the government considered garrisoning it. Breadalbane, who did not want government troops on his lands, had dissuaded them; it was not large enough to house an effective garrison he claimed. However, it proved too tempting a target to the MacDonalds of Keppoch and Glencoe on their way home after the attack on Dunkeld. They burnt it, probably on orders from Colonel Cannon. Today, the castle is badly ruined but the walls on the north and east sides survive almost to their full height. The windows, few, high up and very small, are replaced by pistol holes lower down. The entrance in the south wall was on the first floor for added security and the ground floor could only be reached from inside the tower. It was a stark, grim building, lacking in comfort, mirroring bleakly the surrounding landscape and the violence of contemporary Highland society.

The conference at Achallader must have been an impressive sight for each chief brought his 'tail' of followers to maintain his dignity and emphasize his power. In all several hundred Highlanders assembled there. Around the fire-blackened tower the clansmen camped while their leaders listened to Breadalbane's proposals. At the back of all his offers was the threat that unless a settlement could be negotiated, William would run out of patience and might unleash a full-scale campaign on the Highlands. Fort William had already been established and government frigates were cruising in the Minch. Some of the chiefs, notably Lochiel, were realistic and favoured peace under the right conditions.

During the conference Breadalbane seems to have isolated each chief in turn and persuaded them to agree to a ceasefire. One of the first, surprisingly enough, was the impetuous MacDonald of Keppoch but Breadalbane quarrelled violently with MacIain of Glencoe over some cattle stolen by a party of his men. MacIain left the conference in anger and foreboding. The sums which each leader was to receive as compensation were agreed and eventually on June 30th 1691 a treaty was signed. A three-month ceasefire was to operate during which messengers would be sent to James requesting that the chiefs be released from their obligations to him so that they could take the oath. The chiefs dispersed to their homes agreeing to live peacefully until the messengers returned. Breadalbane hurried to Flanders, where William was campaigning, to get his approval.

THE GOVERNMENT GETS TOUGHER

Breadalbane appeared to have been successful in his peace mission. Many people in William's government, Campbells and Lowlanders, resented this and wanted to take a tough line against the rebels. Some were jealous of Breadalbane or believed that he was in league with the Jacobites. Not without justification they thought that the chiefs were merely playing for time, making false promises, and that they would rise again if conditions were favourable. They considered that William, and his agent Grey John, were being too soft with them. In the months that followed the Scottish Privy Council, ignoring William's wishes, tried to undermine the truce.

Their most successful ploy was to discredit Breadalbane by producing forged sets of 'Private Articles' to which he had supposedly agreed in his bargaining with the chiefs. According to these the ceasefire was to be void if there was a Jacobite invasion or a rising in the Lowlands, if James objected to the terms offered, or if William shipped abroad the troops that he was using to keep the Highlanders in check. The final clause stated that if William did not approve the agreement Breadalbane himself would join the Jacobites with 1,000 men! The copies that were circulated were almost certainly forgeries. MacDonald of Glengarry, who was hostile to any settlement and who refused to attend the Achallader meeting, was thought to have produced them out of spite against Breadalbane but more recently suspicion has fallen on an agent of the Privy Council itself. Grey John strenuously denied the existence of any 'private articles' yet while the documents may have been forged it was probably true that he had come to some arrangement with the Jacobite chiefs. The Privy Council indignantly sent the copies of the articles to the King. William was philosophical about the accusations. He did not trust Breadalbane either but the man had done him a useful service. 'Men who manage treaties must give fair words' was his comment.

Due to delays caused by Breadalbane's journey to Flanders, the deadline was extended until the end of the year. In mid August William signed an order requiring all those who had been in arms against him to take an oath of allegiance by January 1st 1692. Meanwhile James hesitated over sending the message which would release the chiefs from their promises: the French might organize an invasion in which case he would need the clansmen once more. With the Treaty of Limerick, which was signed on October 3rd, the Jacobite campaign in Ireland finally ended and the Highland chiefs were dangerously isolated. While they delayed taking the oath to William and the Privy Council worked to wreck the ceasefire, opinion against them hardened.

From a conventional military standpoint the Highlanders were in a hopeless position. They were not capable of fighting yet had refused favourable terms of surrender. Not surprisingly politicians as well as soldiers wanted to take a strong line with them. The most influential man in Scottish affairs was Sir John Dalrymple, William's Secretary of State for Scotland. He was the son of Viscount Stair, one of Scotland's greatest legal minds, who had been driven into exile for his Whig politics by Claverhouse in the last years of Charles II's reign and who had returned with William. Dalrymple was almost as skilled a lawyer as his father but more ambitious and completely ruthless. As the year wore on he became more and more paranoid about the Highlanders' intransigence. Colonel Hill at Fort William continued to advise peaceful negotiation but the tide of opinion was turning against him.

Early in December James eventually consented to release the chiefs from their oaths. His two messengers left Dunkirk with barely a month to reach the Highlands and spread the news. They were delayed when their vessel was captured by an English warship off Dover and they were then detained in London before one of them was allowed to continue to Scotland. James' message barely reached Lochaber in time and it is likely that some of the chiefs who took the oath at the last minute had not received confirmation that James' message had arrived. With barely enough time left to submit they suddenly seem to have realized how tough-minded the government had become. Plans for a winter campaign in Lochaber, including besieging Invergarry Castle, were under way and news of the associated troop movements may have convinced the chiefs that the government meant business. In the last days of December Lochiel hurried to Inveraray to take the oath before the sheriff there, while Keppoch went to Inverness. Even the incorrigible Glengarry sent a message to Colonel Hill at Fort William saying that he was prepared to surrender himself and his castle at Invergarry provided that the government would allow Buchan, Cannon, and a score of their followers, who were staying with him, to travel to France. His conditional offer also included the MacDonalds of Keppoch and Glencoe, though this was unknown to them at the time.

MACIAIN'S DESPERATE JOURNEY

MacIain, chief of the Glencoe MacDonalds, left it to the very last minute, presenting himself at Fort William, according to different accounts, on the night of December 30th or on the following day. Unfortunately, Hill was not authorized to administer the oath. It had to be taken before the sheriff of Argyll, Campbell of Ardkinglas, at Inveraray. MacIain may have been ignorant of this; after all, Hill had earlier given letters of protection to a number of clansmen including the tacksman of Achtriachtan in Glencoe, MacIain's own kinsman. It is equally possible that he knew perfectly well where to go but could not face taking the oath before a Campbell at their capital of Inveraray, where Argyll had once had him imprisoned. In either event it was a dangerous mistake. Hill must have given him an indication of the dim view which the government would take of anyone who failed to take the oath in time. He gave the now thoroughly rattled MacIain a covering letter and the chief hastened southwards through a blizzard on the long journey to Inveraray.

He had some sixty miles of rugged country to cross; down the coast of Appin, round or across Loch Creran, over Loch Etive, through the Pass of Brander, around the head of Loch Awe, and then across the hills to Loch Fyne. Even if he had arrived at Fort William on the 30th, there was little hope of reaching Inveraray before New Year. Fate worked against him though. By Loch Creran his party met some soldiers of the grenadier company of Argyll's regiment, the advance guard of a larger force heading north for Fort William. Suspicious of them, they took MacIain and his men to their captain, Robert Drummond, who was temporarily quartered nearby at Barcaldine Castle. Drummond was not impressed when the chief showed him Hill's letter and he held MacIain and his party for twenty-four hours, presumably out of sheer spite. Once released, MacIain struggled on southwards, probably with mounting anxiety, but he did not reach Inveraray until the 2nd or 3rd of January. Then he discovered that Ardkinglas, the sheriff, had returned home across Loch Fyne to spend New Year with his family. He would not be back until the weather improved.

MacIain and his men had to wait anxiously at their inn until the 5th of January when Ardkinglas returned. At first he refused to administer the oath as the deadline had passed. He was not being hard-hearted — his subsequent letters on MacIain's behalf show him to have been a fair man. He was probably concerned about possible repercussions; he might be accused of leniency to a notorious rebel and in the current climate of opinion he might lose his office. The old man had to forfeit all his pride and, with tears in his eyes, plead with the sheriff for the safety of his people. In the face of this Ardkinglas, himself a Highlander, relented and let MacIain take the oath on the following day, January 6th.

PRELUDE TO THE MASSACRE

Ardkinglas sent the certificate with MacIain's signature on it to Colin Campbell, his sheriff clerk in Edinburgh, along with the letter from Hill and a covering note of his own explaining the circumstances. He then wrote to Hill saying that he had administered the oath to the chief of Glencoe, asking Hill to ensure that the MacDonalds were protected from harm until the Privy Council decided whether or not to accept their chief's submission. Campbell presented a certificate with the signatures of those who had taken the oath at Inveraray to the two Clerks to the Privy Council. They refused to accept it with MacIain's name included because he had missed the deadline. Instead of laying all the facts before the Privy Council, Campbell privately sought the opinions of a fellow advocate, John Campbell, and some members of the Council, including Lord Ab-eruchill (another Campbell) and Viscount Stair, Dalrymple's father. The consensus was that it would be inadvisable to give in either the certificate with MacIain's name on or the additional correspondence. MacIain's signature was, accordingly, struck off.

This has sometimes been interpreted as a Campbell plot against the Glencoe men. Colin Campbell, among others, had suffered from their cattle-raiding in the past. It is more likely, however, that given the hardening of opinion within the government none of the people concerned was prepared to risk their careers by pleading MacIain's case too forcefully. Campbell and his brother Ardkinglas were treading warily as there had been previous complaints that they had exceeded their authority in official matters and they probably decided that it would be safer not to take a stand on this issue.

Even if MacIain's case had been put to the Council it might not have affected the outcome for by this time Dalrymple had determined on some violent action. His orders to the military in Scotland by-passed the Privy Council entirely. In early January, before he knew for certain which chiefs had taken the oath at the last moment, he sent orders to Sir Thomas Livingstone, the victor of Cromdale, who had replaced Mackay as commander-in-chief in Scotland, for an attack on the rebel clans 'with fire and sword'. The main thrust was to be against Invergarry Castle though Appin and Glencoe were also mentioned. The winter weather would, Dalrymple hoped, keep the clans trapped in the valleys and prevent them from scattering to the mountains when attacked. A war was still in progress in the Highlands after all and it was not unexpected that the government should take extreme measures against any clans whose leaders had failed to submit.

Dalrymple seems to have directed his attention specifically towards the Glencoe MacDonalds from January 11th. It has often been suggested that his enmity against them was aroused because as well as being notorious robbers they were also Catholics. The evidence for this is far from conclusive but Dalrymple certainly believed that they were Papists. It is more likely though that he singled the clan out for special attention because it was small and readily accessible from Fort William. In the middle of writing orders for Livingstone the Earl of Argyll called on him with the news that MacIain's signature had not been on the list of those who had submitted at Inveraray. Believing that MacIain had not taken the oath at all Dalrymple added a postscript to the orders recommending that the Glencoe MacDonalds should be 'rooted out' if possible. He added, however, that all those who had taken the oath should be protected.

Dalrymple had met both Argyll and Breadalbane in the first days of January and the two Campbells have been accused of master-minding the plot to slaughter the inhabitants of Glencoe. Even more cynically it has been suggested that when he met Dalrymple on the 11th, Argyll knew that MacIain had taken the oath and that either he did not tell Dalrymple or the Secretary of State deliberately ignored the news. If MacIain had taken the oath on January 6th, however, it is unlikely that the news could have reached Argyll in London by the 11th.

Dalrymple was still primarily concerned with operations against Glengarry but by the middle of the month he had been told of Glengarry's conditional offer of surrender. Because he, his clansmen, and his stronghold at Invergarry were such a tough nut to crack, the government was prepared to negotiate with him in a way in which they would not have done with a smaller, less powerful, more accessible clan like the Glencoe MacDonalds. Dalrymple also seems to have been increasingly aware of the folly of a winter campaign against Invergarry, and Hill at Fort William was given wide powers to negotiate with the chief of Glengarry. Baulked of his prey, Dalrymple turned towards Glencoe once more. The same orders which gave Hill powers to negotiate with Glengarry contained instructions that if MacIain's people could be isolated they should be 'extirpated'. The orders were signed by King William himself; twice rather than once which was usual practice.

Historians have tried to exonerate William from complicity in the massacre by claiming either that he signed the orders without reading them, or that he misinterpreted them and did not understand the significance of 'extirpate'. Admittedly he was a poor administrator and Scottish business was not one of his priorities but as the orders concerned troop movements it seems unlikely that he would not have given them some attention. It is more probable that he approved in outline the scheme for punitive action. William was a professional soldier and used to the brutality of large-scale Continental campaigns. He was perfectly capable of being tough-minded and there is no reason to believe that he was not fully aware of the meaning of the orders.

The orders which William signed and Dalrymple sent to Scotland were nevertheless conditional. The main object was still to negotiate with Glengarry. However, the private covering letters which Dalrymple sent with them placed more emphasis on a punitive expedition against Glencoe and this may have given the military command in Scotland the idea that this was the real priority. Livingstone, who seems to have hated the Highlanders as much as Dalrymple did, could easily have modified the orders, especially as Hill had sent him the full details of MacIain's case. However, Livingstone wrote back to Fort William on January 23rd saying that MacIain's belated oath had not been accepted, and that a raid on the glen would give the garrison a chance to prove its worth. Significantly though, he addressed the letter not to Hill but to Lieutenant Colonel Hamilton, his deputy. Both Livingstone and Dalrymple were convinced that Hill was too sympathetic to the Highlanders and would not carry out the orders without prompting. Threatening to undermine his position by dealing with his ambitious deputy was an effective way of unsettling the old man.

Hill was in a difficult position. The planned action against Glencoe, however it was done, would be unjust at best and at worst an atrocity. Hill had little room for manoeuvre though. He was old and financially insecure with two unmarried daughters to support. To take any action which breached his orders might well have resulted in him being dismissed. In such an unenviable position many men would have sat silent, as he did, with a troubled conscience but taking no positive action to alter the course of events. All he could do was to try and delay matters hoping that Dalrymple, receiving more information on conditions in Lochaber, would appreciate how unnecessary action against Glencoe was. The orders to carry out the attack required Hill's signature: there was no way in which he could escape involvement. At the same time he distanced himself as far as possible by drafting orders which were vague and generalized, leaving Hamilton to work out the details.

SLAUGHTER UNDER TRUST

It was almost certainly Hamilton, an outsider with little sympathy for the Highlanders, who conceived the idea of quartering troops in Glencoe and then setting them to attack their hosts. The reasons for this appalling breach of the Highland traditions of hospitality were practical enough. Any troops marching from Fort William towards Glencoe would be spotted and the alarm would be raised before they could reach the valley. If they were already on the spot the MacDonalds could be caught by surprise. Hamilton seems to have confided details of the plan to Major Duncanson who commanded the seven companies of Argyll's regiment which had been sent north as part of the force to attack Invergarry. Together they had to pick a man who was sufficiently unscrupulous or desperate to obey their orders — someone who could take the blame if things went wrong.

They chose Captain Robert Campbell of Glen Lyon, commander of one of Argyll's companies. Glenlyon, nearly sixty, was a rather pathetic figure. A notorious drunk and gambler, he had frittered away his family's lands in Glen Lyon piece by piece until he was bankrupted several times over. He and his family were already in dire straits in 1689 when the Glencoe MacDonalds and other clansmen raided Glen Lyon and stripped the valley from end to end, ravaging the few lands left to Robert Campbell by his creditors, driving off his livestock and plundering his house. Glenlyon and his family had nearly starved during the following winter. Desperate for even a pittance to keep body and soul together he had taken a captain's commission in Argyll's newly-raised regiment at an advanced age. Hamilton and Duncanson could have chosen other captains from among Argyll's men who had grudges against the Glencoe men, but not one half as desperate.

Superficially one might think that the choice of such a man to command a force billeted in the glen would have aroused the inhabitants' suspicions. However, Glenlyon was bound to MacIain by ties of kinship. His niece had married one of MacIain's sons and it may have been thought that this blood tie would allay the MacDonalds' fears. Glenlyon was given orders to take his own and Drummond's company to Glencoe and await further instructions. It is clear that at this stage he had no idea of what he would be required to do. Had he been privy to the plan it is doubtful if he could have been hypocritical enough to have brazened it out — or else he might have let slip some warning when drunk.

On February 1st the two companies of soldiers were ferried across the narrows of Loch Leven at Ballachulish and then marched towards Glencoe. They were met by one of MacIain's sons with a party of men. When Glenlyon was asked what their business was in the valley he replied that they had been sent to be quartered there for a few days. There was no room in the fort for them, he said, with the concentration of troops being prepared to move against Glengarry. MacIain seems to have accepted Glenlyon's friendly assurances. Ironically the only measure that he took to ensure the clan's safety was to order his men to hide their weapons well away from their homes in case an attempt was made to confiscate them.

For nearly two weeks the soldiers stayed in the glen, scattered in small groups among the various townships. Glenlyon lodged not with MacIain himself but with one of his tacksmen, MacDonald of Inverrigan. During the day the troops drilled and exercised while at night they sat around the peat fires with their hosts, drinking and telling stories. Glenlyon spent a good deal of time gambling and drinking with Inverrigan, and he dined with MacIain on several occasions. Hamilton's original plan had probably been to order the massacre within a couple of days of the soldiers' arrival. The delay was caused by Hill, desperately hoping for fresh orders from the south, hesitating to sign the crucial order. By the 12th of February Hill had received a final sharp letter from Dalrymple and he had to act or risk dire consequences. Reluctantly he signed the order giving Hamilton the go ahead.

Hamilton then sent orders to Duncanson whose men were camped at Ballachulish. He in turn sent a message to Glenlyon. Hamilton had ordered Duncanson to attack at 7am the next morning emphasizing that neither MacIain or his sons should escape and that nobody under seventy should be spared. Duncanson was to march from Ballachulish and seal off the mouth of the glen. Hamilton himself would lead a party of 400 from Fort William, leaving the fort under cover of darkness to prevent their movements being spotted. Historians have disputed whether Hamilton merely planned to attack the settlements at the head of Loch Leven or whether he intended to skirt the northern side of the Aonach Eagach, cross the hills by the Devil's Staircase, the pass over which the military road was later built (Map 4), and come down to the head of Glencoe to block escape to the east. In any case Glenlyon was ordered to post men to cover the passes leading out of Glencoe.

Transmitted by Duncanson, the final message, cold blooded and ruthless, has become notorious. It began: 'You are hereby ordered to fall upon the MacDonalds of Glencoe and to put all to the sword under 70. You are to have a special care that the old fox [MacIain] and his sons do upon no account escape your hands.' The orders to Glenlyon were heavy with threats of what would happen if he did not comply. If he failed to do his duty he could 'expect to be treated as not true to the King or government, nor a man fit to carry a commission in the King's service'. In effect he would be cashiered.

Duncanson made it clear that the operation had been approved at the highest level; in theory this would absolve Glenlyon from all responsibility. If protests were made afterwards he could plead that he was only carrying out orders, as Hill and other higher-ranking officers were to do in their turn at the inquiry. Whether it was a difficult decision for Glenlyon to take is uncertain; possibly not for, once committed, he put on a bluff facade to keep his victims from suspecting anything. In reality he was being set up. Hamilton's orders to Duncanson had mentioned a 7am start; Duncanson's message to Glenlyon required him to begin the killing at 5am and not to wait for reinforcements. The most convincing explanation is that Glenlyon's superiors were covering themselves by ensuring that the dirty work would be done by the soldiers already in the glen and that the killing would be over by the time they arrived.

In the event the plan was completely botched. Most of the soldiers were only warned just before 5am. Glenlyon mustered his men at Inverrigan, in the dark and in the middle of a snowstorm, to give them their orders. He then sent them back in groups to the individual settlements to await the appointed time. This certainly gave some of the MacDonalds a warning. Glenlyon told his host that they were preparing to leave and march against Glengarry but some of the glen's inhabitants were suspicious. There are plenty of traditions of warnings given by the men of Argyll's regiment to their hosts that danger was threatening them. Many of these tales can have little foundation: there was little time for warnings to be given. However, many of Glenlyon's men appear to have been horrified at what they were required to do and to have carried out their work at best half-heartedly, turning a blind eye to escaping clansmen and their families. The use of firearms rather than swords and bayonets to kill the first victims also warned many of the people in the outlying townships, giving them time to take to the mountainsides. Moreover, Glenlyon failed to post men to guard the passes out of the glen to the south.

At the settlements where Glenlyon, his officers, and his sergeants were in command, many of the inhabitants, including women and children, were shot or cut down in cold blood. At Inverrigan Glenlyon had the inhabitants bound, taken outside, and shot, he himself finishing off the victims with a bayonet. Afterwards he seems to have been overcome by remorse, and tried to spare the lives of a young man and a boy. Drummond, the other company commander who had brought the fatal orders from Duncanson, was more hard-hearted and had them shot. MacIain himself, that redoubtable old warrior, died without glory, shot by Lieutenant Lindsay and his men in the act of getting dressed to see, as he thought, his guests' departure. His wife was stripped naked and robbed of her rings; she was later to die of shock and exposure.

The daring escapes of individual MacDonalds, some of them wounded, have passed into tradition. Overall about thirty-six people seem to have been

8 The steep slopes of Glencoe; a refuge but also a trap to the unsuspecting MacDonalds. (Courtesy National Trust for Scotland)

9 The River Coe and the National Trust for Scotland Visitor Centre. (Courtesy National Trust for Scotland)

killed by the soldiers. It was fairly easy for many of the glen's inhabitants to escape to the mountainsides for Glenlyon did not follow them and the blizzard rapidly hid them from sight. Fearing further pursuit, however, most of them, including MacIain's two sons, scrambled up through the snowy passes leading south towards Appin. An unknown number died of exposure on the way. Predictably, Duncanson arrived when the slaughter was over, while Glenlyon's men were rounding up the livestock and burning the houses. One contemporary account claimed that 900 cattle, 200 horses, as well as many sheep and goats were driven to Fort William and there sold cheaply.

Hamilton arrived even later. His excuse was a reasonable one. He had much further to march than Duncanson and over rougher ground. Halted by the driving snow only a short way south of Fort William his men had been forced to camp for the night. They moved on at first light, but warning of their approach went before them. The account of Hamilton's movements is vague and it is unclear whether or not he crossed the hills to the head of Glencoe. If he had done so, weather conditions over the Devil's Staircase, in the teeth of a blizzard, must have been grim. By the time that they arrived, whether at Kinlochleven or the head of Glencoe, it was mid-morning and most of the inhabitants had fled. Their sole contribution to the day's atrocities was to kill a helpless old man. They burnt the houses, drove off the livestock, and returned to the fort.

THE AFTERMATH: REACTION AND REVULSION

The massacre had fallen short of Dalrymple's intention of wiping out the Glencoe MacDonalds. Only a small proportion of the clan's fighting men had been killed. Including those who died of exposure no more than 50-60 out of a total population of around 500 had perished. In the long term it neither destroyed them as a clan nor curbed their Jacobite leanings. They played an active part in both the 1715 and 1745 rebellions. This continuity is evident if you visit the small island of Eilean Munde in Loch Leven off Ballachulish. MacIain was laid to rest in the burial ground of the MacDonalds of Glencoe at the eastern end of the island. Within the small enclosure is a triangular stone pediment dated 1706. It came from the house of MacIain's eldest son, who rebuilt it on the site of his father's ruined home. At the opposite end of the island are the ruins of a small, simple medieval chapel and in its burial ground is a fine tombstone showing a Highlander cutting down a dragoon on horseback. It commemorates the feats of one of a later generation of local Jacobites at Prestonpans in 1745.

In the short term, however, the loss of their livestock and homes brought the people of Glencoe to the edge of starvation. The government's brutal action destroyed its credibility in the Highlands making those who had been at Achallader cynical. They saw Breadalbane's negotiations as having been insincere from the start. Breadalbane lost most credit in the aftermath of the massacre and the more he protested that he had not been involved in planning it the less anyone believed him.

The earliest accounts of the massacre to reach the outside world were brief and inaccurate, suggesting that the Glencoe men had been caught in an ambush. The horrifying details gradually leaked out and copies of the incriminating military orders began to circulate. It was excellent propaganda for the Jacobites who seized upon it with glee. By mid-April a proclamation by James, who was at La Hogue with a planned French invasion force, specifically excluded Duncanson and Glenlyon from any amnesty. Pressure for an investigation mounted. In part this was from a genuine desire to bring the murky events of the winter of 1691-2 out into the open. Also, both Dalrymple and Breadalbane had political enemies for whom an inquiry into the massacre was an ideal weapon. The only problem was how to get at them without implicating the King himself! The Scottish Parliament, increasingly annoyed at William's lack of interest in Scotland other than as a source of men and money for his campaigns against France, threatened to appoint a commission to examine the events and William was forced to forestall them and set up one of his own.

Colonel Hill and Hamilton, his deputy, were summoned to appear before the Commission; the latter refused but Hill told his version of the story with calm dignity. Sir Thomas Livingstone was also examined, as were Ardkinglas and the clerks of the Privy Council who had objected to MacIain's signature being accepted. Ten Glencoe men, including MacIain's sons, also gave evidence. It was unfortunate, however, that Glenlyon, his officers, and men, were in Flanders on active service and were not available to testify.

The outcome of the Commission's deliberations was predictable in part. William was absolved from having had any hand in the Glencoe affair. A scapegoat was needed though. With so many enemies, it was hardly surprising that Dalrymple was blamed for exceeding his orders. Livingstone was cleared, which was surprising considering that he had admitted in one of his letters that he knew MacIain had taken the oath. Hill had not told the whole truth about this and it is possible that a deal had been arranged which would clear both Hill and Livingstone. In some ways the Commission's examination of the evidence was one-sided and erratic. It suited them to believe in a plot and they concluded that the matter of the removal of MacIain's signature from the papers presented to the Privy Council was the result of malicious designs against the Glencoe men by a group of Campbells.

The Scottish Parliament immediately demanded a copy of the Commission's report. They debated it enthusiastically and re-examined the evidence for themselves. Their own conclusions were more emphatic than those of William's commissioners. The killing of the Glencoe men had been unlawful murder, they concluded. William was blameless (of course!) as was Livingstone whom they mistakenly believed to have been unaware of MacIain's submission. Hill was also cleared. The blame was placed on Dalrymple for exceeding his orders and initiating the chain of events. Parliament concluded that he had known full well that MacIain had taken the oath and had initiated the massacre in spite of it. As we have seen this may have been untrue. Blame also fell on the junior officers — Hamilton, Duncanson, Glenlyon and his subordinates — who had carried out the orders and moves were made to prosecute them. Parliament even arrested Breadalbane for the matter of the 'Private Articles' and he was imprisoned in Edinburgh Castle.

William was annoyed at the Scottish Parliament's temerity in arresting Breadalbane although he was slow to have him released. He was more concerned with conducting the war against France than with defending his own servants. After some months in prison Grey John was set free, suitably frightened. He retired to his estates and kept a low profile thereafter. If the Scottish Parliament had shown unusual independence in their deliberations, the limitations of this short-lived freedom — extinguished within a few years by the union of the Scottish and English parliaments — was demonstrated by the fact that nobody was ever prosecuted for the massacre. William publicly defended Dalrymple's conduct but pressure of opinion forced the Secretary of State to retire from public office a few months later. He remained in the political wilderness until after William's death. His successor, Queen Anne, brought him back to the forefront of politics and he took a leading part in pushing through the Union of England and Scotland in 1707. The strain of this proved to be too much and he died suddenly in the middle of his labours.

Meanwhile the Highlands were at peace. All troops apart from Hill's regiment were withdrawn. The dislocation caused by the earlier campaigns, a heavy burden of taxation, and the example of what had happened in Glencoe kept the chiefs quiet and inactive. However, as several politicians realized, a successful French invasion in the summer of 1692 might have changed the situation overnight. Many of the chiefs who had submitted to William would probably have renounced their allegiance a few months later if a suitable opportunity for action had arisen. Although in the Highlands large-scale raiding had almost ceased, a plague of small-scale robbery and cattle stealing showed how impoverished the area had become. Quiet the Highlands may have been; pacified they were not.

THE SIEGE OF THE BASS ROCK

The last episode in the Jacobite struggle against William took place not in the Highlands but in a much more unlikely location, off the coast of East Lothian. The Bass Rock is an impressively steep plug of volcanic lava offshore from North Berwick. In the seventeenth century it was a notable attraction for curious travellers, mainly because of its colony of gannets, large black and white seabirds with an angry, predatory appearance. Thousands of them still nest on ledges and on the sloping summit of the island. In summer they wheel around the rock like a snowstorm, plunging vertically into the sea to catch fish. They were eaten as a local speciality. 'A most delicate fowle' wrote John Taylor, the Water Poet, though he admitted that roast gannet went down best when followed quickly by two or three glasses of sherry or canary sack! There had been a castle on the island in late medieval times, belonging to a local family, but in 1671 the government acquired it for use as a state prison. A number of ultra-Protestant covenanting ministers were incarcerated here during Charles II's reign, a bleak and rather smelly existence among the gannets for both them and their jailors.

In 1689 the governor held the castle for King James but, lacking supplies, he was forced to hand it over in 1690. After the rout at Cromdale the Bass was used as a prison for some of the captured Jacobite officers. The rock is sheer on all sides save the one facing North Berwick and even here the rocks drop steeply to the only landing place, immediately below the castle. Trips around the rock can be made in summer from North Berwick and from a small boat the fortress-like appearance of the rock is especially impressive. Landing on the Bass is still difficult today and even when the sea is calm the scramble on to the rocks can be awkward. The lighthouse keepers whose quarters occupy the site of the prison governor's house are sometimes forced to remain on the island for an extra day or two when due to go on leave if there is a heavy swell running.

The Jacobite prisoners noted that when supply vessels called most of the garrison had to help land the provisions. It happened that on one occasion a boat arrived with a load of coal when the governor and many of the guards were on the mainland. Every remaining soldier had to scramble down to the sea to land the coal. The prisoners, possibly helped by a sympathizer among the garrison, seized the opportunity to shut the gates on the guards and train one of the castle's guns on them. Completely overlooked by the ramparts they had no option but to retreat to North Berwick.

The four Jacobites were joined by a boatload of sympathizers but at no time did the defenders number more than about twenty. Despite this they held out for nearly three years defying all attempts by William's forces to dislodge them. The French government helped by sending a frigate with provisions for them, and a boat mounting two small cannon. Using this they led a semi-piratical existence, rowing ashore to the mainland for quick night forays and intercepting coasters which sailed too close to the island. So successful were they that at one time the supply of grain to Edinburgh was threatened. All attempts to attack them failed despite the fact that the castle was not particularly strong. As the contemporary sketch (Plate 10) shows, it consisted merely of a curtain wall crossing the south side of the island with small batteries for cannon at either end. Today the eastern end of the castle has been altered by the construction of the lighthouse and its associated buildings but the crumbling remains of the western end are still quite well preserved. Nevertheless, a landing could only be made by a few men at a time right

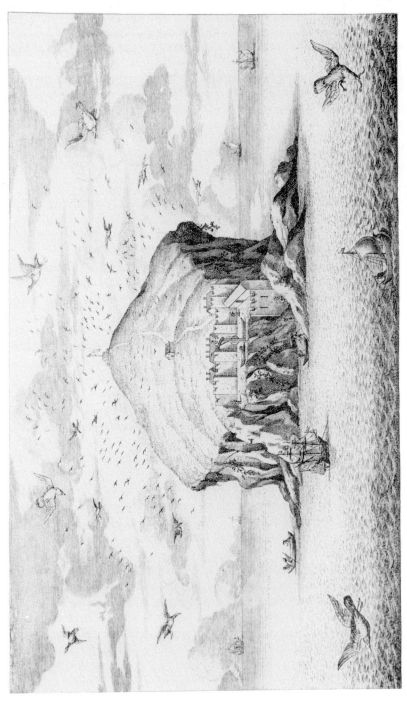

10 The Bass Rock around the time of the siege, showing the difficult landing place under the guns of the castle.

under the castle's guns and a direct assault never seems to have been tried. Two government warships bombarded the castle but to no effect, while the castle guns damaged their rigging so badly that they were forced to sail off for a refit. After this ships were used to blockade the island and this curtailed the garrison's raiding activities.

On one occasion a man called Trotter was caught running provisions out to the Jacobites. He was ordered to be hanged on the shore in sight of the rebels. When this was tried a cannon shot from the Bass broke up the party and the hanging was quickly moved out of range! The garrison eventually capitulated when they ran out of food but even then they surrendered in style. They invited the commissioners who were negotiating the surrender out to the island for talks and entertained them lavishly with most of their remaining food. By this ruse they convinced their guests that they could hold out indefinitely and as a result they were allowed to surrender on the most favourable of terms which allowed them to sail off to France with their arrears of pay provided by William's government!

4

UNION, UNREST, AND THE HOUSE OF
HANOVER

THE COURT IN EXILE

In his later years James became increasingly introverted and concerned mainly
with religion although he still indulged in his favourite sport of hunting as
late as 1699, when he was sixty-six. He never seems to have recovered from
the collapse which he suffered in 1688. He lost all determination to recover
his throne and was quite content to live quietly in France as a pensioner of
Louis XIV. In 1701 he had a stroke and died three weeks later leaving his
son, James Francis Edward Stuart, to head the Jacobite cause. Known as the
Chevalier de St George in France, James Francis Edward has gone down in
British history as the 'Old Pretender' to distinguish him from his son, Charles
Edward Stuart, the 'Young Pretender'. This designation is misleading as it
makes him seem prematurely old; it is important to remember that he was
only thirteen when his father died. He was still a young man when efforts
were made to restore him in 1708, 1715, and 1719.

James grew up at St Germain in an atmosphere of piety, austerity, gloom,
and frustrated hopes. He inherited a rigid series of rules which his father had
prescribed for his education and an ill-assorted group of advisors and
hangers-on. Growing up under these circumstances it is not surprising that he
inherited his father's inability to judge people and his tendency to place faith
in unsuitable counsellors. It is, indeed, remarkable that he turned out as well
as he did. With the right luck, the right decisions, and proper support he
might have made a reasonable monarch. He could hardly have been less
endearing than the first Hanoverian king of Britain, George I! In his teens
James had served with the French army in its campaigns against Marlborough. He fought with some distinction in the grim slaughter of Malplaquet,
where he had been wounded in the arm during a charge. Despite this he
seems to have inherited little of his father's military flair. While pleasant
enough in many ways he lacked the ability to inspire his followers. Although
he lived to the age of seventy-eight, dying in 1766 when the Jacobite cause
had long since perished, his health was always precarious and apt to let him
down at critical moments.

60

'BOUGHT AND SOLD FOR ENGLISH GOLD'

There had been intermittent pressure for a full union of Scotland with England ever since James VI of Scotland had succeeded Elizabeth I of England in 1603. Since then Scotland had remained nominally independent although in practice English influence had been paramount in determining matters such as foreign policy. The need for some kind of closer link became more urgent in the early years of the eighteenth century as the split between Scottish and English interests widened. William's intervention in Continental wars demonstrated his lack of concern for the interests of his northern kingdom. Higher taxation to pay for the enlarged army and navy had affected almost everyone in Scotland. War with France had severed links with one of Scotland's major trading partners. Moreover, it had brought swarms of French privateers down to prey on unprotected shipping in Scottish coastal waters. As if this were not enough, the start of the new century saw the disastrous collapse of the Darien Scheme, the ill-advised Scottish colonial venture in Central America, in which many nobles as well as large numbers of lesser people, had invested money. Resentment against the English who, fearful of a possible challenge to their own trading monopolies, had obstructed the Scheme, ran high.

Over the same period the Scottish Parliament was enjoying, and exploiting, a greater degree of independence than it had known hitherto, and it obstructed William on a number of occasions. One possible solution to the deteriorating relations between the two countries was separation. This England would not countenance, however, for under such circumstances the Scots would almost certainly have offered the crown to James Francis Edward, the Old Pretender. Such a situation would have been of little benefit to Scotland as war with England would have been the almost inevitable result, seeing that James was unlikely to give up his claim to the throne of that country.

The crisis eventually revolved around the the question of the Hanoverian succession. William died in March 1702, only six months after his father-in-law, and was succeeded by James II's youngest, Protestant daughter, Anne. Anne, however, weakened by a succession of miscarriages, was in poor health and had no heir. The Protestant house of Hanover had the most direct and acceptable claim to the throne. The Scottish Parliament indicated that they might not be prepared to accept a Hanoverian sovereign unless some of their major grievances were dealt with. In 1704 they passed the 'Act anent war and peace' in which they stated that, after the death of Queen Anne, their express permission should be required before Scotland was dragged into another major war, or committed to a peace treaty. Two could play at that game though and the English Parliament knew how to respond. In 1705 they threatened to pass an Alien Act which would make all Scots not actually living in England aliens unless negotiations for a union of the two countries were under way by Christmas 1705.

Since 1603 all Scots had been treated as English citizens. Ending their freedom to live and work in England would have had serious implications for many Scots at all social levels. However, the threat was aimed primarily at Scottish nobles, the group with the power to push through a treaty of union. Many Scottish magnates had lands and business interests in England. They would also have been seriously affected by the accompanying proposal to ban all Scottish imports into England which was by now Scotland's major trading partner. Many Scottish nobles were directly involved in the trade in cattle, grain, and textiles to England while others would suffer indirectly through the effects of a disastrous trade slump on their incomes from rents.

There was little enthusiasm for such a union among the ordinary people of England who disliked and distrusted their northern neighbours. Neither did the Scots like the idea of losing their independence. However, as relations between the two countries deteriorated the negotiators who had been appointed became convinced that some sort of union was the only way of avoiding disaster. The English government favoured a full or 'incorporating' union between the two countries. Many Scots preferred the idea of some kind of federal system but they were not able to agree on a detailed plan of how such a scheme could work.

The English government, determined to push for a union, produced a package in 1706 which they then tried to force through the Scottish legislature. The deal was aimed at placating the Scottish nobles who dominated Scotland's Parliament and Privy Council. They would be represented in the House of Lords at Westminster and were to retain their traditional legal jurisdictions over the inhabitants of their estates. A substantial sum of money was set aside to compensate people for their losses in the Darien venture; again this benefited those nobles who had been major subscribers to the scheme. The Scottish church and legal system would retain their distinctive identity. Customs duties on exports from Scotland to England would be abolished. Scotland's royal burghs would retain their old privileges and much publicity was directed at trying to persuade Scotland's burgesses, as well as the nobles, that trade would flourish as a result of the Union.

Many people in Scotland saw flaws in these promises. A substantial group of nobles was opposed to the idea while many of the gentry and most of the merchants disliked the proposals. The bulk of the population, who had no say whatever, did not favour the idea either. Nevertheless the Union was pushed through by Scottish career politicians like the Earl of Seafield and the Earl of Mar who genuinely saw little practical alternative. It was widely suspected that the Scottish commissioners who negotiated the Union treaty, and who had been nominated by Queen Anne rather than by the Scottish Parliament, had been bribed. A substantial sum of money was transferred from England to Scotland but most of this was accounted for by overdue, unpaid salaries for those nobles who were holding, or had held, government posts. Doubtless the payment of these arrears made some of the recipients more amenable but part of the money at least went to men who stoutly opposed the Union. The allegations of bribery are probably unfounded. Nevertheless, the taint still clung to the commissioners, the 'parcel of rogues' as a later Jacobite song described them, who were widely thought to have sold their country for English gold.

It rapidly became clear that the Union would do Scotland little immediate good, whatever the long term advantages might be. The new 'British' (but in fact English-dominated) government soon began to infringe the spirit and even the actual wording of the Treaty. In addition to insensitive, heavy-handed treatment of Scottish concerns by Westminster, Scotland's economy was still too primitive to respond positively to the potential advantages of the Union. The result in the short term was a surge of anti-English, anti-government feeling and nationalist sentiment upon which the Jacobites seized and tried to capitalize.

THE FAILED RISING OF 1708

It was under these conditions that the rising of 1708 was planned. In the previous year Jacobite agents had been active in Scotland. One in particular, Colonel Nathaniel Hooke, came back to St Germain with a glowing vision of a country whose population was ready to rise en masse. Unfortunately, Hooke was over optimistic. He had contacted a number of Lowland nobles, mostly indirectly via intermediaries. Several had made vague promises of support which stopped short of a firm commitment. Hooke, trying to ingratiate himself among Scotland's great families, ignored the Highland chiefs who were the most likely source of armed recruits.

On the strength of these misleading reports Louis sanctioned the assembly of an invasion force. 6,000 French troops were to be sent to Scotland to form the nucleus around which a Jacobite army would rally. A fleet of thirty Dunkirk privateers, light and fast, along with some other vessels, was assembled to transport them. Throughout February the force was being prepared at Dunkirk and St Omer but just as James was about to embark he came down with measles and was so seriously ill that the expedition was postponed. Word of the planned invasion force reached Britain and a fleet was sent to blockade it in port and prevent it from sailing but eventually, on March 6th 1708, contrary winds forced the blockading warships off station. James, still weak, quickly embarked and the French fleet was able to escape.

Combined operations between army and navy often have a history of unhappy relations and this one was no exception. Neither the Comte de Gace, in charge of the troops, nor the Comte de Forbin, commanding the fleet seem to have been at all enthusiastic about the expedition. They had some justification. From a strategic point of view, France was backing this venture as a diversion to reduce pressure on their armies which were fighting the British and the Dutch in the Low Countries. The expedition's commanders were concerned that there had been no preliminary rising in Scotland and there was, indeed, no certainty of support at all. They shrewdly suspected that if anything went wrong they and their men would be expendable.

The fleet reached the Firth of Forth and anchored off the Isle of May. Signals to the shore produced no reply. They made a landing at Pittenweem in Fife, but found only a handful of supporters rather than the army that had been promised. At this point sails were sighted to the south for Sir George Byng's fleet had pursued them northwards from the Channel. The fast-sailing Dunkirk vessels made off northwards although one ship was captured. The French fleet hove to off the Aberdeenshire coast where, again, there were no signs of a welcoming party. In vain did James plead with the admiral that if he would not disembark the troops he should at least set him on shore, alone if necessary, to try and organize a rising. The admiral refused and the reappearance of Byng's fleet caused them to sail further northwards. They returned to France round the west of Britain having achieved nothing and the expedition ended in general recrimination.

The campaign had been a fiasco but it is intriguing to speculate what might have happened if the French commanders had shown more determination and made a landing. Scotland had been denuded of troops and the authorities, having word of the intended expedition, were ready to abandon the country and retreat to Berwick. Yet although the arrival of the fleet was expected not a single nobleman came out in open support. It seems that Hooke's distorted report made the French, as well as the Jacobites, misjudge the degree of ill feeling in Scotland resulting from the Union, or at least the extent to which it could be translated from passive grumbling into active rebellion. Certainly conditions were not as favourable for a Jacobite success as they were to be in 1715 when the groundswell of opposition had grown significantly.

THE HANOVERIAN SUCCESSION

Historians have pointed out that the dynastic changes in Britain between 1688 and the death of Queen Anne in 1714 were more in the nature of a family squabble, as the Stuart dynasty had not really been supplanted. William's wife, Mary, was the daughter of the deposed James VII of Scotland and II of England while William himself, the son of the eldest daughter of Charles I, was half a Stuart. They ruled together as joint monarchs. Anne, who succeeded him in 1702, was James' other daughter by his first, Protestant, wife, Anne Hyde. It was only when Anne was on the throne, without any immediate heir (her last surviving son had died in 1700), that the question of the succession became vital. That whoever succeeded Anne should be a Protestant was agreed by the vast majority. Had James Francis Stuart, the Old Pretender, been prepared to change his religion he might have found widespread support within British society, and even from Queen Anne herself. But he refused to revoke Roman Catholicism and a Protestant successor had to be found.

There were various potentially acceptable candidates but the rulers of the Electorate of Hanover were favoured by William and Anne because of their staunch opposition to Louis XIV of France. The mother of the Countess Sophia of Hanover had been the eldest daughter of James VI and I. In 1701 the English Act of Settlement had made her Anne's successor although it was widely recognized that, as she was already elderly, her son George was more likely to inherit the throne. But would the Jacobites in exile or in Britain allow this to happen?

Politics in early eighteenth-century Britain were dominated by the conflict between the Whigs and the Tories. Although there were many shades of opinion within each party the Whigs were, broadly speaking, supporters of the principles of the Revolution of 1688. They were staunchly anti-French and favoured military intervention in Europe. Their interest was allied to those of religious dissenters and the traders and financiers of the City of London. The Tories supported the monarchy, the Church of England, and the landed interest. They were against intervention in Europe.

In 1710 the Tories came back into power. Historians have argued about the extent of Tory involvement in the Jacobite cause at this period but they agree that it was significant. The Tories were led by Robert Harley, Earl of Oxford. Although Harley was a moderate, a number of men in the new government had overt or covert Jacobite sympathies. It was widely believed that another leading Tory, Henry St John, Viscount Bolingbroke, was determined to prevent the Hanoverian succession and restore James, with Anne's tacit support. Events did not move in the Jacobites' favour though. In order to end the long and expensive war with France the Tories were forced to agree to Whig pressure and require Louis, as one of the provisions of the Treaty of Utrecht, to expel James and his court in exile from France. This Louis did and James took up residence at Bar-le-Duc in Lorraine, then a separate duchy.

In 1706 it was agreed that a group of state officers nominated by Hanover should take over as regents on the death of Anne to administer the country until the Hanoverian successor was able to take over the throne, thus avoiding a vacuum of power which the Jacobites could exploit. Countess Sophia died in April 1714, and only a few weeks later Anne herself died. The sealed letter from Hanover was opened immediately and it became clear that almost all the regents were Whigs. The Whigs assumed power with remarkably little fuss, and invited George to come and take over the throne. The failure of those Tories with Jacobite leanings to do anything positive at this critical stage was due in part to the fact that the party was riven by internal dissension. Many Tory leaders, whose Jacobite activities had been uncovered, or who had been smeared by vicious Whig propaganda, were discredited.

'THE WEE, WEE GERMAN LAIRDIE'

George arrived at Greenwich on the 18th of September 1714. He must have been one of the least likeable characters ever to have sat on the throne of Britain. In his middle fifties, he was dour, reserved, and shy. He was narrow-minded and not particularly bright and this made him suspicious and cunning. He did not inspire affection, apart perhaps from the two German mistresses who accompanied him, the ugliness of whom was the subject of Jacobite lampoons. George made little effort to accommodate himself to his new kingdom. His command of English was poor and during the thirteen years of his reign he rarely left London. He was dubbed 'The wee, wee German lairdie' in one particularly cutting Jacobite song whose comments on the Hanoverian take-over were summed up in the scathing line 'The very dogs of England's court, they bark and howl in German!'

George's affinities were naturally with the Whigs who had backed the Protestant succession so vigorously and there was little surprise when he chose his new ministers almost entirely from their ranks. A general election in 1715 returned a large Whig majority and sent the Tories into opposition. One of the Whigs' first acts was to move the impeachment of former Tory leaders. Harley was imprisoned and Bolingbroke, scared by Whig threats to his life, fled to France and eventually to the Jacobite court in exile. A final disaster for the Jacobites was the death of Louis XIV in September 1715. As long as Louis, with his grandiose schemes to dominate Europe, was alive France was a potential source of aid for the Jacobites but the Duke of Orleans, regent for Louis XV, was less sympathetic and more concerned with maintaining peace with England.

The accession of George I was so peaceful that he and his new ministers could be forgiven for being complacent. Nevertheless, storm clouds were starting to gather. The growing unpopularity of the new regime was manifested by increasing popular discontent as 1714 gave way to 1715. There were riots in many English towns. Much of this ill-feeling was anti-government without necessarily being pro-Jacobite. But the fact that local authorities did little to intervene may indicate that there was passive Jacobite support throughout England. Even if this were so, Jacobite agents made the mistake of over-emphasizing it and believing that this indicated that the population at large was ready to rise against the Hanoverian regime. Events were to show how mistaken this assumption was.

5

THE REBELLION OF 1715:
THE SCOTTISH CAMPAIGN

BOBBING JOHN GOES NORTH

It was during this period of seemingly growing discontent with the new regime that the Jacobites laid the foundations of the 1715 rebellion. The plan was for the main rising to be in south west England, close to France so that men, supplies, and James himself could be landed easily. Simultaneous risings planned for the Scottish Highlands, the Borders, and northern England were merely diversions to confuse the government. The authorities were not so easily confused though; they had details of the Jacobite plans from their own spies and from careless talk among the Jacobite leaders. The Duke of Ormonde was appointed to organize the western rising but his Jacobite sympathies were too well known and after Parliament had voted to impeach him he panicked and fled to France. Command of the rising then passed to the Marquis of Lansdowne who was assembling arms and supporters around Bath. Unfortunately, Ormonde had fled without passing on his plans and when the government quickly occupied Bath, Bristol, and other centres of potential Jacobite support, the rising collapsed. It took some time for news of this to reach James in France. Ormonde actually sailed back from St Malo to Devon and then on to Cornwall before realizing that there was no hope of rallying support. Jacobite hopes now shifted to the more remote areas where diversionary activity had been planned: Northumberland and Scotland.

The 1715 rebellion in Scotland was created by one man: John, Earl of Mar. Arguably it was also created largely for his own benefit. Mar was known to contemporaries by the nickname of 'Bobbing John'. One suggestion is that this derived from a nervous habit of twitching his head. Another, more cynically, claims that it reflected his ability to survive changes of political leadership unscathed. He was not an established Jacobite leader like Ormonde. He was a career politician who had served under William, then Anne, and who would happily have continued under George. Unfortunately his career had unexpectedly crumbled. He had helped to push through the Union in 1707 and had worked hard to ensure the accession of George I. George had shown his gratitude by deliberately snubbing him, for Mar was a Tory and as far as George was concerned all Tories were potential Jacobites. It had been made abundantly clear to Mar that there was no place for him in British politics. He might have retired to live peacefully on his estates but instead he took the gamble of returning to Scotland to raise a rebellion. If there was no political future for him under the House of Hanover he would try to bring in a monarch who would reward him suitably. Like most of his contemporaries he had probably been secretly in touch with the Jacobite court in exile but his sudden transformation into the leader of the Scottish Jacobites took many people by surprise. Mar's principal shortcoming as a leader, as events were soon to show, was that while he was a capable enough administrator he was no soldier.

On August 1st, almost a year after George had first snubbed him, Mar attended a royal levee in London. George pointedly turned his back on him. Perhaps this was the last straw — or perhaps Mar had already decided on a desperate gamble and had attended the levee purely as a cover, for there are indications that his arrival in Scotland was not completely unexpected. In either case he slipped away from London that evening. He sailed north on a collier to Newcastle and transferred to another ship which landed him at Elie in Fife. Once back in Scotland he sent out messages to known Jacobites.

Having warned potential supporters, he set off on August 10th for his Highland estates in upper Deeside where he hoped to start recruiting forces. From Blairgowrie he travelled north, stopping for the night at the inn at Spittal of Glenshee. He had intended staying with Farquharson of Invercauld, one of his feudal vassals, at his house near Braemar. Farquharson, a shrewd man, demanded to see Mar's credentials. Where was his commission from King James appointing him as commander and authorizing him to raise men? Mar had acted independently and did not have a commission. Farquharson slipped away, having refused to support Mar until James landed in person. He subsequently joined the rising and was taken prisoner at Preston. He was able to plead at his trial that he had been forced to take up arms by his feudal superior. In the meantime Mar, while waiting for his commission to arrive from France, resorted to the temporary expedient of forging one; an 'anticipatory draft' as some historians, presumably with their tongues in their cheeks, have called it.

As a cover for starting the rising he invited potential supporters to a great hunt or 'tinchal' on his lands. It is not certain how many people attended; the official list of nobles and lairds from all over Scotland who gathered at Braemar is suspiciously long. The hunt may have been in part a blind but it seems likely that Mar's guests did enjoy some sport during their visit. In Glen Quoich a large hollow in a rock in the middle of the stream is still known as Mar's (or the Devil's!) punch bowl, supposedly being a place where punch was mixed to drink the health of King James and success to the rising. Over the next few days Mar made visits to other landowners in the area to get pledges of support. He went to his lands at Kildrummy at the head of the Don, staying with his baillie as the castle, destroyed during the first Jacobite rising, was still ruinous. He also went down Deeside to Aboyne where the Marquis of Huntly, heir to the Gordon estates, met him.

Back at Braemar on September 6th he raised James' standard on a hillock beside the local courthouse; the rebellion had officially begun. The spot where Mar is supposed to have done this is marked by a plaque on the wall of the Invercauld Arms Hotel in Braemar. It was unfortunate that when the standard was unfurled the gilt ball on top of it fell off, an event which many Highlanders considered to be a bad omen. Mar's actions took the Jacobite court in exile by surprise and it was some time before James adjusted to the new strategic situation. From being a sideshow Scotland had suddenly become the main Jacobite hope.

A week or so later Mar began to head south, gathering forces as he went. The response of his own tenants to his call to arms had been disappointing. In a frequently-quoted letter to 'Black Jock' Forbes, his baillie at Kildrummy, he threatened to burn the homes of those of his tenants who would not join him. The letter has often been cited — by Whig contemporaries and historians — as an example of bullying brutality. In fact under Scots law Mar, as a feudal superior, was strictly within his rights in requiring his tenants to support him although his actions were rather harsh.

An advance party of horsemen under Colonel John Hay captured Perth. As soon as Hay's men appeared on the far side of the Tay, local Jacobite sympathizers seized boats and ferried them across to the town. Mar had no hand in this bold stroke but was quite ready to claim the credit for it. Perth made a good temporary headquarters for the Jacobites as bodies of men continued to come in from the Highlands, the north east, and the surrounding Lowlands.

Mar soon had an army of around 12,000, the largest and potentially the most formidable force that the Jacobites ever raised. Although Mar's army is sometimes portrayed as an exclusively Highland one, support for his rising was more broadly based than in 1689 or 1745. In 1715 the clans of Lochaber and the Isles played a comparatively minor role, partly because the action was centred well away from them in the Lowlands. The Grampian Highlands provided a sizeable proportion of the Jacobite forces, but so did the north east and the Lowlands from Perth to Aberdeen. Some Jacobite landowners, like the Earls of Southesk and Panmure, had estates in both the Highlands and the neighbouring Lowlands and brought in mixed contingents of troops.

There was also a lot of passive Jacobite support in the east-coast burghs, whose inhabitants were disenchanted with the failure of the Union to improve trade. Indeed, apart from Campbell territory in Argyll (even there some Campbells came out to fight for the Jacobites) and the far north, most of

11 Perth at the end of the seventeenth century; the Earl of Mar's headquarters during the 1715 rebellion.

Scotland north of the Firth of Forth was pro-Jacobite. Glasgow and the south west, solidly Whig as ever, supported the government as did Edinburgh but it only needed decisive action and some early success for Mar to have all of Scotland at his feet.

This should not have been difficult for there were few government troops in Scotland to oppose him. After the end of Marlborough's wars against the French the British army had been rapidly run down and the forces available to counter the Jacobites were woefully few. General Wightman concentrated all the available regular troops at Stirling. When the government in London realized the seriousness of the threat in the north they appointed John, second Duke of Argyll, commander-in-chief for Scotland. 'Red John of the Battles', as he was known to his Gaelic clansmen, was an accomplished soldier who had gained a considerable reputation fighting under Marlborough at Ramillies, Oudenarde, and Malplaquet. After a final interview with George I on September 8th Argyll hurried north. Six days of hard travel saw him at Edinburgh where he halted briefly to inspect the Castle before continuing to Stirling. The magistrates of Glasgow had raised a regiment of around 600 volunteers commanded by Colonel Blackadder, an old Cameronian officer, but even with these Argyll had little more than 2,000 troops. Many of these, even in the regular regiments, were newly raised and inexperienced. It was little wonder that Red John of the Battles was despondent about his ability to hold back the Jacobite army. His position was precarious, and he knew it.

THE ATTACK ON EDINBURGH CASTLE

One of the most interesting offshoots from the main campaign in Scotland was an attempt by a party of Jacobites within the city to capture Edinburgh Castle. In retrospect the attempt has within it a strong element of farce but this was only because it failed: it is sometimes forgotten that it failed by only a very little. Like many of the operations during this Jacobite rising the plan itself was sound; it was the execution which was faulty.

The leader of the band of Jacobites who hatched the plot seems to have been Thomas Arthur, once a lieutenant in the regular army. The plan was simple enough. Arthur had bribed three soldiers in the garrison, two privates and a sergeant, William Ainslie. At a pre-arranged time, when they were on sentry duty, they would lower ropes from the battlements down the crag to the waiting party below. The Jacobites would tie makeshift ladders on to the ropes which the sentries would haul up and secure so that the Jacobites could climb up, overpower the garrison, and take over the fortress. The attacking party included Lord Drummond, the son of the Jacobite Duke of Perth, with some of his retainers and a mixed party of Edinburgh citizens including former officers, clerks, and apprentices. In all there may have been up to ninety of them.

Many ambitious wartime plans have been ruined by careless talk and this was an example. Arthur made the mistake of telling his brother, an Edinburgh doctor, about the plot. He in turn passed the story on to his wife. Arthur's sister-in-law seems to have been a staunch Whig for she promptly sent a message to Sir Adam Cockburn of Ormiston, the Lord Justice Clerk, saying that an attempt was to be made on the Castle that night. Cockburn got the Lord Provost of the city to increase the town guard's patrols. General Preston, the governor of the Castle, was in England at this time. Cockburn warned his deputy, who seems to have dismissed the affair as a mere rumour. He increased the number of sentries, warned his junior officers to be on their guard and then went to bed!

Some of the party went out drinking in Edinburgh taverns on the evening that the escalade was scheduled. Like Arthur they couldn't resist boasting about what they were going to do. The other customers seem to have taken remarkably little notice of them; like the deputy governor of the Castle they thought that it was all talk. Nevertheless, at around 11pm they met in the churchyard of the West Kirk, at the west end of where Princes Street now stands, and moved to a spot below where the bribed sentries were on guard. One of the sentries lowered a rope and called out softly to find out if they were ready. They replied that they were not. Charles Forbes, the man who was bringing most of the ladders, had failed to turn up! They decided to have a go with the ladders they had brought. They called to the sentries to haul in the rope and pull up the ladders, which proved to be too short. Time was passing while they blundered about and suddenly the sentries heard the officer of the guard with a patrol approaching.

They called a frantic warning to the Jacobites below, then, to divert suspicion from themselves, they threw the ropes down the crag, and fired their muskets as if they had just discovered the attackers. A party of the Town Guard, patrolling the base of the crag, was alerted by the firing and hurried over. The Jacobites dispersed in confusion, running round the edge of the Nor' Loch and escaping across Bearford's Parks, the fields which are now covered by the New Town of Edinburgh, north of Princes Street. The pursuers found the ladders and a dozen muskets which had been thrown down in panic. In their flight, some of the attackers met Charles Forbes, arriving too late with the rest of the scaling ladders.

Only three or four Jacobites were captured, including one who had fallen on the rocks and injured himself. There was only circumstantial evidence against them though and none of them was brought to trial. It was a different matter with the sentries. A confession was forced out of them. The two privates were lucky to escape with a flogging but Sergeant Ainslie was court martialled and sentenced to be hanged — from the battlements of the Castle at the spot where he had tried to help the Jacobites scale the cliff. The deputy governor of the Castle was also dismissed for negligence. The attack had been badly mismanaged, becoming one of history's might-have-beens. With better organization and less talk the attempt could well have succeeded. The Jacobites had arranged to fire a cannon, once they had secured the Castle, to alert supporters in Fife who were to carry the message to Mar. Mar was then to have marched on the capital immediately. Had he done so, tackling Argyll's army on the way, the rebellion might have taken a different and more dangerous turn for the Hanoverian government.

THE CAMPAIGN IN THE WEST

Having assembled a substantial army at Perth, presumably with a view to invading the Lowlands, Mar decided that the Jacobite clans in the west needed some support. While the Duke of Argyll was assembling the government forces at Stirling his brother, the Earl of Islay, was at Inveraray rallying the Campbells. Islay, another politician, was as inefficient a commander as Mar, but the latter may have been worried about the Campbells launching some kind of pre-emptive strike into Atholl behind his back.

Mar sent General Alexander Gordon to rally the western clans. Gordon was an experienced soldier who had served his apprenticeship in King William's wars with France at the end of the seventeenth century and then risen to high command in Russia under Peter the Great, only returning to Scotland in 1711 to succeed to the family estates on the death of his father. His orders were to capture Inveraray then march into the Lowlands and possibly occupy Glasgow. Late in September he travelled westwards and met MacDonald of Glengarry at Achallader in Glen Orchy. This was the same Glengarry who had held out against William after Killiecrankie and he was ready once more for action — and plunder.

A contingent of Clanranald MacDonalds appeared early in October. With Glengarry's men and some MacGregors Gordon had some 1,300 men; hardly an impressive army but enough to cause considerable nuisance. The MacGregors were a dubious asset. Their notoriety as robbers and thieves, out of all proportion to their numbers, exceeded that even of the Glencoe MacDonalds. So bad was their reputation that in 1603 the Scottish government had outlawed the entire clan and banned the use of the name 'MacGregor'. The ban was lifted in 1661 but King William re-imposed it. Mar persuaded them to come out by promising to have their name and identity restored. The MacGregors had become a broken clan, deprived of most of their ancestral lands by the expansion of the Campbells and other neighbours, and forced into banditry, preying on all and sundry.

Their most famous leader at this time was the notorious Rob Roy MacGregor. Rob Roy was not chief of the MacGregors, only the head of one of their leading branches, the MacGregors of Glengyle. He was in his mid-forties at the time of the 1715 rising. At the age of eighteen he had fought with Dundee at Killiecrankie and had been active in raiding into the Lowlands later on in the first Jacobite campaign. He became a cattle drover on a large scale, supplementing this by offering protection from cattle raiders to other landowners. They paid him money known as black mail ('mail' being a Scots word for rent), from which the modern term for extortion is derived. However, as the government was unable to stop cattle raiding they condoned this protection racket. In 1711 Rob was bankrupted when his deputy absconded with a large sum of money. His business partners, notably the Duke of Montrose, sued him then had him outlawed and evicted from his lands at Craigroystan, east of Loch Lomond. He found refuge in the Earl of Breadalbane's territory and used it as a base from which to raid Montrose's lands. He had become a professional outlaw with nothing to lose. His movements at this time are obscure; the MacGregors had been raiding the Lowlands, as far south as the outskirts of Dumbarton, but the contingent that came to Glen Orchy was led by Rob Roy's nephew.

In mid-September Gordon headed for Inveraray, the heart of Campbell territory. Today Inveraray is a neat, whitewashed little community on a promontory south of Inveraray Castle. The town was laid out as a planned settlement on a new site later in the eighteenth century when the present castle was built. The original burgh, less well built, was close to the gates of the old castle. The Earl of Islay, expecting the Jacobites, had raised around 1,000 men who had dug entrenchments around the little town. Despite experience of besieging major continental cities, Gordon camped a mile away and did not venture to attack. There were a few skirmishes between the Campbell outposts and the attackers and on one occasion the MacGregors made an unsuccessful raid on Inveraray. However, both sides seemed to have lost all initiative when a message from Mar ordered Gordon back to Perth, probably to support a planned advance on Stirling. The Jacobite campaign in the west Highlands effectively petered out.

CROSSING THE FORTH: BORLUM'S DIVERSION

Mar remained at Perth issuing edicts when he should have been taking positive action. He even failed to fortify the town against possible attack. Early in October he was joined by a contingent of Mackintoshes under the command of Mackintosh of Borlum, a tough old professional soldier. Borlum was about sixty, a tall, fair man with grey eyes and beetle brows according to a rather unflattering contemporary description. Another was even less complimentary: 'a brute beast who was as obstinate as a mule and as savage as a tiger'. Borlum had his cultivated side though: during long years of imprisonment in Edinburgh Castle, after the rising had failed, he devoted his time to writing on agricultural improvement, one of the first Scottish landowners to do so. With Borlum came Farquharson of Invercauld, now reconciled with Mar. The day after Borlum arrived the rising in Northumberland started and the English Jacobites asked Mar for help, particularly for a detachment of infantry to support their small force of horsemen.

Mar decided to send Borlum off on detached service with around 2,000 men. It is not entirely clear what Mar's intentions were as his orders to Borlum were vague. Probably even Borlum was unsure of what he was supposed to do. The plan was for Borlum to march into eastern Fife, assemble all the small boats that he could gather, and cross the Firth of Forth to East Lothian. From there he could threaten Edinburgh, take Argyll in the rear, or march southwards to help the English Jacobites.

Operations which involve transporting troops by sea, especially in the face of enemy naval forces, are always difficult and frequently end in disaster. Borlum's was a well-organized triumph. The Master of Sinclair, who knew Fife well, was sent to collect as many boats as he could find in Anstruther, Crail, Elie, and Pittenweem. Borlum's force, along with an additional 500 men who were to create a diversion, left Perth on October 9th. The diversion involved sending the 500 men to Burntisland, where the Forth was relatively narrow, to make the Hanoverians think that this was the embarkation point while Borlum led his men further east. The plan worked: the men of war guarding the Firth bore down on Burntisland and opened fire on the boats in the harbour, and on the town itself. The Jacobites returned the fire with a battery of cannon which they had mounted by the harbour. Meanwhile Borlum was embarking his men in open boats for a sea crossing of between fourteen and twenty miles.

Some historians have assumed that Borlum got his men over the Forth in a single night but it seems more likely that the flotilla of boats needed two trips under cover of darkness. On the second night they ran out of luck. Landing at Aberlady and North Berwick, Borlum's advance guard pushed on to Haddington and someone sent a message to warn the commanders of the warships what was going on. They sailed down the Firth and captured one boat with about forty men on board. Some other boats, under the command of the young Earl of Strathmore who was later killed at Sheriffmuir, evaded the warships by landing on the Isle of May, a small island in the mouth of the Forth. After a day or two they were able to sail back to Fife and rejoin the main army.

These setbacks were only minor ones though. Borlum had crossed the Forth with over 1,500 men, an impressive achievement. His first action was to march on Edinburgh to see how well it was guarded. The city authorities, hearing that the Jacobites had landed in East Lothian, had sent an urgent plea for help to Argyll and were desperately trying to strengthen their defences. Coming in sight of the city Borlum noted all this activity and opted for a softer target, the undefended port of Leith. This was a mistake as a determined assault would almost certainly have carried the city, though probably not the Castle, and improved the Jacobites' position. Borlum's men broke open Leith's tolbooth, or prison, and released the forty men who had been captured during the crossing. They took money from the customs house and cannon and supplies from vessels in the harbour. On the outskirts of the port was an old fortress, a square citadel with corner bastions for artillery which had been erected in Cromwell's day. Since then the fort had stood empty but its walls were intact and it made a good base once Borlum had got his men to block up the entrance and mount cannon on the walls. Today most of the citadel has been demolished but you can still see one of its arched gateways in Dock Street.

Receiving the message from Edinburgh, Argyll reacted swiftly. With 500 dragoons he rode hard for the city and the following morning he sallied out, his small force augmented by a large body of Edinburgh volunteers. Optimistically he called on the Jacobites in the citadel to surrender. Borlum's reply was along the lines of 'come and get us'. It was a stand-off: Argyll did not have the equipment to besiege the Jacobites while Borlum was gaining nothing by staying in Leith.

Argyll withdrew to Edinburgh while Borlum marched back into East Lothian. Late that night he arrived at Seton House, east of Prestonpans, a strong old castle owned by the Earl of Winton who was at that moment with the Lowland Jacobites on the Border. The house had been in the hands of the Seton family for generations and was known as Seton Palace on account of its size. The palace was demolished later in the eighteenth century and Robert Adam built the present house on the site in a mock-castle style. Borlum hurriedly threw entrenchments around the building in case Argyll attacked him there.

As soon as Argyll heard that Borlum was fortifying Seton House he had some artillerymen sent from Stirling in order to besiege the Jacobites. Then came the news that he must have been dreading. Mar had left Perth and was moving south towards Stirling. Argyll hurried back to rejoin his army before the Jacobites brought them to battle. Fortunately for him, and quite inexplicably, Mar failed to press his advantage and returned to Perth. Given that he had detached some of his best men under Borlum he should have used them to divert attention from Stirling and attack with his main force while Argyll was still trying to contain the threat in his rear. Mar's failure to co-ordinate the movements of his two armies underlines his incapacity as a soldier. Argyll had left General Wightman in Edinburgh with about 250 men and Wightman set out with these and 300 Edinburgh volunteers to probe the defences at Seton. After exchanging a few shots with the defenders he decided that they were too well entrenched for a successful attack. It was another stand-off. Wightman returned to Edinburgh. Borlum received further orders from Mar to march south and join the English Jacobites. Borlum slipped off to cross the Lammermuir Hills en route for the Border.

THE ROAD TO SHERIFFMUIR

If you stand on the battlements of Stirling Castle on a clear day the strategy of the Jacobite and Hanoverian commanders in Scotland during the 1715 rebellion becomes clear. The crossing of the River Forth, under the guns of the Castle, was the gateway to the south. From the Castle you can look east to the steep front of the Ochil Hills, and the winding estuary of the Forth. To the west, between Stirling and Glasgow, lie the Campsie Fells while a long line of Highland peaks forms the skyline to the north.

In the early eighteenth century the routes into southern Scotland were even fewer than today. At that time most of the Forth valley above Stirling was a

12 The crossing of the River Forth at Stirling Bridge, seen from Stirling Castle, the key objective in the manoeuvres leading to the Battle of Sheriffmuir.

77

huge expanse of peat moss. It was shunned by settlement which clung to the higher ground around the margins of the moss. Only towards the end of the eighteenth century did improving landowners start reclaiming these carse-lands as they were called. There were only a couple of feasible routes through the mosses. One led to the Fords of Frew, eight miles above Stirling, just north of Kippen. This route was used by cattle drovers but was not an easy passage for an army. Rob Roy, alone among the Jacobite leaders, knew this route but nobody trusted him and Argyll was also believed to have booby-trapped the crossing by sinking rows of iron spikes attached to beams of wood in the river bed.

Having failed to profit by Borlum's diversion, Mar remained in Perth, gathering more reinforcements and working far harder at raising finances to pay his army than at planning the next moves in his campaign. However, once the Marquis of Huntly and his Gordons, and the Earl of Seaforth, had joined him there was no excuse for further delay. On November 9th Mar called a council of war. There was unanimous agreement for a move across the Forth to secure southern Scotland. The plan was a complicated one, probably unnecessarily so. The main body of the army was to cross the Forth above Stirling. 1,000 men were to make a diversionary attack along the causeway leading directly to Stirling Bridge. Another 1,000 were to attempt to cross at the Abbey Ford a mile below Stirling and another 1,000 at the ferry of Drip further upstream. There was no way that Argyll with his meagre forces could cover all these crossing points. The army moved out of Perth on November 10th and at Auchterarder they were joined by General Gordon's clansmen who had marched from Inveraray. In all Mar had over 6,000 infantry and 1,000 horsemen.

All this presupposed that Argyll would sit at Stirling and wait to be attacked. He was too old a campaigner for that though. He had heard the details of the Jacobite plan from his spies and immediately moved north. His army had received some reinforcements but it was still only a quarter or a third the size of Mar's forces. He had only about 2,200 infantry and 1,000 cavalry. He could not guard all the potential crossing points of the Forth and with the winter turning cold there were fears that the river might freeze, allowing the Jacobites to cross almost anywhere. Moreover, a defensive position along the river would fail to make use of his cavalry, the only respect in which his army was stronger than Mar's. Accordingly, his decision to march out and meet the Jacobite army north of the river was a sensible one. Some of his regiments contained a fair proportion of veterans but many of the newly raised regiments were filled with inexperienced recruits. However, a number of his officers had, like him, served under Marlborough and knew their job. Argyll's small army was probably better equipped than the Jacobites and Red John was a popular commander with a reputation for looking after his men, something he had probably absorbed from 'Corporal John' Marlborough.

The valley of the Allan Water which leads northwards towards Perth is dominated by a dark ridge of moorland on its eastern side. This moorland, an outlier of the higher Ochil Hills which lie beyond, was known as Sheriffmuir. From the little cathedral town of Dunblane the ground rises steadily towards the crest of the moor in a long, gradual slope. To the south of the ridge the land drops gently into the valley of the Wharry Burn whose actual course is deeply cut. Beyond this stream the land climbs more steeply towards the Ochils. In the early eighteenth century the area was open moorland, boggy in places, with small farms scattered along the lower slopes. The moorland crest dominated the approach from Perth and gave Argyll full scope for deploying his cavalry. Having pushed forward to occupy Dunblane he moved eastwards and uphill so that he could quickly move on to the crest of the ridge the following day.

Mar had intended to halt for the night at Dunblane. News of Argyll's advance caught him by surprise and filled him with consternation. The Jacobite advance guard stopped at Kinbuck, a small hamlet two miles north of Dunblane, where they were later joined by the main body. Here they were so closely packed together and so disorganized that the Master of Sinclair wryly commented that 'it cannot be properlie said we had front or rear more than it can be said of a barrel of herrings'! They were vulnerable to attack but with his small forces Argyll was not going to risk a premature engagement, especially at night. Instead he kept to the high ground above Dunblane. His men had to spend the night in the open in their battle positions without tents. Some of them got shelter in the buildings of the scattered farms which lay east of the town and Argyll himself slept in a building on the site of the modern farm of Dykedale. It was mid-November and the men's fears about the coming battle must have been balanced by relief at seeing the dawn mark the end of a long, cold night.

'THERE'S SOME SAY THAT WE WON AND SOME SAY THAT THEY WON'

Early on the morning of November 13th the Jacobite army formed up on the low moors above the Allan Water just east of Kinbuck. At sunrise they could see a group of horsemen on the crest of Sheriffmuir some two miles to the south. It was Argyll and his officers reconnoitring the area. For much of the morning neither side did anything. Sinclair, waspish as ever, believed that Mar had not expected the Hanoverian army to advance and was stunned at their appearance. Mar held another council of war and made a rousing speech, something he did to perfection. There was general agreement that they should bring the Hanoverian army to battle.

To understand why the Battle of Sheriffmuir was such a confused mess it is necessary to study the preliminary manoeuvrings of both armies. The

Master of Sinclair's personal history of the rising provides a vivid account of how the Jacobite army was formed up. The various divisions were originally organized into two lines with the cavalry on each wing. When Mar ordered the advance uphill he, or more probably one of his senior officers, moved the army from line into column, thinking no doubt that it would be difficult to keep them in order if they marched them uphill in ranks. When they got close to the enemy the army would have to be reformed into two lines. These manoeuvres, from line to column and back again to line, would not have been easy over rough ground with trained and disciplined regular troops. It was potentially dangerous with untrained Highlanders.

General Hamilton divided each line into two columns but sent them off one after the other rather than all together so that the leading column, with the right-wing cavalry, was well up the slope before the last column started to move. The men in the last three columns then had to hurry uphill trying, unsuccessfully, to catch up with the leading troops. As the infantry in the first column reached the crest of the slope and formed back into line they could see Argyll's men hurrying across their line of march to get into position. Originally the Jacobite cavalry had been split between the two wings of the army but due to some misunderstanding of orders the horsemen on the Jacobite left moved round towards the other wing, ending up somewhere in the centre of the infantry and leaving the foot soldiers on the left unsupported. It was a mistake which was to have important consequences for the course of the battle. Mar stayed with the right wing while General Hamilton commanded on the left of the new line.

The course of the battle was determined by the fact that on the gently swelling moorland neither commander had a clear view of all of his opponents as the two armies approached each other. Even worse, once battle was joined neither general could see the whole of his own forces! Red John made some errors in the disposition of his troops which neatly balanced those made by Bobbing John. When Argyll realized that the whole Jacobite army was marching towards him he rapidly moved his men uphill from the valley of the Wharry Burn to occupy the boggy crest of Sheriffmuir. He planned to hold the high ground with his smaller army and let the Jacobites come up the gentle slope. It was unadventurous but, given the smallness of his army, probably the wisest course of action. However, he left his decision to move his men to the crest of the ridge almost to the last moment. The men who were to form the right wing of his battle line got off first and had time to form up properly in their new positions. There, by good fortune rather than skill, they overlapped the left wing of the Jacobite line. These were the men of the rear two columns who had left the valley last and who had hurried uphill arriving at the top in disarray and confusion. However, the Hanoverian troops who moved off last, forming the left wing of Argyll's line, had not got into position properly before the Jacobites from the first two columns came over the crest of the hill a mere 150 or 200 yards away and formed into line ready for battle. The Highlanders outflanked their opponents just as the Hanoverians were doing on the opposite wing.

The result of this last-minute disorganization was that when the Jacobite attack came, the soldiers on Argyll's right wing were ready for it while those on the left were not. Even Mar, useless soldier that he was, could appreciate that the troops opposite him were disorganized and that a first class opportunity was being offered to him. He ordered the Highlanders to charge and sent a message to the other wing telling Hamilton to do likewise.

The Highlanders on the right surged forward. They dropped flat when the government troops opened fire and then charged on, firing as they ran before throwing down their muskets and drawing their swords. For an instant they faltered when the captain of the Clanranald regiment was shot dead but Glengarry rallied them with a shout of 'Revenge!' and on they surged. In a few minutes, as at Killiecrankie, the government troops broke and fled. The only exception were the government dragoons who managed to delay the Highlanders' onslaught sufficiently to give the fleeing infantry some breathing space. As at Killiecrankie the battle disintegrated into a disorganized melee of pursuers and pursued, stretched out along the road back to Stirling where the fastest runners brought news of total defeat.

Unfortunately for the Jacobites things were different on their left. The Highlanders charged here too but Argyll's regiments of regular soldiers were ready for them. The government troops managed to keep the Highlanders at bay with volleys of musketry. Then Argyll sent in his horsemen. They rode across an area of marshy ground which had been frozen by the overnight frost and took the Jacobites in the flank. This checked the Highlanders who retreated downhill, but then reformed and charged again. This happened several times but gradually the Jacobites were forced back down the long slope to the River Allan at Kinbuck where some were drowned trying to escape across the stream. Even so, casualties among the Highlanders were light compared with Killiecrankie and the story that they were protected for part of their retreat by boggy ground, which had frozen enough to allow them, but not the pursuing horsemen, across may be true.

One man who missed the battle was Rob Roy. Although some of the MacGregors fought under their chief on Mar's left wing, Rob had been sent off to scout the Fords of Frew with a party of 250 MacGregors and MacPhersons. Hearing that a battle was imminent they hurried east and reached the Allan Water just in time to meet the Camerons and Appin Stewarts being driven across it by Argyll's dragoons. According to the Cameron leader he asked Rob to join him in crossing the river to attack the horsemen but the MacGregor refused. This story may have been an excuse on the Cameron's part, however, for another eye witness claimed that when the MacGregors met the fleeing clansmen they all turned to confront the dragoons who then drew back from the pursuit. The oft-repeated story that

Rob Roy and his men stationed themselves on a hill a little way from the battle without intervening is not true. It has been used to claim that Rob was either waiting to see which side gained the upper hand before deciding who to join or was merely poised to plunder the losers. The story appears to have emanated from the Reverend Patten's history of the rising and as Patten was at that time with the English Jacobites in Preston, fighting bravely (according to him), his version of events at Sheriffmuir should not be accepted uncritically.

Both commanders were guilty of being preoccupied with part of the battle and ignoring what was happening elsewhere. In the early afternoon Mar rounded up his infantry and horsemen and brought them back to join the Master of Sinclair's cavalry who, having got out of position before the battle, had played no significant role in the fighting. Mar moved to the top of a small hill at the eastern end of Sheriffmuir, north of where Stonehill farm stands today. At much the same time Argyll, having discovered that half of his army had been shattered, checked the pursuit of the Highlanders, reformed his men, and brought them back. Mar was waiting for him with about 4,000 men to Argyll's 1,000. The two armies advanced to within about 500 yards of each other. Red John halted somewhere south west of the Gathering Stone, a little lower down the hillside than the Jacobites. His small force prepared for a last stand behind some turf dykes and waited for annihilation. It never arrived. Mar stood immobile on his hill for half an hour or so and then, as the light began to fail, he led his men off northwards without firing a shot, leaving Argyll, relieved and puzzled, to return to Dunblane. Argyll had lost as many as 600-700 men according to some estimates; a substantial proportion of his little army. Jacobite casualties were rather fewer.

Sheriffmuir was a disorganized, untidy fight from which neither commander emerged with much credit. Nevertheless, it was the turning point in the rebellion. Argyll had done well merely to survive it. It is sometimes portrayed as an indecisive battle; tactically this was true. In terms of Jacobite strategy, however, it was a disaster. It is another of the great 'What ifs' of Jacobite history, perhaps the most important turning point of all. What if Mar had been a better soldier and a more decisive man? His army greatly outnumbered Argyll's and notwithstanding the rout of the Jacobite left wing he should still have been able to overwhelm the Hanoverians and force his way across the Forth. A decisive victory would have given Mar almost total control of Scotland and would probably have brought in a wave of new supporters. This could have given him an army which, moved south to the Border, might have brought the Jacobites of northern England out in open support and could have seriously threatened the Hanoverian regime. At the end of the day Argyll, with barely 1,000 men waiting grimly for a last, devastating attack which never materialized, must have scarcely believed his good fortune. It was little wonder that Gordon of Glenbucket, who had been at Killiecrankie, is said to have exclaimed 'Oh for an hour of Dundee!' as he saw Mar throw away his last opportunity of a decisive victory. At almost the same time as Mar was hesitating the Jacobite army was surrendering in Preston. The rising was starting to collapse.

SHERIFFMUIR TODAY

Today the site of the battle is still partly open moorland as it was in 1715 although areas of it, including much of the crest of Sheriffmuir, are covered with plantations of conifers. The difficulty lies in deciding just how the two armies were deployed in this rather featureless country. There is general agreement that Argyll's initial observation post from which he watched the Jacobite army form up was at the eastern end of the ridge in the middle of Sheriffmuir Big Wood, near a spot marked as the Gathering Stone on modern Ordnance Survey maps. The Gathering Stone is merely a small clump of boulders protected by an iron grille, difficult to find among the conifers and hardly worth the effort of searching for.

Before the battle Argyll probably had his men south and west of the crest of the ridge, above the Wharry Burn around Stonehill farm and from there he marched them up to the crest. The left wing of the Hanoverian army was probably formed up fairly close to the Gathering Stone. Historians have differed in interpreting how the two armies were orientated from this point. Some place Argyll's line as running from the Gathering Stone eastwards up the gently-sloping crest of the ridge to a point somewhere just beyond the Sheriffmuir Inn where the Ordnance Survey actually mark the site of the battle. Others have Argyll's line formed up almost at right angles to this, running from near the Gathering Stone down towards the Wharry Burn with the Jacobite army facing it across the line of the minor road from Dunblane to Blackford, a little way west of the Sheriffmuir Inn. The various contemporary accounts of the battle are, naturally enough, vague as regards place names and topography. However, we are inclined to favour the former interpretation and have reconstructed the battle on this basis. It is difficult to believe that Argyll would have failed to occupy the crest of the ridge which was by far the best place to form up his army. Also, if the two armies were facing east–west to the south of the ridge when they fought it makes it harder to work out how Argyll drove the Jacobite left back to Kinbuck as this would have involved pushing them back over the top of the hill in a three-quarter turn. If the Hanoverian right was located close to the deeply cut Wharry Burn it is also hard to see how Argyll's cavalry could have had room to operate effectively.

From the road above the Sheriffmuir Inn, near the empty farmstead of Lairhill, you can get a good view of the whole battlefield with the Highland peaks beyond. The ground to the north of the road is used as a rifle range and is fenced off with danger signs but even from the road you will appreciate how wet the ground is and the difficulties which this must have posed for the two armies. The only monument on the battlefield stands beside the road 1km

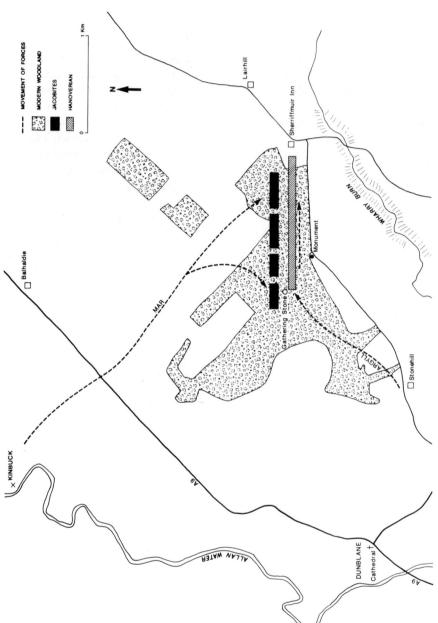

Map 5 The Battle of Sheriffmuir.

13 The abandoned cottage of Lairhill stands at one end of the battlefield at Sheriffmuir.

west of the Sheriffmuir Inn. It is a tall cairn commemorating the McCraes who were part of the Earl of Seaforth's contingent on the Jacobite left and who suffered particularly heavy casualties from the Hanoverian muskets. At the inn itself some rusty broadswords and a musket picked up on the battlefield can be seen.

THE OLD PRETENDER ARRIVES

After Sheriffmuir the mood of the Jacobites shifted from optimism to despair. Large contingents began to leave Mar's army and return home. Huntly, who had never been really enthusiastic, was one of the first, returning to the north east and making his peace with the government. Seaforth also left as did the Atholl men. With the end of the rising in England reinforcements for Argyll began to come north while the Jacobite army dwindled.

It was at this stage that, on December 22nd, James landed at Peterhead from a French ship. One might ask, as many of his followers did, why it had taken him so long to reach Scotland. Had he arrived before Sheriffmuir he might have boosted Jacobite morale more effectively. This is unfair though. James had left Bar-le-Duc in Lorraine at the end of October and travelled to Brittany narrowly escaping assassination by Hanoverian agents on the way. He remained in Brittany for some time, expecting to be landed in Devon to

14 The monument to the clan McCrae at Sheriffmuir.

lead the western rising which never materialized. It took time for news of Mar's rebellion to reach him. Once it was clear that Scotland was the focus of operations, the best way to get there seemed to be from Dunkirk to the east coast rather than the longer, more risky journey from St Malo to the West Highlands. However, travelling across France from St Malo to Dunkirk in winter, with the roads barely passable, was not easy. James did not reach Dunkirk until mid-December and made a remarkably quick passage to Scotland considering the time of year and the fact that British warships were trying to intercept him.

Mar's troops were encouraged when they heard of James' arrival but their enthusiasm faded when they found that he had not brought any reinforcements. James had not been in the best of health. He was always rather sickly and the rough sea passage had not helped. He did not make a particularly favourable impression on his supporters. They saw a tall, thin, pale man who looked dejected and discouraged. He had little to say and he rarely smiled. If they were disappointed in him the feeling was mutual and neither was able to animate the other.

From Peterhead James moved on to Monksholme, a house of the Earl Marischal's near Newburgh. From there he passed through Aberdeen in disguise and reached Fetteresso Castle, the principal residence of the Earl Marischal. There he was struck down by illness — a bad cold or a virus of some sort — for nine days. The bedroom which he occupied can still be seen. At Fetteresso he was joined by Mar and some of the other Jacobite leaders. Once he had recovered he made a rather unconvincing royal progress southwards. He made a ceremonial entry into Dundee and then carried on to Scone, just outside Perth, where the ancient kings of Scotland had been crowned. He reviewed the Jacobite army in Perth while arrangements were made for his coronation at Scone on January 23rd.

SCORCHED EARTH

Meanwhile, Argyll was building up his forces at Stirling. Soon he would march on Perth. By now it was January, a time when regular troops were usually in winter quarters. The roads north of Stirling were covered with snow and difficult to travel but Argyll was determined to come to grips with the Jacobites as soon as he had a large enough army. On January 21st an advance party of dragoons set out to reconnoitre the road to Perth causing panic among the Jacobites. Having done nothing to protect the town for weeks they hurriedly set about fortifying it. Unfortunately they did not have a skilled military engineer to design the trenches and ramparts. Monsieur La Pange, a French dancing master, to whom the task was entrusted, made a ridiculous botch of it although hacking away at the frozen ground may at least have kept the troops warm.

Three days later Argyll moved to Dunblane, sending advance parties further north towards Auchterarder. It was at this stage, with the campaign all but lost as far as morale went, that James, probably influenced by Mar, authorized a particularly cynical and brutal move. In order to make things difficult for Argyll a scorched earth policy was adopted which involved burning a number of villages between Stirling and Perth to deny Argyll's men shelter and supplies.

On January 24th 1716 a party of Clanranald MacDonalds and Camerons left Perth and marched overnight to Auchterarder. Arriving in the small hours of the morning, and believing that Argyll's army was only a short distance away, they immediately roused the inhabitants and started burning their homes after taking their horses and any other useful booty. The luckless people were turned out into the snow. Only the church and the house of a Mrs Paterson, where local Jacobites had used to meet, were spared. The next day the same party burned Blackford and the day after Crieff. The proprietor of Crieff, Lord Drummond, was a Jacobite, as was his factor, or steward, who grimly helped the clansmen in their work. The inhabitants of Crieff had not supported their lord's political views and were now suffering for it.

On January 28th young Lord George Murray, the man who was to become the Jacobite's general in 1745, led a party of 300 to burn Dunning's thirty or so houses. The weather was bitterly cold and some sources claim that several people died of exposure as a result of being made homeless. Muthil and Dalreoch received the same treatment and then Auchterarder received a second visit to burn down a few houses which had survived the previous conflagration.

THE LONG RETREAT

This wanton destruction was particularly unnecessary as it seems that Mar had already decided on a retreat from Perth. By the end of January Argyll had received an artillery train and had an army three times as large as at Sheriffmuir. Mar held another council of war. Many Jacobites wanted to stay and fight. They pointed out that even their depleted army was more than strong enough to defend Perth. Argyll could not dig siegeworks in the frozen ground and, if forced to camp in open country outside the town, he could scarcely remain for more than a day or two in the bitter weather. Had James been more determined and ignored Mar's advice he might have made a stand at Perth and rallied his supporters. However, he was surrounded by Mar's friends and did not get the opportunity to hear the views of the more steadfast of his men who were determined to make a fight of it. Mar ensured that the more aggressive leaders were excluded from the final vote. The decision to retreat and, effectively, to abandon the rising was taken. On the last day of January the army left Perth, marching across the ice-covered Tay. The following day Argyll's men entered the town. The burnt villages had made their march harder but had not slowed them. The inhabitants had suffered for nothing.

The remainder of the campaign consisted of an orderly retreat by the Jacobites through the eastern Lowlands, via Dundee and Brechin to Aberdeen and on towards the Spey. Argyll followed them closely enough despite the intense cold and snow. That he did not catch up with them was largely due to the traditional mobility of the Highlanders. However, by this time Argyll was in increasing difficulty with the government who thought that he was treating the rebels too leniently and was not pursuing them vigorously enough. Ignoring the difficulties of campaigning through a hard Scottish winter they claimed that he was letting them escape. There is no indication that Red John was deliberately delaying but, equally, he was a Scotsman and might well have preferred to give the Jacobites an opportunity to disperse to their homes without a final battle. Suspicious of his loyalties the government sent General William Cadogan, supposedly to assist him but in practice to take command of the army. At the end of February Argyll handed over to Cadogan and returned south. His opponents succeeded in engineering his disgrace and he was stripped of most of his offices and responsibilities.

The Jacobite army diminished as the march continued until, in mid-February, the last remnants gathered at Ruthven in Badenoch, a place which seemed fated to be the scene of crucial events in Jacobite history. From there they dispersed to their homes. James had already abandoned them. On February 5th he had sailed from Montrose on a small French vessel. With him went Mar and one or two other Jacobite leaders. The Earl Marischal, whom James had asked to accompany them, refused to leave his men and steadfastly commanded the Jacobite rearguard during the rest of the march northwards. The captain of the *Marie Thérèse* successfully evaded patrolling men of war and reached France six days later. James' departure was eminently sensible — given that no French aid was likely there was little that he could achieve by remaining in Scotland. However, the manner in which he slipped away in secret without the army knowing — they only found out when they got to Aberdeen — disillusioned many of his supporters. Several leading Jacobites got away to France from harbours in the north east while others went north to Orkney to find friendly skippers willing to carry them into exile. Others merely returned home to await events.

6

THE REBELLION OF 1715:
THE ENGLISH CAMPAIGN

THE NORTHUMBERLAND RISING

After the rebellion the government claimed that the rising in northern England had been plotted well in advance. Although Jacobite agents were active in the area, the evidence points to the rising having been spontaneous. What precipitated it was a heavy-handed attempt by the government to arrest known Jacobites. This forced into rebellion some key figures who, with more sympathetic handling, would happily have stayed at home. After the failure of Ormonde's efforts in the south west, the north east was the most favourable part of England for a rising. Many landowners in the area were both Catholics and Jacobites. Their religion debarred them from lucrative political offices or military careers while rapidly rising taxes had reduced their income from rents. Many had interests in mining and the fact that the coal trade was going through a bad patch made their position worse. Most were heavily in debt, some close to bankruptcy and desperate enough to attempt anything. It was also believed that there was a broader base of opposition to the Hanoverian regime from the industrial workers of Tyneside, particularly the keelmen.

One leading Jacobite whose arrest was planned was Tom Forster, MP for Northumberland, who actually initiated the rising. Aged thirty-six, fattish, stooping, and hard-drinking, he was a man without any organizational or military talents. Forster was reliable only in his consistent failure to face the demands of any situation which confronted him. He seems to have initiated the rising out of blind panic. Hearing that a warrant had been issued for his arrest, he kept on the move. The messenger who had been sent to take him into custody got within half a mile of Bywell, a house belonging to the Fenwick family, which stood beside the Tyne downstream from Corbridge. At this point someone managed to get a warning to Forster, giving him just enough time to slip away.

Having sent messages to potential supporters, Forster held a meeting of Northumbrian Jacobites on October 6th at a place called Greenrig. Greenrig was 20km north of Corbridge, just east of the main road to Carter Bar and Jedburgh which, built on the line of the Roman Dere Street, runs

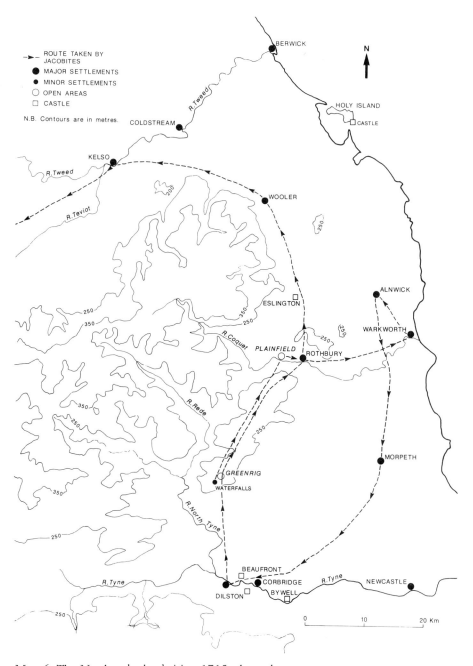

Map 6 The Northumberland rising 1715: the early manoeuvres.

straight across the broken topography, climbing then swooping sickeningly down over a seemingly endless succession of blind summits. An unfenced minor road leaves the main road and heads eastwards towards the wood fringed lake of Sweethope Loughs. Greenrig is merely a low ridge of moor between two shallow valleys draining into the lake. Forster had only a handful of followers plus three Jacobite agents: Colonel Henry Oxburgh and two Irish captains, Charles and Nicholas Wogan. Forster moved his small group to the top of Waterfalls, a low hill, rocky on its south side, a kilometre away across the shallow valley south of Greenrig. Today the name is attached to a farmstead which nestles at its foot. Here he was joined by the Earl of Derwentwater, the first of the Northumbrian nobility to declare for James, with a party of friends and servants, some of them mounted on the Earl's coach horses.

James Radcliffe, third Earl of Derwentwater, joined the Jacobites with reluctance, unlike Forster who was bankrupt and had nothing to lose. Despite the disadvantage of being Catholic, his family had built up a large and profitable estate in the valleys of the Tyne and its tributaries. Their lands also included lead mines on Alston Moor in the Pennines. When he was thirteen, Derwentwater had been sent to the Jacobite court at St Germain where he had been a companion to the young James, only a year older than himself. Derwentwater succeeded to the family estates in 1705 at the age of sixteen but until 1709 he remained abroad.

Returning to Northumberland he decided to rebuild the cramped tower house of Dilston with its limited Jacobean extension. The old house stood in an attractive setting beside Devil's Water near where it enters the Tyne a short distance below Hexham. He had a much larger house laid out around the old tower with three ranges of buildings enclosing a courtyard. In 1715 work on the west range with the main reception wings was still unfinished. Eighteenth-century drawings show the enlarged house to have been plain and rather barrack-like but, curiously, the only surviving remains are of the earlier castle and chapel which, overshadowed with trees, form part of a modern residential centre. After the rebellion, when the estates had been forfeited, they came into the possession of the Commissioners for Greenwich Hospital. They leased the house to tenants who so neglected the place that in 1765 the Commissioners had most of it demolished, leaving only the ruins of the earlier tower which you can still see today.

Derwentwater had recently married and although they had lived at Dilston for only a short time he and his young bride had become popular figures in the area. He was related to local Catholic landowners with Jacobite sympathies and, through their influence, had travelled to Lancashire and met some of the Jacobite gentry there. Unfortunately his wife seems to have encouraged him to join the rising although almost certainly the factor which pushed him into open rebellion was the issuing of a warrant for his arrest.

15 The ruins of Dilston Hall near Hexham, home of the third Earl of Derwentwater, one of the leaders of the Northumberland rising in 1715.

16 Greenrig, where Tom Forster held the first meeting of Northumbrian Jacobites.

On his way to join Forster, Derwentwater had called at Beaufront Castle, north of the Tyne between Hexham and Corbridge, the home of the Errington family, with whom he had stayed while Dilston was being renovated. Thomas Errington the heir came along with him. By now the party numbered around sixty horsemen. Forster was chosen as their leader for the simple reason that he was a Protestant. The embryo army consisted entirely of local Catholic gentlemen and their retainers. For the rising to succeed they needed the support of a broader spectrum of high church Tories in the north and they hoped that a non-Catholic leader would help in this. Forster had nothing else to recommend him but in fairness to this inadequate man it has to be said that none of the other gentlemen who joined the Northumbrian rising had any military experience or were any more decisive.

From the initial gathering at Waterfalls, Forster and his party moved northwards across the bleak moors of Harwood Forest and dropped down into the valley of the River Coquet to a place called Plainfield 7km to the west of the small market centre of Rothbury. Today the low-lying moor has been enclosed but the name survives attached to a farmstead and a couple of cottages. As they went they called at the mansions of known Jacobite sympathizers. By the time they reached Plainfield, late in the afternoon, the party had swelled to nearly 150. The fact that Forster's band were all mounted gave them considerable mobility which they failed to exploit. They were a curious-looking force; 'an army of fox hunters armed with light dress

17 The site of the Jacobites' rendezvous at Plainfield, near Rothbury.

swords' as one Scottish commentator described them. They even turned away potential recruits because they were short of weapons and couldn't use slower-moving infantry!

Plainfield was an open, uninviting spot so the party moved on to the little town of Rothbury for the night. Rothbury nestles in an attractive site beside the Coquet where its valley narrows between two blocks of moorland. It is hard to visualize it as the venue for the launching of a rebellion. Its main street, set on two levels around an elongated green shaded by mature trees, is one of the most peaceful in Northumberland. There, remote and temporarily beyond government reach, Forster's supporters must have felt pleased with

18 The entrance to the Three Half Moons Inn at Rothbury, the Northumbrian Jacobites' first headquarters.

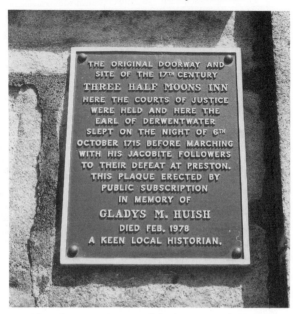

THE ORIGINAL DOORWAY AND
SITE OF THE 17TH CENTURY
THREE HALF MOONS INN
HERE THE COURTS OF JUSTICE
WERE HELD AND HERE THE
EARL OF DERWENTWATER
SLEPT ON THE NIGHT OF 6TH
OCTOBER 1715 BEFORE MARCHING
WITH HIS JACOBITE FOLLOWERS
TO THEIR DEFEAT AT PRESTON.
THIS PLAQUE ERECTED BY
PUBLIC SUBSCRIPTION
IN MEMORY OF
GLADYS M. HUISH
DIED FEB. 1978
A KEEN LOCAL HISTORIAN.

19 The plaque at the site of the Three Half Moons Inn.

themselves and exhilarated by the enterprise they had set in motion. Forster and the other leaders took over the Three Half Moons inn while the rest found quarters in the Black Bull and elsewhere in the town. Of the Three Half Moons only the doorway remains today, sandwiched between the parish church and the National Park information centre, but a plaque commemorates the inn as the site of the planning of the rising. Realizing that he needed more rank-and-file to swell his force Forster wrote to Mar asking for reinforcements of 2,000 infantry and 500 cavalry.

The next day, October 7th, they moved on to Warkworth, near the mouth of the Coquet and only a kilometre from the sea. Warkworth, set within a sharp bend of the Coquet, is one of the most attractive and dramatic villages in Northumberland. If you approach it on foot from the north, you cross a fourteenth-century bridge with a fortified gatehouse at the end and enter the main street which climbs up to the dominating mass of an impressive ruined medieval castle. Warkworth also boasts the most complete Norman church in Northumberland, set beside the river at the bottom of the main street. Close to the church is the market cross. Warkworth has the dubious distinction of being the first place in England at which James III was proclaimed king. The local vicar, called upon by Forster to pray for James, refused indignantly, and a Jacobite chaplain took his place. Like Rothbury, it seemed an unlikely base for a rebellion. The reason for the move to Warkworth is not clear: presumably it was not completely aimless! At least on the coast they could

20 Warkworth, dominated by its imposing castle, provided the Jacobites with a temporary base.

intercept any vessels with reinforcements coming from France. At Warkworth the Jacobites were joined by a band of horsemen from Scotland. The latter had mustered at Coldstream, proclaiming James king in the market place, before moving over the Border to Wooler. Worried about the possibility of being attacked by troops from the garrison at Berwick-on-Tweed, they moved south to join Forster.

Undoubtedly Forster's best hope for an early success to bolster the rising would have been a quick move on Newcastle. Its medieval walls were crumbling and the ironwork of the gates was so rusty that they would hardly close. Local Jacobites considered that with a little help they could easily take over the town and there were high hopes of widespread support from the Tyneside keelmen. However, the leading Newcastle Whigs acted fast, throwing up barricades and mustering the town's trained bands while Forster delayed until the Whig supporters in the city had been reinforced by government dragoons and infantry.

THE CAPTURE OF LINDISFARNE CASTLE

After five days at Warkworth the Jacobites moved on to Alnwick — further from Newcastle! A few more recruits came in but otherwise they achieved nothing. They may have been hoping for reinforcements, supplies, or at least

21 The old parish church at Warkworth where James Francis Edward was proclaimed James III of England.

news from France but none came; for the moment they were on their own. During this period of inactivity there occurred a startling piece of individual enterprise which showed that despite the incapacity of their leaders on both sides of the Border, the Jacobites still had men of initiative and action. This event was the capture, almost single-handed, of Lindisfarne Castle.

Lindisfarne, or Holy Island, lies off the Northumberland coast but is accessible over the sands at low tide. Famous for its Dark-Age monastery, victim of the first recorded Viking raid in the north and its medieval abbey, Lindisfarne also had a small castle, built on a low but prominent crag, an outcrop of volcanic lava, at the south eastern tip of the island. Seen from the mainland it is Lindisfarne's most prominent feature, its steepness accentuated by the low, even silhouette of the rest of the island. The castle had been built at the end of the 1540s from stone taken from the medieval abbey. It was designed to guard the island's harbour as part of Protector Somerset's campaign against the Scots. Although it mounted two batteries of cannon, one facing the open sea the other covering the harbour, its garrison was small; a mere twenty men or so. It continued in use into the early nineteenth century but was then left to fall into ruin. It was restored early in the present century by the famous architect Sir Edward Lutyens, who retained most of the castle's original layout. Today it is open to the public and if you climb the steep flight of stairs which leads up beside the lower battery to the entrance you get a view which has changed little from the Jacobite period.

In 1715 it was held by a small party of government troops detached from the garrison at Berwick. Lancelot Errington, captain of a merchant vessel based at Newcastle, knew the coast well. As he had been employed in landing provisions for the garrison he also knew its size. An active Jacobite, he determined on a piece of private enterprise. On October 10th he called with provisions. He invited the sergeant in charge of unloading the cargo, along with most of his men, on board for a drink and soon had them paralytic. Then, helped by his nephew, he coolly walked into the castle and overpowered the couple of remaining sentries. James' flag was soon flying from the battlements.

With reinforcements, the castle might have been a useful holding point where vessels from France could land, but Errington had no time to let Forster know what he had done. Next day the Governor of Berwick, hearing what had happened from the shamefaced and hungover troops, sent a party of thirty soldiers along with fifty local volunteers to recapture the fortress. Errington and his nephew sensibly decided that forty to one was rather long odds and when they saw the party approaching they scrambled down the crag and hid among the nearby rocks intending to sneak across to the mainland when darkness fell. Unfortunately for Lancelot he was spotted and was wounded in the thigh by a musket ball. He was taken to Berwick but, resourceful to the last, he escaped by tunnelling through the wall of his room. Shortly after the castle was recaptured, two French vessels did appear off the island but, failing to receive any friendly signals, they sailed away.

THE ARRIVAL OF THE SCOTS

Having moved north to Alnwick, on October 14th, Forster returned southwards to Morpeth, a larger market town, and then on to Hexham the following day. He had about 300 men but he received news that Newcastle was now so strongly held that an attack was out of the question. General Carpenter, an experienced soldier, had arrived to take command there and two more regiments of dragoons were on their way to join him. At the same time he got word that a group of Jacobites from south-western Scotland had arrived at Rothbury. Joining up with them allowed Forster to move away from Newcastle without seeming to be retreating!

The Scots were a small party led by Viscount Kenmure, the Earl of Nithsdale and the Earl of Carnwath. The area they came from was strongly Whig in character and their small aristocratic group was out of step with the general feeling in Dumfries and Galloway. Like many other Jacobite leaders they had been pushed unwillingly into rebellion by government attempts to take them into custody. Gathering at Lochmaben they planned to take over the town of Dumfries. They were joined by the young Earl of Winton, whose lands lay east of Edinburgh, and some of his followers. The combined force, numbering about 150 horsemen, decided that Dumfries was too strongly held by the local Whigs for them to attempt an attack. Instead they rode through the Borders towards Kelso, another town which they considered capturing but decided was too strongly held. Having received messages from Forster, they turned south to join him.

At Rothbury Forster spent another convivial night at the Three Half Moons with his new allies. The combined forces then went north to Wooler. Here they were joined by the Rev. Robert Patten who became Forster's chaplain. Patten was later to turn King's evidence and testify against his former colleagues but in doing so he wrote the most detailed and interesting account of the English rising. Hearing that Mackintosh of Borlum with his High-landers was at Duns, they rode north and the two groups met just outside Kelso. A local landowner had organized Whig supporters to barricade the town, mounting some cannon taken from Hume Castle, but when the two Jacobite forces approached from opposite directions they quietly slipped away. The Highlanders arrived with bagpipes playing. Borlum, at their head, made an impressive figure but the Scots were bedraggled from their long march in the rain. The next day Patten preached a sermon in the town's main kirk and the following day the whole army formed up in the market place to proclaim James as their lawful king.

The Jacobites now had an army of around 2,000, albeit a rather oddly structured one, large enough to achieve something useful. But what were they to do? None of the English or Scottish nobles had any military experience; their decision to give command of the army to Kenmure while in Scotland and Forster when in England demonstrates this amply. Their only professional soldier was Borlum who, although he had brought in the greater part of the army, was not given much say. Not surprisingly, Borlum was almost permanently at odds with the other Jacobite leaders; a blunt and single-minded man, he did not suffer fools gladly.

Borlum's advice was characteristically straightforward: advance on Carpen-ter, bring him to battle, and defeat him. Borlum was probably right. While the Jacobites were at Kelso, Carpenter had marched north from Newcastle with one regiment of infantry and two of dragoons — around 1,000 men. Two days later he was at Wooler, only a day's march away. Carpenter's dragoons were mostly raw recruits; they were tired after their long march and many had dropped out on the way. Despite the Highlanders' traditional aversion to fighting horsemen the government forces, if tackled directly, would probably not have constituted very serious opposition. A decisive victory at this point might have brought in support from throughout northern England as well as providing Mar with encouragement.

Borlum was overruled though and other possibilities were discussed. Winton and other Scottish nobles proposed marching into western Scotland, via Dumfries and Ayr towards Glasgow. This would create a useful diversion in Argyll's rear. Forster and the English leaders, however, favoured moving

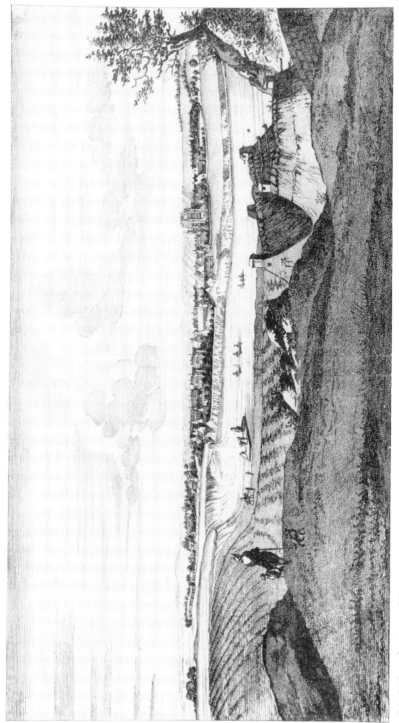

22 Kelso, dominated by its ruined abbey, where the Northumberland Jacobites joined forces with Borlum and his Highlanders.

into Lancashire for they had received letters from Lancashire Jacobites promising substantial support. Several of the Northumberland landowners had relatives in Lancashire who had made extravagant claims of how many men they could raise. Disagreement within the Jacobite army was heightened by antipathy between the Scottish and English components which more than once nearly came to blows. As Patten commented, 'there was a fate attending all their councils for they could never agree to any one thing that tended to their advantage'.

A compromise was reached whereby the army would march westwards through Scotland parallel to the Border so that they could postpone the decision as to whether to turn south into Cumbria or continue towards Dumfries. From Kelso they marched to Jedburgh and then on to Hawick where the Scots flatly refused to march into England. The Northumberland horsemen surrounded them to try and force them to agree and the Highlanders cocked their muskets ready to fight them if necessary. The quarrel was patched up and the army continued its aimless progress along the Border. At Langholm a party of horsemen was sent ahead to establish the strength of Dumfries but once more they concluded that the town was too well defended. This was used by the English leaders as the clinching argument in favour of turning south towards Lancashire. The Scots believed that they could easily force their way into Dumfries which would make a useful base but no one would listen. 20,000 Lancashire men were ready to rise for King James — or so the letters they had received claimed — and the decision was taken to go south. Most of the Highlanders were persuaded to stay but a body of about 500 marched off in disgust to try and rejoin Mar. They had a long journey through country whose inhabitants mostly supported the government and few of them managed to evade capture on the way. Nevertheless, they probably came off better than their compatriots who stayed with Forster.

THE MARCH INTO LANCASHIRE

The Jacobite army marched from Langholm to Longtown and on to Brampton, avoiding Carlisle. The town and castle were not strongly held but lacking any artillery it would have been difficult for them to have attempted an assault on the city. Cumbria produced only two recruits. This cannot have helped morale but on the positive side was a bloodless success against the Cumberland militia, assembled by the Lord Lieutenant of the county and the Bishop of Carlisle, and strengthened with forces raised by the local sheriff. They gathered on Penrith Fell to oppose the Jacobite army but thought better of it and disbanded in confusion as the Jacobites approached.

From Penrith they continued south by Appleby to Kendal which they reached on November 5th. The winter weather was bad and the journey a hard one; it was a bedraggled and downcast body of men who entered the 'auld grey town', mud splattered, with six sodden pipers playing at their head. Borlum led his men, looking grim according to an eyewitness, as well he might for it had rained for several days and his troops were soaked. The Highlanders, wearing their coarse woollen plaids woven in reds, blues, blacks, and greens, must have presented an outlandish spectacle to the citizens of Kendal. In an age when it had ceased to become normal for Englishmen, even in the north, to carry arms, the clansmen, armed to the teeth with broadswords, targets, dirks, pistols, and muskets, would have looked alien and frightening.

They proclaimed King James at the Cold Stone or cross in the main street and dispersed to find comfortable quarters. The base of the cross still stands outside the modern Town Hall. Derwentwater lodged at the White Lion, other officers at the Kings Arms nearby. Forster moved into the house of Alderman Simpson then went to pay his respects to his godmother, a Mrs Bellingham. She lived in a house in Stramongate which is now a bookshop. A staunch Whig, she refused to have anything to do with Forster and when he went upstairs to see her she boxed his ears and threw him out calling him a rebel and a popish tool!

The following day they marched a relatively short distance to Kirkby Lonsdale. It was a Sunday and Patten preached in the parish church with its fine Norman arcading. On the 7th of November the Jacobites continued to Lancaster. They made a more impressive entrance into Lancaster than they had done at Kendal, swords drawn, drums beating, colours flying, and bagpipes playing. From Lancaster they were entering territory which should have produced more recruits. These did indeed begin to come in but they were almost all Catholics. There was disappointingly little response from the local High Anglican Tories.

Lancaster, though a small town, was prosperous, a river port trading actively with the New World. Sir Henry Hoghton, in charge of the local militia, had proposed demolishing the bridge over the Lune but the townsfolk had protested. They claimed that this would damage their trade to no purpose as the river could easily be crossed a short way upstream. Hoghton also tried to force a local merchant who had a large vessel moored at Sunderland Point, Lancaster's modest outport at the mouth of the Lune, to hand over its cannon in case the rebels seized them. The merchant refused, scared that if he did this the Jacobites might burn his vessel as a reprisal. Hoghton had about 600 local militia, too small and inexperienced a force to challenge the Jacobites, and he prudently withdrew southwards towards the Ribble leaving the Jacobites to enter the town. They took what money they could find from the customs house on the quayside. They also removed the cannon from the vessel in the river and mounted them on makeshift carriages using wheels taken from Hoghton's abandoned coach.

23 The house in Stramongate, Kendal, where Tom Forster's godmother lived. A staunch Whig, she threw him out as a rebel.

THE SIEGE OF PRESTON

On the 9th the cavalry reached Preston where the infantry joined them the next day. The army went through the by now customary ritual of proclaiming James at the market cross. They received a good deal of support from the inhabitants of the town and the surrounding countryside which boosted morale. After a long day's march over muddy and difficult roads they felt they had earned a rest. They found the ladies of Preston so attractive and attentive that for a short time the main purpose of the campaign was forgotten.

Forster intended to push on to Manchester where he expected large numbers of supporters, High Church Tories as well as Catholics, to join him.

24 Timber-framed houses in Kirkland, Kendal showing what the rest of the town was like at the time of the 1715 rebellion.

Unknown to him, however, General Wills, commanding the government troops in Cheshire, had marched north by Manchester and Wigan to intercept him. Carpenter, who had crossed the Pennines in pursuit of the Jacobites, was now approaching Preston from the east. The swift approach of Wills' men seems to have caught Forster by surprise. He had been keeping his eye on Carpenter but he appears to have been relying on local Jacobites for warning of troops coming from the south; a warning which they never gave. On the night of November 11th Forster held a meeting of the Jacobite leaders in his inn, the Mitre, overlooking the market place. They decided to stand fast in Preston until they saw what Wills would do.

Preston was larger than Lancaster, being a market town of around 6,000 inhabitants which acted as a local social centre; many landowners from the surrounding countryside had town houses there. Although the Ribble provided access to the sea the town stood away from the river to the north on a plateau overlooking the valley. From the east of the town the main road southwards dropped down to the Ribble, crossed it at Walton le Dale and ran on towards Wigan. From the bottom of Fishergate, to the west of the town, another road descended to a ford then climbed again through Penwortham heading towards Liverpool.

The market town of the Jacobite era was transformed in the nineteenth century, and was the model for Dickens' 'Coketown', the epitome of industrial squalor. Yet despite this the layout of the town centre has not changed greatly. The Ribble still defends Preston to the south, the two bridges at Penwortham and Walton le Dale causing rush-hour traffic bottlenecks. If you approach the town by the new by-pass west of Walton le Dale, which joins the old road near the Ribble bridge, you get a fine view of the skyline of the town centre. This is dominated by a cluster of tower blocks among which it is difficult to pick out the spire of Rickman's nineteenth-century parish church which replaced the one on the same site used by the Jacobites as an observation post. Nevertheless you can still get a good impression of the steep slope up from the river which made an attack on the town from the south a difficult proposition.

The following day Forster rode across the Ribble bridge to reconnoitre and almost ran into an advance party of Wills' dragoons. He galloped back to Preston to give the alarm. Farquharson of Invercauld had been ordered to guard the bridge with a party of Highlanders but as Wills approached these men were withdrawn. Some historians have argued that this was a fatal error; if the bridge had been held against Wills the Jacobites could have prevented themselves from being surrounded. However, Borlum favoured abandoning the bridge and defending Preston from close in. His argument was that there were other fords by which the dragoons could cross the Ribble and that the Jacobites did not have enough men to guard all of them effectively.

Instead they began to barricade the streets leading into the town. It was sensible to concentrate on the town centre because the outskirts formed too wide a perimeter for effective defence. This would force the dragoons to dismount and fight on foot while reducing the risk of exposing the Highlanders to horsemen. Wills had no artillery to blast his way through the barricades though Borlum cannot have been sure of this when the Hanoverians first approached.

Plate 26 shows the Jacobites' plan of defence. The main roads leading up from the bridge and the ford at Penwortham — Church Street and Fishergate — were blocked off, as was Friargate which ran north-westwards from the town centre. Another barricade to the east of the Market Place prevented a flank attack on Church Street. The street layout has not altered much despite the later industrial developments but the eighteenth-century streets were

25 The nineteenth-century parish church of Preston on the same site as the church used by the Jacobites as an observation post. The main barricade down Church Street stood just to the left.

probably narrower and easier to block. Beyond the main barricades outer defences were thrown up, probably designed to delay the government forces and to be abandoned at need. The Jacobite horsemen commanded by Kenmure were mustered in the churchyard and the tower of the parish church was used as a lookout post.

Wills arrived at the Ribble in the early afternoon, moving his men down to the bridge cautiously, suspecting a trap. An ambush during the Civil Wars in the deeply hollowed road leading from the bridge to the town had given Cromwell some nasty moments when he found the hedges above the sunken lane lined with musketeers. Wills was surprised to find the bridge unguarded.

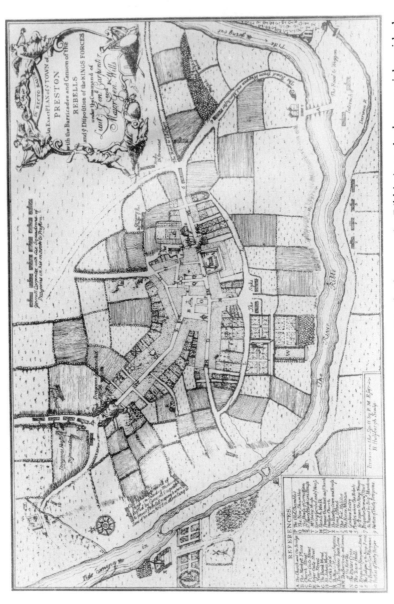

26 A contemporary plan of the battle of Preston. The bridge over the Ribble is at the bottom right with the sunken lane leading up towards Church Street. Around the parish church and the market place you can see the location of the Jacobite barricades.

At first he thought the Jacobites had retreated northwards but he soon discovered that they had dug in. Riding too close to the town his party was fired on and two men hit so he did not bother to make a formal request for surrender. Instead he prepared to attack the town, sending his men forward to probe the Jacobite defences. The first regiment to attack was known as 'Preston's' after its colonel but in reality it was the Cameronians. It was an ironic reversal of the situation at Dunkeld in 1689 for here were the Cameronians attacking a town strongly defended by Highlanders!

The first attack by the Cameronians was made up Church Street. The barricades here were being defended by Borlum, commanding a mixed force of Northumbrians, Lowland Scots, and Highlanders. The government troops met a withering fire from the Highlanders manning the outer barricade. Some had been posted in houses overlooking the barricades, particularly the town house of Sir Henry Hoghton which overlooked the foot of Church Street and the lane leading to the bridge. The height of this building gave it a commanding position and its flat roof provided an ideal vantage point for some fifty Highland sharpshooters. Borlum's defences allowed his men to make the most of their marksmanship and government losses were heavy. One estimate suggests as many as 120 casualties and the Cameronians were eventually beaten back.

Borlum thought it prudent to abandon the outer defences and strengthen the main one. Hoghton's house was abandoned and quickly occupied by government troops who set fire to the houses and barns between it and the main barricade. Later that day Forrester's dragoons mounted another attack up Church Street. At the main barricade Borlum had mounted two cannon from the vessel at Lancaster but because of a lack of trained gunners they proved to be of little use. Lord Forrester mustered his men in a side alley then stepped out into Church Street to see how the land lay, calmly ignoring the musket fire aimed at him. His men then rushed the barricade but this attack was also beaten back with significant losses on the government side and only a few casualties among the Jacobites.

According to one source Forster ordered Borlum to sally out after this attack and pursue the government troops. Borlum refused: he was ready for a fight but he was not prepared to expose his Highlanders to an attack by mounted dragoons unless he was supported by the Jacobite cavalry. He may well have suspected that these, had they been given the opportunity, might have galloped off to save themselves.

Other attacks were made on the barrier north of Church Street commanded by Lord Charles Murray which protected Borlum's flank. When the fighting became fierce the Rev. Patten, acting as a messenger, brought over some fifty of Derwentwater's gentlemen volunteers to help, and had his horse shot from under him in the process. Attacks were also mounted on the Friargate barricade by dragoons who had ridden around to the north of the town and then dismounted to fight on foot. The Mackintoshes were defending this barrier and they opened up a murderous fire on the dragoons causing many casualties, including their brigadier who was shot in the leg. The attacking troops were mostly raw recruits but, encouraged by their officers, they advanced bravely. The result was the same; Wills' men were beaten back with significant losses. As the government troops retreated they set fire to the buildings around the barricades.

An attack directly up the slope from the river towards the town was also beaten back. As night fell sniping continued but though there were many false alarms there was little real action. Wills had not surrounded the town completely and in the darkness many of the men who had recently joined the Jacobites — mere rustics who Borlum had decided were not worth the expense of feeding — slipped away down Fishergate into open country. They were wise.

The following morning Wills mounted another attack up Church Street against Borlum's barricade but, like the previous ones, it was unsuccessful. This was the end of serious fighting though. A short time later Carpenter arrived with his three dragoon regiments and a substantial number of militia and volunteers. Forster had taken no active part in the fighting so far and had remained at the Mitre Inn. Although the Jacobites' defence of Preston had been spirited and effective, Forster became convinced that their position was untenable and that they were lost. Lord Widdrington, Colonel Oxburgh, and some of the other leaders agreed with him, though the Highlanders were all for carrying on fighting despite the fact that they were running out of gunpowder.

The arrival of Carpenter with over 2,000 reinforcements was the last straw and from that time on Forster was only concerned with negotiating the best possible terms for surrender. In the afternoon Colonel Oxburgh was sent to the government headquarters to discuss terms. With the town completely surrounded now, Wills held all the aces and he took a tough line, offering only unconditional surrender and giving the Jacobites an hour to make their mind up. An hour later one of his officers, Colonel Cotton, rode into town and up to the Mitre to ask for their reply. In the meantime the Scots, realizing that they were being sold out, had sent a separate envoy to discuss capitulation. They asked for a truce until 7am the following morning. Having received no firm answer, Cotton rode back but as he left the town his drummer, who had come to beat the call for a parley, was shot by a sniper, possibly a Highlander. This did not improve the feelings of Wills and his men but eventually they agreed to give the Jacobites until the following morning provided that they gave up hostages. Derwentwater and Colonel Mackintosh, one of Borlum's officers, then surrendered themselves.

The Jacobites were in a state of high tension. The Scots, particularly Borlum, wanted to cut their way out and escape northwards. Unfortunately the terms of the ceasefire ruled this out if they were to retain their honour. Had Forster come out of the Mitre and appeared in the street he would probably have been set upon. Prudently, he remained indoors. This did not stop an enraged Highland officer from charging in and attempting to shoot Forster with a pistol. Patten, Forster's chaplain, narrowly averted a possible murder which few would have regretted by deflecting the firearm. The ball embedded itself in the panelling instead of in Forster!

The next morning at 7am the Jacobites surrendered; the officers handed over their swords in the churchyard while the nobles were allowed to do so with more privacy inside the Mitre. Government casualties are hard to estimate as Wills played down his losses but about 150 killed and as many wounded is probably not too wide of the mark. These losses may help to explain the tough attitude which the Hanoverians took with their captives, some 1,500 of them. The rank and file prisoners were herded into the church and kept there for a month in overcrowded and very uncomfortable conditions. Six prisoners who had held commissions in the regular army were court-martialled and four of them, who did not have enough influence to gain a reprieve, were executed by firing squad. Meanwhile the more important prisoners had been sent to London. The Whigs clearly thought that a few show trials would impress upon those with latent Jacobite sympathies the folly of rebellion.

THE PRISONERS IN LONDON

Over 100 leading members of Forster's little army were brought to London. They had plenty of time to ponder on their follies during the journey. On being told where they were to be imprisoned, Derwentwater ruefully suggested that the most suitable place to lodge them would be Bedlam! They reached the outskirts of the capital on December 9th. There their arms were tied and their escort increased for the final parade through the city. It was felt that a pro-Jacobite mob might try to release them; moreover, this treatment also robbed them of any dignity they had left. If they had been hoping for a sympathetic reception and possible rescue they were disappointed: the London Whigs had turned out in force to jeer at them and wise Jacobite supporters kept a low profile as the prisoners were paraded through the streets.

The Jacobite peers were lodged in the Tower and other important prisoners, including Forster and Borlum, in Newgate. Forster protested at this attack on his dignity. He felt that he should have been in the Tower too. The Marshalsea and Fleet prisons took the remainder. The peers were charged with high treason after being brought to Westminster for preliminary examinations. Their situation was a bad one but they did not lack comforts entirely. On one occasion the keepers who were returning them to the Tower allowed them to stop for dinner at the Fountain Inn in the Strand and then to buy snuff at the shop next door before returning them to their prison.

All the peers save the Earl of Winton pleaded guilty. When asked to explain their conduct Kenmure and the Earl of Carnwath had the sense to merely admit their guilt and plead for mercy. The others produced a set of lame excuses. They had been forced into rebellion. They had joined the rebels unwittingly without realizing what was going on. They had been forcibly detained with the rebel army and had not been able to escape. This only made them look like liars or idiots — or both. Derwentwater's statement that he had joined the rising on impulse because many of his friends and neighbours had done so, and that he had not engaged in any preliminary plotting, at least rings true.

Faced with these unconvincing testimonies and given that the Whigs were out for blood, it was not surprising that all six were sentenced to death: to be hanged by the neck but cut down before death, to have their bowels removed and burnt in front of them, to be beheaded, and then have their bodies cut into quarters. In a society which was brutal in many ways this medieval punishment still had the power to shock even the most hardened. However, because of the rank of the prisoners, the sentence was commuted to straightforward beheading. Winton was tried later and, given that the dice were loaded against him and that he had no real hope of winning, he put up a spirited defence. A quirky and unconventional character who was only twenty-six at the time — quite mad according to many contemporaries — he nevertheless showed great skill in the courtroom and proved that he was far from stupid. In the end he too was found guilty.

While the peers were being tried the other prisoners were being dealt with. Most pleaded not guilty and asked for adjournments to give them time to prepare their defences. Most who were tried were found guilty but some were acquitted. Invercauld, who had been at odds with Mar at the start of the rebellion, successfully claimed that he had been forced to join the rebels by his feudal superior. Two Lancashire Jacobites, Robert Towneley and Edward Tildesley, were also acquitted though there was ample evidence of their involvement with the Jacobite army. The government might be keen to take a tough line but there was more sympathy for the rebels among the ordinary people who sat on juries.

On February 24th Derwentwater and Viscount Kenmure were taken from the Tower to Tower Hill and beheaded in front of a large crowd. Derwentwater seems to have been expecting a reprieve right up to the last moment. He made a speech in which he recanted his former admissions of guilt and acknowledged James as his true king though he wistfully remarked that had he been reprieved by King George he would have been content to live in peace thereafter. Kenmure met his fate with more coolness and dignity, and less oratory. The executions had a marked effect on public opinion which began to turn against the government's harsh attitude. It was probably due to this that the remaining four peers were reprieved. Indeed there were only four more executions in London. Colonel Oxburgh was one and, not being peers, they had to suffer the full barbarity of being hanged, drawn, and quartered at Tyburn.

JACOBITE ESCAPES

A surprising aspect of the aftermath of the rebellion in England is how many leading prisoners managed to escape from prison and get out of the country. It is worth remembering though that the prison system operated differently in eighteenth-century England than today. Prisons were less secure, turnkeys more easily bribed. The system at Newgate and in many other prisons was designed to squeeze as much money out of the prisoners as possible in return for various privileges. Anyone who was committed to Newgate and had no funds was thrust into the Black Hole where they were lucky to survive until their execution. On the other hand money could buy all sorts of concessions. Alcohol was easily obtained, provided that turnkeys and fellow inmates were also supplied. A drunken stupor was probably the best state in which to endure Newgate. Women were readily available too; female prisoners were allowed to mix with the men and those women who had been condemned to death were often eager to get pregnant so that they could 'plead their bellies' and save themselves. Money could buy fresh air in the exercise yard while visitors could come and go freely. Many Jacobites had sufficient private means to ameliorate their conditions and in addition many sympathizers provided them with funds.

In a situation like this bribery was easy. It was probably partly by these means that Forster escaped from Newgate just before his trial. One night he was drinking with the prison governor. Having got the man well stewed Forster sent his servant out for another bottle. When the servant failed to return Forster announced that he would go and see where he had got to. Taking a duplicate key which had been made by the local blacksmith on his estate, according to one story, he locked the governor in and made his escape. The plot had been carefully arranged for there was a vessel waiting to take him to France. Had Forster shown the same energy and initiative in command of his army the Northumberland rising might have taken a different course! Borlum also escaped from Newgate in a characteristically direct manner. With a group of prisoners he rushed the guards one day and escaped into the street. Several prisoners were recaptured but, despite a price on his head, Borlum reached France. It was only later that, on returning ill-advisedly to Scotland, he was recaptured and imprisoned once more — this time in Edinburgh Castle from where he did not succeed in escaping, dying in captivity at the age of eighty-seven.

The Earl of Nithsdale got out of the Tower even more improbably by the hoary old dodge of exchanging clothes and walking out dressed as a woman. After lying low in London for a while he got away to the Continent dressed in the livery of a servant of the Venetian ambassador (who knew nothing of the plot). Winton too escaped from the Tower, supposedly by sawing through the bars of his room, though it is likely that his guards had been bribed to look the other way.

The rank and file prisoners who had been left in Lancashire were eventually moved from Preston parish church to Lancaster Castle and prisons in Liverpool and Chester. Over seventy were tried in Liverpool and most were found guilty but the majority never came to trial. A number died in prison awaiting trial. Most of the remainder had the sense to petition for deportation before trial thus avoiding the chance of the death penalty. Most were probably shipped to the Caribbean. Over thirty of those who were convicted were executed and the authorities clearly set out to strike fear into the hearts of Lancashire Jacobites by spreading the executions out between the main towns. Lancaster, Preston, Garstang, Wigan, Manchester, and Liverpool all received their share. The men executed in Preston and Garstang were mostly locals, some of them labourers and tradesmen but most of them gentlemen like Richard Shuttleworth whose head was ordered to be fixed on the town hall. It was a grim warning to the inhabitants of this potentially volatile area. Memory of the executions may have helped reduce support from Lancashire in 1745. Unlike London there were few escapes though one enterprising group, en route for the colonies, succeeded in taking over the ship that was carrying them to the American plantations and sailing her to France.

In Scotland there were fewer prisoners as most Jacobites had retired from Mar's disintegrating army in good time and were safely back in the Highlands. In addition, public opinion was far more strongly in favour of leniency than in England and any attempts by the authorities in Edinburgh to emulate the trials and executions that had taken place in London would probably have been stopped by major riots. Many of the leaders who had submitted in good time before the rising ended, including Huntly, were released. The government at Westminster then decided that to prevent undue leniency the remaining prisoners should be brought across the Border to Carlisle for trial. This was in direct contravention of the articles of Union and drew howls of protest from the Scottish judiciary. Nevertheless they moved over seventy prisoners south. In the end they achieved little by it. Over thirty prisoners were released without trial and most of the rest, although found guilty, were never sentenced and were later released. On the other hand, although no peers had been executed in Scotland a substantial number of landowners who had supported James and who had fled to France had their estates forfeited.

The story of the 1715 rebellion does not make very edifying reading, which is perhaps why it is less well known than the more spectacular rising of 1745. It was a botched job from start to finish, largely due to the poor performance of the leading figures. Had Ormonde moved faster and not panicked he might have been able to unite enough support in the west of England to constitute a real threat. Had Mar possessed any military ability and had he moved south from Perth sooner he could have wiped out Argyll's forces and made himself master of Scotland. This would probably have brought in many more supporters enabling him to mount an invasion of northern England on a larger scale than Charles Edward Stuart did in 1745. This in turn might have prompted more English Jacobites to declare themselves. Had Forster acted decisively he might have turned the Northumbrian rising into a more serious affair than the tragi-comic effort which emerged. One cannot escape the conclusion that the government was extremely lucky. It had run down the regular forces in Britain to such a low level that they were unable to act fast when the rebellion started. The government response after the rising was inconsistent, probably because they had to change their course of action in response to public opinion. In Scotland the forfeiture of the estates of Jacobite supporters deprived them of the power of raising forces for King James in the future but, as we shall see, the measures which the government took did little to remove the threat of the Highlands as a potential gathering ground for a future rising.

7

BETWEEN THE 'FIFTEEN AND THE 'FORTY-FIVE

THE 1719 REBELLION: THE SPANIARDS INTERVENE

Despite the failure of the 1715 rebellion the Jacobite cause remained active, particularly in Scotland where the rising had fizzled out rather than been defeated. The prospect of military aid from France had faded with the death of Louis XIV but the possibility of help emerged from another source. Spain was drawn into war with Britain in 1718 for various reasons. These included dissatisfaction with the terms of the Treaty of Utrecht, under which they had lost territory in the Netherlands and Italy, and anger at British interference in the Mediterranean. Philip of Spain's chief minister, Cardinal Alberoni, who was sympathetic to the Jacobite cause, devised a scheme to cause Britain maximum annoyance with minimum resources. The plan was to assemble an invasion fleet commanded by the Duke of Ormonde who, despite his shortcomings as a leader during the 1715 rising, was still well regarded. The expedition, consisting of 5,000 regular Spanish troops, a train of artillery, and arms for a further 15,000 men, was to land in England and form the nucleus of another Jacobite rebellion. Ormonde proposed that, as had been intended in 1715, the main rising should be in western England but that a diversion should also be staged by landing a small force in Scotland. This would encourage another Highland rising which would tie down government troops as far from the main landing as possible.

Ormonde proposed young George Keith, hereditary Earl Marischal of Scotland, who had served creditably under Mar in the 1715 campaign, as leader of the diversionary attack which was to consist of only two frigates and about 300 Spanish infantry, with 2,000 muskets and ammunition. The Jacobite court in exile had moved from France to Lorraine, then to Avignon, and finally to the small hilltop town of Urbino in Italy as a result of British diplomatic pressure. The Old Pretender, who was to accompany the main fleet, set out for Spain to join the expedition at the northern port of Corunna. First, however, the ships had to be assembled at Cadiz, where the troops were to be embarked. They were to sail to Corunna for final provisioning before heading for England.

The fleet duly left Cadiz but on its way northwards it was struck by a severe storm which scattered the ships and nearly sank several of them. The battered vessels limped into various Spanish ports; only ten reached Corunna. Conditions for the soldiers, crammed below decks in the darkness, with the ships rolling violently and leaking badly, can be imagined. Several of them died and the rest were in no condition to fight. Nor was the fleet able to transport them to England. The Spanish authorities were forced to cancel the expedition. Once again the elements had intervened to wreck Jacobite hopes!

A DIVIDED COMMAND

Unfortunately, the smaller diversionary expedition sailed from San Sebastian at about the same time the main force had left Cadiz and George Keith did not realize that the invasion had been abandoned. They pressed on, dodging British men-of-war, to make a landfall in the Outer Hebrides. The Earl Marischal's brother James Keith had gone to France to recruit other Jacobite exiles to join the expedition. He hired a small vessel and sailed from the mouth of the Seine. With him was the Earl of Seaforth, in whose territory the landing was to be made, Cameron of Lochiel, MacDonald of Clanranald, and the Marquis of Tullibardine, the popular but ineffectual eldest son of the Duke of Atholl. Unfortunately the leading Jacobite exiles had split into two factions, centred around Ormonde and Mar. In bringing some of Mar's supporters on an expedition planned by Ormonde, James Keith was merely storing up trouble for his brother.

Sailing around Land's End in the darkness the party from France blundered into a large fleet. Optimistically, they hoped that these were Ormonde's vessels en route for the West Country. In fact they were British men-of-war escorting a convoy of transports bringing troops back from Ireland to counter Ormonde's expected landing! The Hanoverian government had got wind of the planned invasion well in advance. The small Jacobite vessel was lucky to escape notice in the darkness. They caught up with the two Spanish frigates at Stornoway on the east side of the island of Lewis. The Earl Marischal had proposed an immediate landing on the mainland and a quick overland strike at Inverness, which was known to be held by a garrison of only 300. He held a council of war with the leaders who had arrived from France and Tullibardine produced a commission as commander-in-chief of Jacobite forces in Scotland which had been granted directly by the Old Pretender. This, he claimed, gave him precedence over the Earl Marischal, whose appointment had only been made by Ormonde. George Keith reluctantly gave way as far as command of the troops was concerned but insisted that the ships had been given into his personal charge by Alberoni and that he had no intention of relinquishing control over them.

Tullibardine at first suggested that they should wait in Lewis until they received definite news that Ormonde had landed with the main invasion force. Although this fitted his vacillating character it was, as it turned out, sound advice. Despite the change of command the original proposal for an immediate descent on the mainland was kept to, though not the plan for attacking Inverness. After some delays due to contrary winds the expedition rounded Skye and anchored in Loch Alsh, the narrow strait which separates Skye from the mainland. The Jacobites set up camp at the castle of Eilean Donan.

Eilean Donan is one of the most picturesque and photogenic of Highland castles. It stands on a small island a short distance offshore, where the waters of Loch Alsh divide into Loch Duich and the narrower Loch Long. That there was a fort here in prehistoric times is suggested by finds of vitrified rock. The name of the island records the presence of an early Christian hermit, Saint Donan, but by medieval times the hermit's cell had been replaced by a strong tower house. The castle came into the hands of the Mackenzies of Kintail, as the surrounding district was known, and was garrisoned by the MacRaes, hereditary bodyguards to the Mackenzies. The castle which you can see today is something of a fake because it was almost totally rebuilt and restored during the early years of the present century, at tremendous cost, by a descendant of the MacRaes. However, the restoration sticks fairly closely to the original design. Parts of the castle are open to the public and on display are a number of Jacobite relics from various risings. Today a bridge links the castle with the mainland but in 1719 it could only be reached by boat.

THE BOMBARDMENT OF EILEAN DONAN

The Jacobites stayed in the vicinity of Eilean Donan for several weeks, waiting for news that Ormonde had landed. The leaders occupied themselves in endless wrangles. What the Spanish soldiers and their officers thought, stranded in a strange country with an abominable climate and barbaric inhabitants, has not been recorded but one can imagine that they were not particularly happy! Meanwhile Tullibardine sent messages to rouse the clans and the Lowland nobles. Most of the replies were cautious; everybody was sitting tight until the arrival of the main expedition. At last word reached them that Ormonde's venture had been called off. Tullibardine, not unreasonably, proposed that they re-embark and return to Spain. The Earl Marischal was more belligerent and, to prevent a retreat, he sent away the two Spanish frigates. Without any means of retreat they were now committed.

The frigates left just in time. A few days later five British warships appeared off Skye. Three of them came into Loch Alsh and anchored close under the walls of Eilean Donan. Forty-five Spaniards had been left there to guard the expedition's ammunition and supplies. The warships opened fire with their cannon and bombarded the castle for several hours. The Jacobites had thought themselves safe from immediate attack by government forces. It would have been extremely difficult to bring siege artillery overland to such a remote site. They had left the Royal Navy out of their calculations though. It was far easier to transport guns by sea! After several hours of pounding the castle's thick walls were still standing but badly battered and it was an easy matter to send in a couple of boatloads of sailors. They quickly overpowered the dazed garrison. The ammunition was blown up and the castle wrecked by the landing party. One vessel sailed further into Loch Duich to bombard a supply dump which the Jacobites had established at a place they called the 'Crow of Kintail' — probably at the mouth of the River Croe near the head of the loch. The Spanish guards blew up the ammunition there to prevent it from being captured.

The bombardment galvanized Tullibardine into belated action and he made more determined efforts to rally the clans. Not surprisingly, following the failure of Ormonde's expedition there was a distinct lack of enthusiasm! Government measures to disarm the clans following the 1715 rising had also deprived some of them of weapons. Seaforth brought in the largest contingent, some 500 men from the nearby glens of Kintail. Lochiel arrived with a smaller party, as did the redoubtable old Mackintosh of Borlum who had sneaked back to Scotland once more. Lord George Murray, Tullibardine's younger brother, came with a few followers.

The irrepressible Rob Roy also turned up with a party of MacGregors. After the collapse of the 1715 rising Rob had sought protection by approaching the Duke of Argyll. He surrendered to Campbell of Fonab, one of Argyll's supporters, and received a formal letter of protection. Despite this his old enemy, Montrose, had enough influence in government circles to have him chased and harried. In 1716 a party had burnt his house at Inversnaid and Rob retired to Campbell territory, building a house high in Glen Shira from where he planned raids on Montrose's property. His exploits thereafter had included carrying off £3,000 of rents which had been paid by Montrose's tenants and holding to ransom the steward who had been collecting the money. Montrose had been lucky enough to capture Rob by a quick strike at Balquhidder, where his family were staying. Rob was taken south on horseback, and was thought to be securely bound, but crossing the River Forth at the Fords of Frew he managed to free himself and by diving into the darkly flowing water he made his escape. On another occasion he was tricked into capture by the Duke of Atholl and was locked up in the Duke's prison at Logierait above Dunkeld while a military escort came from Perth to collect him. With some help from well-wishers among the Duke's tenants he was able once more to stage a daring escape and make his captors look silly. Though he was at odds with the Duke of Atholl he was on good terms with his Jacobite sons and it was Lord George Murray who recruited him into the rising. Rob had been specifically excluded from the government's general

27 Statue of Rob Roy MacGregor in Stirling, minus the blade of his broadsword!

amnesty of 1717 so that he had nothing to lose by joining the rising, while there was also the possibility of plunder!

THE BATTLE OF GLEN SHIEL

Cut off from the sea, the Jacobites were now threatened by land. General Wightman, a veteran of Sheriffmuir who commanded the Inverness garrison, had assembled what forces he could and, rather than wait to be attacked, he moved out boldly to challenge the Jacobites. He had barely 1,100 men, most of them regular infantry with a few dragoons and some Highlanders from Whig clans like the Mackays and Munros. He also had four light bronze mortars, called Cohorns after their Dutch inventor, which fired grenades. Wightman left Inverness in early June. He marched his men down the Great Glen to Fort Augustus and then up Glen Morriston to Loch Clunie.

The Jacobites, hearing of Wightman's advance, took up defensive positions in Glen Shiel, the deep, narrow valley which runs back eastwards from the head of Loch Duich. The valley provided the most direct route to the Great Glen and Inverness, but also the most ready access to Kintail for the government forces. Glen Shiel is a wild and empty valley today, more sparsely inhabited than in 1719 as many small settlements in the lower part of the glen have been deserted. Narrower than Glencoe it is almost as rugged, if perhaps less spectacular. To the north the valley is shut in by the steep slopes of the mountain ridge known as the Five Sisters of Kintail. To the south is another long wall of mountains, most of them rising above 3,000 feet, culminating in the rocky peak called the Saddle. Although some parts of the valley have been planted with conifers Glen Shiel is probably the least altered of all Jacobite battlefields and if you walk over the ground today you will readily appreciate what a strange and unlikely battlefield it was.

Tullibardine's men moved five miles or so up the glen to a point where the valley narrowed sharply at the foot of a steep spur running down from the ominously named peak of Sgurr na Ciste Dubh, the peak of the black coffin. The drove road which followed the glen ran close beside the tumbling stream and was easily blocked with a barricade. The Jacobites also threw up rough entrenchments on the slope above. Tullibardine had over 1,000 Highlanders plus the Spanish infantry and he was making a stand on ground which was well suited to the Highlanders' traditional fighting tactics.

As Wightman advanced down the valley, Lord George Murray, in command of the outposts which had been keeping the government troops under observation, fell back towards the main Jacobite force. When he saw his opponents lining the crest of the ridge and clustered in the valley floor Wightman halted and made his own dispositions before beginning the attack in the early evening.

The thin Jacobite line stretched up the ridge for nearly half a mile. Seaforth and his clansmen, with the Earl Marischal, were posted highest up the slope with the Mackintoshes, MacGregors, and Camerons lower down. Tullibardine stationed himself near the centre of the line. The Spanish infantry, with their black cocked hats and distinctive whitish uniform coats and breeches made from undyed wool, were placed a short way above the river. The Spanish commander was joined by Borlum. Lord George Murray and about 150 men were stationed south of the river on a steep bluff forming the left wing of the little army. Wightman opened the attack by sending some of his troops against Lord George Murray's contingent, after a preliminary bombardment

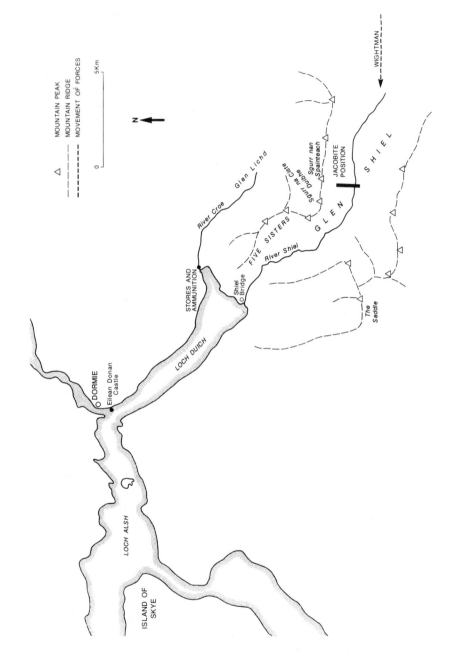

Map 7 The rebellion of 1719 and the Battle of Glen Shiel.

with his mortars. Although they were not heavy-calibre weapons the mortars seem to have caused a degree of confusion disproportionate to their size. The Jacobites beat off the first attack but when Wightman reinforced the troops on his left wing Murray pulled his men back across the river where they were protected by a steep bank.

Meanwhile, Wightman's main force had been moving across the steep, rocky slope towards the Jacobite entrenchments. The Mackays on Wightman's extreme right got high enough up the mountainside to move round the end of Seaforth's defences while at the same time a force of 200 grenadiers assaulted the Highlanders directly. Grenadiers were, at this time, an elite group. One company in each regiment was composed of grenadiers who were specially picked for their height and strength. As well as muskets, carried on a sling to leave both hands free for throwing their missiles, they wore large pouches which held three round grenades as well as cartridges for their muskets. Most of the time they fought like ordinary infantrymen with musket and bayonet. However, they were specially trained for siege warfare and were usually the first troops sent in to clear a breach with their grenades. Wightman launched them against the Jacobite entrenchments with devastating effect. The fierceness of their charge combined with the explosions of the unfamiliar grenades seem to have shaken the Highlanders, and Seaforth himself was wounded in the arm. In vain did the MacGregors hurry uphill to reinforce them; the Highlanders began to pull back and disperse upwards across the mountainside to safer ground.

With the Jacobite left now in disordered retreat, Wightman concentrated his efforts on breaking their centre. The Spanish regulars here came under heavy fire from the mortars but they stood firm and their commanding officer even suggested that they should attack. However, the Highlanders, whose hearts may not have been in a fight which was clearly not going to gain them much even if they won, were already rattled. The explosions of the grenades had set the heather on fire and the drifting smoke added to the confusion. The Jacobite leaders lost heart and they too began to disperse into the mountains. The Spaniards retreated uphill towards the crest of the Five Sisters ridge. The next morning they were the only remnant of the Jacobite army in sight. As prisoners of war they were sure of eventual repatriation so that afternoon they surrendered to Wightman. After a few months of confinement they were sent home, thankful no doubt to return to a more civilized climate. The only monument to their brave but futile stand is better known to mountaineers than to historians. The easternmost peak of the Five Sisters is still called in Gaelic 'Sgurr nan Spainteach', the peak of the Spaniards.

Casualties in the battle were light. The government forces lost 21 men and around 120 were wounded. Jacobite casualties are unknown but were probably of a similar order; most people managed to escape and, apart from the Spaniards, few prisoners were taken. Wightman had achieved a remarkable success fighting in terrain which, in theory, gave his opponents every advantage. Today there is little to mark the battlefield apart from a small cairn just north of the modern road. You can see the impressive topography of the battlefield quite well from the road but the view improves if you climb some way above the river and, if you feel sufficiently energetic, you can continue upwards towards Sgurr na Ciste Dubh and search the crest of the ridge for traces of the fortifications thrown up by the Jacobites.

GENERAL WADE'S REPORT

Following the rebellions of 1715 and 1719 the Hanoverian regime did little to tackle the problem of the Highlands as a source of Jacobite support. Forfeiting the estates of the major rebels did not alter the basis of Highland society or integrate the area more closely with the rest of Britain. Public opinion and vested interests in Scotland were still too strong, so soon after the Union, for the Whigs to implement major changes. Efforts were made to defuse potential trouble by passing a Disarming Act in 1716 requiring the Highlanders to hand over their weapons. All that this produced was a thriving import trade in broken, rusty weapons from the Low Countries. These were handed over and the good weapons carefully concealed! Perhaps the fact that Jacobite military operations in 1715 and 1719 had been so hopelessly inept reduced the perceived scale of the threat. Yet the government realized that the Highlands were still a security risk which required attention.

The wily Simon Fraser, Lord Lovat, whose political stance was murky and suspect, sent George I a report on the state of the Highlands. But Lovat was biased and George needed a more objective viewpoint. In 1724 he sent Major General George Wade to the Highlands to assess conditions there. Wade, an Irishman, was in his early fifties at this time. First commissioned in 1690, he fought in King William's campaigns in Flanders and had risen to the rank of Brigadier General by 1708. In 1715 he had suppressed the embryo western rising by occupying Bath and seizing the caches of arms that the Jacobites had hidden there. This had given him experience of security work and it was perhaps for this reason that George chose him for the mission to the Highlands. After spending five months in Scotland Wade reported that there were, according to his estimate, some 22,000 potential fighting men in the Highlands, over half of whom were, potentially, disaffected to the government.

To counter this threat Wade made a number of practical suggestions which, taken together, formed a sensible policy for policing the Highlands at a modest cost. First he proposed re-forming independent companies of locally-raised troops commanded by Gaelic-speaking officers loyal to the government. The first six companies were raised in 1725 and four more were added in 1739. The total numbers of troops involved was not great but with their mobility and knowledge of the country they could go freely into areas that regular troops could only penetrate with difficulty and give an early warning of trouble. In 1739 the companies were formed into a new regiment which, because of the dark colour of the tartan which the men wore, and their job of watching the glens, became known as the Black Watch. Wade also instituted a new disarming act which brought in some more firearms.

NEW FORTS IN THE HIGHLANDS

Another element in Wade's plan was to establish more garrisons in the Highlands. Following the 1715 rising new forts had been built at the southern end of Loch Ness and elsewhere but Wade planned to rebuild and extend them into a proper system of defence. Fort William had successfully deterred the clans in 1690-2. Although isolated from the centre of action in 1715 it nevertheless restricted the activities of the surrounding chiefs. Wade recommended that stronger forts should be established at Inverness and mid-way down the Great Glen between Inverness and Fort William. This would create a chain of posts cutting the Highlands in two. These forts were to house substantial garrisons but Wade also suggested that smaller outposts should be constructed. These were not designed to be proof against full-scale attack but were to act as 'listening posts' in the heart of potentially hostile country, whose garrisons could give an early warning of potential trouble.

Fort William was already in being. Wade merely upgraded its defences which, having been left to fall into disrepair, required a good deal of renovation. At Inverness, Cromwell had built a small pentagonal citadel with corner bastions and water defences a little way downriver from the medieval royal castle. After the Restoration it had been dismantled although traces of one of its bastions still remain. In the early 1690s Mackay, while occupying Inverness, ignored it and chose to strengthen the old castle. When Wade came to Scotland this was a substantial tower house, at the top of a steep bank overlooking the main bridge across the River Ness. Wade had the defences remodelled and improved so that cannon could be mounted, while additional barrack blocks and other buildings were added to the core of the earlier fortress. The present Castle occupies the site of Wade's fort but the buildings which you can see today date from the mid-nineteenth century and their Scottish Baronial style is mere sham.

There had also been an earlier fort at the place now called Fort Augustus but originally Kilcumin, a name commemorating an early Celtic saint. It was located too far from Loch Ness to be easily supplied by water though and Wade had a more substantial fort built beside the loch to replace it. All that remains of the earlier fort is a section of loopholed walling in the back yard of the Lovat Arms Hotel. The new fort was larger with more massive ramparts on which artillery could be mounted. This did not make it proof against attack: like the fort at Inverness it was captured during the 1745 rebellion with remarkable ease. The remains of Wade's fort were later incorporated into a Benedictine abbey, which can be visited by arrangement.

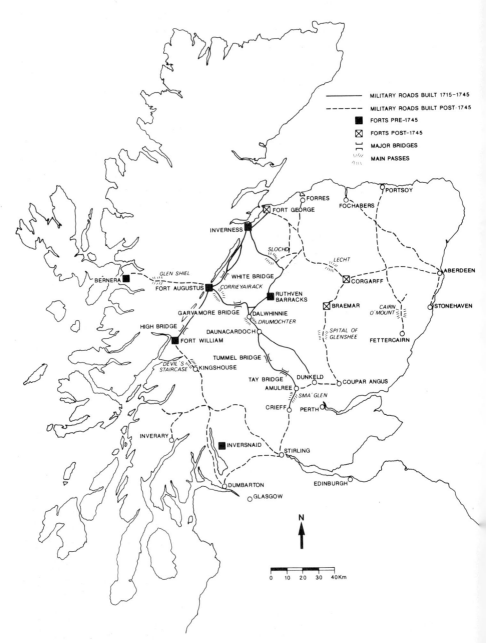

Map 8 Military roads, forts, and outposts in the Highlands.

Fort Augustus was not finished until 1742, just in time for the last Jacobite rising. A thirty-ton vessel armed with light cannon, capable of carrying sixty men down the loch in three or four hours, was maintained to supply Fort Augustus and patrol the shores.

The most accessible and complete of the smaller forts is Ruthven Barracks on the south side of the Spey just outside the town of Kingussie. Although captured and burnt during the 1745 rebellion the remains, which are open to the public, are still impressive, and quite different in appearance from a traditional Scottish castle, even when viewed on a grey day through sheets of driving rain, as the isolated garrison must often have seen it. The barracks were built on top of a mound, probably a natural feature which has been artificially sculpted so that it resembles a Norman motte. A medieval castle once stood here belonging to the infamous Wolf of Badenoch, an illegitimate son of Robert II, whose achievements included the burning of the town and cathedral of Elgin in 1390 following a quarrel with the bishop. A later castle on this site was burnt by MacDonald of Keppoch during Dundee's campaign in 1689. It was from here that the Jacobite army finally dispersed in February 1716 after its long retreat from Perth. In 1721 the main part of the barracks was built using stone from the old castle. Two gaunt three-storey barrack

28 Ruthven Barracks, on a hillock dominating the Spey valley near Kingussie. Loopholes for musketry can be seen in the curtain wall. The ruined building on the far right was the stable block.

29 The courtyard of Ruthven Barracks with the well
and one of the barrack blocks.

blocks face each other across a courtyard containing a deep well. They have
large windows looking into the courtyard but only small openings on the
outside, adding to the barracks' dour appearance. The buildings are surrounded by a wall with a parapet walk, pierced with loopholes for musketry.
Angle towers at two of the corners, which might have been constructed to
provide enfilading fire along the walls served, in fact, as a guardroom and a
bakery. The post could accommodate around 120 infantrymen but after
completion of the military road down Speyside the stable block to the north
of the barracks was added to allow a detachment of 30 dragoons to patrol the
road.

The barracks of Bernera, at Glenelg on the west coast facing Skye, was the
most remote outpost. The buildings are similar in design to Ruthven though

less well preserved. The main difference is that the barracks at Bernera are larger double blocks. Up to 200 troops could be housed here though the garrison can rarely have been so large. Bernera commands one of the most important routes to Skye via the Kylerhea ferry but this must have been a lonely spot for it was only linked to the other forts after the 1745 rebellion by a military road, whose line is closely followed by the modern road from Shiel Bridge to Glenelg. The other major contrast with Ruthven is its site. Ruthven, on its steep little hill, is more convincing as a mini-castle while the barracks at Bernera, in the middle of the flat coastal plain at the mouth of the short, shallow Glen Bernera, seem more like a ruined country mansion in an alien setting. Compared with state-of-the-art fortifications on the Continent these outposts were mere toys; it was not considered that in any future Highland rising the rebels would have the artillery to besiege even these modest fortresses.

The smallest of the garrisons was built between 1718 and 1719 at Inversnaid on the east side of Loch Lomond, partly as a result of continuing raids by Rob Roy and his MacGregors, and ensuing pressure from neighbouring landowners, notably Rob's old adversary the Duke of Montrose. Incensed at the building of a fort in MacGregor territory Rob delayed its construction by various means including, on one occasion, kidnapping all the masons provided by the government's contractor. Nevertheless, the fort was eventually finished. Today the fort is badly ruined but parts of it have been incorporated into a later farmhouse and outbuildings.

THE MILITARY ROADS

The difficulty of moving regular troops through the Highlands, with the rugged, boggy, almost unmapped topography, had long been appreciated. Yet in 1719 Wightman had shown the advantage of rapid mobility in this region for containing Jacobite military threats. What was needed, Wade believed, was a system of roads in the Highlands to link the main forts and to allow troops to penetrate the region quickly in the event of a further rebellion. Wade went on to become a Field-marshal and Commander-in-chief of the British army. He earned himself a place in Westminster Abbey and a verse in the contemporary version of the National Anthem. But he is best remembered as a road builder.

In 1725 Wade started improving the most obvious link, the sixty-mile stretch of road from Inverness to Fort William via Fort Augustus. The original road ran well above the eastern shores of Loch Ness where the ground was less steep but it proved to be exposed and easily blocked by snow. In 1732 a new stretch of road was made close to the lochside and a considerable amount of blasting was required to clear the ground for it. A contemporary writer has left a vivid description of how the miners who carried out the blasting operations had to hang over the cliffs on the ends of ropes in order to bore the holes for the gunpowder. With the three Great Glen forts linked Wade turned his attention to connecting the system to the Lowlands.

In the early eighteenth century even Lowland Scotland had few stretches of road which had been deliberately constructed rather than merely worn by repeated use. The Highlands were traversed by networks of drove roads but these were merely grassy trackways over which lean, wiry Highland cattle were driven to Lowland markets. Nothing like Wade's roads had been seen before and he began the process of opening up the Highlands. This was, however, a process which could operate in both directions for the new road system proved as useful to the Jacobite army in 1745 as it did to the government forces. There is no record of what Wade thought of this!

Wade's main road through the Highlands, 102 miles long, linked the strategic centres of Perth and Inverness. It began at Dunkeld, following the Tay and then the Garry through the gorge of Killiecrankie and past Blair Castle. A short section of it can be seen adjacent to the National Trust for Scotland visitor centre at Killiecrankie. It then crossed the bleak pass of Drumochter and cut across rolling moorland to reach the Spey at Ruthven Barracks. A little beyond Aviemore the road left Speyside and turned north westwards through the Slochd gorge towards Inverness. To improve access to the Inverness road from Central Scotland Wade had a branch built running north from Crieff via Amulree and the Sma' Glen. It crossed the Tay and then the Tummel by impressive bridges and joined the main road north of Blair Castle at Dalnacardoch.

Wade's main road linked the eastern end of the Great Glen to the south but there was also a need for a road that turned more towards Lochaber. Wade's most famous road, made notorious by the descriptions of faint-hearted eighteenth-century travellers, branched off from the main road in upper Speyside and led to Fort Augustus over the Monadhliath mountains via the Corrieyairack pass, climing to an altitude of 2,543 feet. Like many of the military roads it followed the line of an existing drove road, a pass used by the Marquis of Montrose's small but mobile Highland army through the grim weather of January 1645, in his cross-country march to surprise a Campbell army at Inverlochy. The Corrieyairack road was built in a single summer between April and October. If you follow it today, its course westwards from the Spey leads into the steep armchair-shaped hollow of Corrie Yairack, with crags and broken rocky slopes all round. The road escapes from this dead-end by a side valley to the west climbing steadily by means of eighteen zig-zag traverses at a gradient which, though steep, was practicable for wheeled vehicles. Part of the way up this steep section a spring beside the road is still known as the General's Well. The only feature which detracts from the remoteness of the setting is the power lines which follow the line of the road closely!

In some respects Wade's bold decision to drive a direct route over this high pass was a mistake. The road was blocked by snow for long periods in winter.

In the first year of its use eleven soldiers are believed to have died on the pass, victims of exposure, though one suspects that the impact of low temperatures, severe weather, and snowdrifts was often aggravated by the effects of too much alcohol on the journey! In an age before mountain scenery became fashionable the Corrieyairack road had a grim reputation and it was perhaps for this reason that, unlike many of Wade's routes, it is not followed by a modern road. As a result, it is the longest stretch of military road in the Highlands surviving more or less in its original state. The dozen miles from Melgarve, where the modern motorable road ends, to Fort Augustus is one of the classic through walks in the Central Highlands. The zig-zag traverses, faced with stone retaining walls and only slightly modified by later traffic, can still be seen and although the scenery of the Monadhliath, the 'Grey Moors', is bleak rather than spectacular it emphasizes how alien and how hostile was this country to the Hanoverian army.

The roads were laid out by army surveyors and built by ordinary soldiers working between April and October. Living under canvas, on basic army rations, with the rain and the midges to contend with, their life must often have been arduous. However, they received double the normal rate of pay, a tribute to Wade's concern for their welfare. Working parties normally consisted of around 100 men and a couple of officers. Up to 500 soldiers were employed on the roads at any time. The speed at which they worked was impressive. The road from Dunkeld to Inverness was completed in two summers and during the building of the Corrieyairack road each soldier was expected to complete a yard and a half of road per day.

The roads were driven straight across country, like Roman ones, where topography permitted. They had a maximum width of sixteen feet although where the ground was difficult they were often narrower. The ground was first cleared of large boulders and dug out until a solid bottom of rock or gravel was uncovered. The excavated material was piled into banks on either side of the road and large stones were set up on them at regular intervals to mark the road during snowy conditions. They were the ancestors of the modern guide posts which mark Highland roads today. The banks and markers were a characteristic feature of Wade's roads and still be seen clearly today in some places. A layer of stones was laid over the bed of the road and then gravel was beaten down on top. On sloping ground a drainage channel was generally dug on the uphill side with a stone revetment downhill. On soft ground the road might be floated on layers of brushwood.

The major problem faced by the builders was not so much the rugged topography but drainage difficulties caused by the high rainfall. In the early stages of construction, water was channelled across the road by open drains, and streams were crossed by cobbled fords wherever possible but these proved too vulnerable to sudden floods and required annual repairs. Eventually it was decided to carry small streams under the roads through culverts while larger ones required bridges built with distinctive narrow stone arches, a number of which still survive. Their arches were often too small to cope with floods, leading to bridges and sections of roads being washed away, but in fairness to the builders they were not used to such an extreme climate.

Major rivers required more substantial bridges, several of which still carry traffic. The road from Inverness to Fort William crossed the River Spean by High Bridge, 280 feet long with three arches, but the structure is, sadly, badly ruined today. Still complete, with a high single arch, is Whitebridge, beside the modern road south of Foyers on the eastern side of Loch Ness. The most imposing and stylish Wade bridge, built of dressed stone rather than rubble masonry, crosses the Tay at Aberfeldy. 300 feet long, with five arches, it is ornamented by four classical-style obelisks, the result of a design by the architect William Adam. An inscription on the bridge in Latin and English extols Wade's achievements; evidently he was particularly proud of this bridge! The nearby Weem Hotel was used by Wade as his headquarters while the bridge was being built and his portrait still hangs outside it. Other Wade bridges are more functional but equally effective like the one at Tummel Bridge, or the two-arched bridge at Garva, carrying the Corrieyairack road over the upper Spey.

It is not clear to what extent the planning of the roads was done by Wade himself but he took a keen interest in the work and regularly visited the road gangs; his 'highwaymen' as he affectionately called them. On the road to Drumochter from Blair Castle, south of Dalnaspidal Lodge, a tall stone stands beside the southbound carriageway of the modern A9. It was originally a marker stone on Wade's road, now moved slightly from its original position. It bears the date 1729 and is known as the Wade Stone. It is eight feet high and the story goes that Wade, a tall man, once surreptitiously placed a gold coin on top of the stone. A year later when he revisited the site he reached up and found that it was still there!

By 1736 Wade had overseen the construction of around 250 miles of new road with 40 major bridges. This was a great achievement, particularly in such difficult terrain. The lines chosen by Wade's surveyors were often followed by later road engineers, including Thomas Telford, who sometimes merely upgraded the road surface and the bridges. However, some stretches of Wade roads have been little altered and form attractive and interesting walks including the central section of the Corrieyairack road and the road between Dalwhinnie and the head of the Spey.

By no means all military roads in the Highlands were the work of Wade. When he left Scotland in 1740 the system that he had established was extended under his successor in the task, Major William Caulfeild, who had been Wade's chief surveyor. 750 miles of new military roads were built following the 1745 rebellion. These new roads included the route across the edge of the bleak wasteland of peat and bog known as Rannoch Moor, and on past the head of Glencoe to Loch Leven by a series of traverses known as the Devil's Staircase. Another of the later roads ran from Perth via

Blairgowrie to Braemar and on by the Lecht pass to cross the Spey at Grantown and continue to Fort George, east of Inverness. These later roads, which were similar in character to the ones built for Wade, are also shown on Map 8.

The sites of many of the original soldiers' camps along the new roads became inns. Known as 'King's houses', they were spaced out at intervals of about ten miles. A number of modern Highland hotels originated as King's houses like the one at Whitebridge. The Amulree Hotel in the Sma' Glen bears the date 1714 and may have been an even earlier inn on the drove road whose line Wade followed. Sometimes the original name has survived to the present day, the best known example probably being the Kingshouse Hotel on the military road at the head of Glencoe. At Garvamore, on the road to the Corrieyairack, you can still see one of the original King's houses, dating from about 1740, in an attractive setting where the valley of the upper Spey narrows between two steep-sided hills. The inn is a long, unadorned range of two-storey slate-roofed buildings. At one end is a stable with a loft above which probably once accommodated soldiers but in recent times has provided welcome shelter to walkers and climbers. It continued to function into the nineteenth century as a 'stance', or resting place, for drovers and their herds.

As enmities caused by the 1715 rising slowly died it seemed that the Jacobite cause might fade away. Even the redoubtable Rob Roy eventually made his peace with the authorities, submitting formally to Wade in 1725. He was granted some land on the Duke of Atholl's estates, possibly due to the influence of the Duke's sons, and Rob built himself a stone house at Inverlochlarig, a few miles east of the head of Loch Lomond, the remains of which can still be seen. Rob returned to his earlier lifestyle combining farming, cattle droving, and an income from blackmail with a little small-scale rustling. His chequered career ended peacefully in 1734 when he died in bed at his home. He is commemorated by a modern statue in Stirling, a town whose inhabitants would have been extremely wary of him in real life (see Plate 27). His grave can still be seen in the churchyard at Balquhidder, a short distance from Lochearnhead. His tombstone is a recumbent slab on which is carved a weathered figure with a two-handed sword. It is a re-used medieval grave slab but it is an appropriate memorial to a larger-than-life character, a legend in his own lifetime, whose mode of living had become anachronistic by the time of his death. Henceforth the future of the Highlands seemed to be one of slow improvement, with Jacobites like Donald Cameron of Lochiel and Lord George Murray in the vanguard of progress as much as Whig leaders like the Duke of Argyll. The Jacobite movement was, however, to prove more resilient than many people expected.

1745: THE DARING GAMBLE

THE ORIGINS OF THE '45

In the 1720s and 1730s most people, Jacobites included, considered that the Stuart cause was dead. As he grew older James became less healthy and less active, surrounding himself with advisers and plotters but doing nothing positive. He and his supporters were convinced that the only hope of a Stuart restoration lay in massive French aid and this was not forthcoming. Meanwhile James had married, in 1719, Clementina Sobieski, the grand-daughter of a king of Poland and a wealthy heiress. In 1720 she bore him a son, Charles Edward, and five years later another named Henry.

The children were brought up in the claustrophobic atmosphere of the Jacobite 'court' in exile at Rome. Henry was more academic but his elder brother Charles was the despair of his tutors. Headstrong and wayward, petulant and thoughtless, he was redeemed by good looks, charm, and self-assurance. Whatever his faults he had personal charisma and knew how to exploit it. James kept a close hold on him during his teens and did not allow him much independence. At fourteen he was allowed to spend a few weeks as an observer at the siege of Gaeta, a town between Naples and Rome. Charles showed himself to be cool and brave under fire but this was hardly a real training in military affairs. Charles was a good linguist who spoke French and Italian as well as rather heavily accented English; although no scholar, he was far from stupid. He excelled at hunting and horsemanship and his energy and fitness were to stand him in good stead during the '45 rising.

Jacobite support was still active in Scotland. Many leading figures of 1715 vintage were dying off and new ones were succeeding them. Among them were John Murray of Broughton, two years older than Charles and a close friend, who acted as a messenger between Scotland and France, and became the Prince's secretary. Donald Cameron of Lochiel, managing his estates for his exiled father, was another along with the Duke of Perth, and Simon Fraser, Lord Lovat, whose labyrinthine intrigues with both Hanoverians and Jacobites made him an object of universal suspicion.

The Jacobites' position changed in 1740 when the War of the Austrian Succession broke out in Europe, a conflict into which Britain and France were inevitably drawn. Once again Louis and his ministers considered using the Jacobites to divert British troops from the battlegrounds of Flanders and the Low Countries. By 1744, although Britain and France were still not officially at war, the conflict had become such a drain on the French exchequer that Louis was considering invading Britain as a potentially speedy way of ending the conflict. He began to have a fleet assembled in secret. The plan was to land 12,000 men in Essex, within easy striking distance of London, and a further 3,000 in Scotland as a diversion. The main expedition was to be commanded by Marshal Saxe, the most outstanding general of his day, with Charles Edward as the nominal leader.

Charles travelled from Rome to Paris and then to the Channel coast to join the fleet. It proved impossible to organize such a major expedition without the British government getting word of it. The Royal Navy was being mobilized to blockade the assembly ports when a storm struck, destroying many of the French transports and drowning large numbers of troops. A second storm a week later wreaked further havoc and the expedition was abandoned.

Instead of returning to Rome, Charles remained in Paris, trying to persuade Louis to mount another expedition. It was his first taste of independence and he revelled in it, running up large bills. He also began to form his own circle of friends who were very different in character from the older supporters on whom James relied. One important group was a circle of Irish officers in the French service who had strong Jacobite sympathies. Another was a set of wealthy shipowners and privateers operating from the ports of western France, Frenchmen of Irish extraction with Jacobite leanings.

Charles decided that French assistance would only be forthcoming if he pushed matters by initiating a rising on his own with the backing of his new friends. With Antoine Walsh, one of the shipowners, he began to plan a private expedition. James knew nothing of what was going on; nor did the leading Jacobites in Britain. The French government knew what was afoot for Walsh leased one of the vessels for the expedition from the French navy and had to obtain official permission to raise a company of volunteers to sail with the Prince. However, they turned a blind eye to the preparations, doubtless thinking that if the venture failed there would be little cost to France and if it succeeded they could provide official support at a later date.

A quarter of a century after the last abortive Jacobite rising, how strong was Jacobite sympathy in Britain? The question is easy to pose but harder to answer. The traditional interpretation is that the Hanoverian dynasty and the Whig government were firmly established with a broad base of support throughout Britain. This interpretation makes those with Jacobite leanings seem like marginal groups of malcontents, too few and too diverse to constitute serious opposition. More recently some historians have questioned the apparent stability of the Whig regime and suggested that their position was weaker than it appeared. On this interpretation, there was a large and frustrated Tory opposition which had been denied office for many years. Among the Tory ranks there was a substantial Jacobite element whose latent support might become active under the right circumstances.

For years Scotland had been managed for the Whig leader, Sir Robert Walpole, by the Duke of Argyll, the victor of Sheriffmuir, and then by his brother the Earl of Islay. Anyone who was not in with the Campbells was excluded from power and preferment. There were a good number of Scottish nobles who had crossed swords with the house of Argyll who were, potentially, disgruntled enough to back a Jacobite rising. Nearly forty years after the Union there was still a good deal of opposition at a grass roots level to rule from Westminster, particularly regarding the customs and excise regulations.

THE VOYAGE TO SCOTLAND

Charles' plan to land in Scotland with only a token force, lacking official French backing, was an enormous gamble. Previous expeditions, more massively funded and carefully planned, had failed. There seemed little reason to suppose that the '45 would be any more successful than the disastrous expedition of 1719. The difference lay in the character of its leader. Charles had the determination, the drive, the sheer blind optimism which his father had lacked in 1715 and his grandfather in 1688. Admittedly it was an optimism grounded in arrogance and the willingness to use and deceive people but the result was that this expedition, considered mad and ill-judged by both Jacobites and Whigs at its outset, came nearer to shaking the British throne than any previous efforts.

Things got off to a poor start. Antoine Walsh had provided a small sixteen-gun frigate, the *Du Teillay*. He had also hired from the French navy an old sixty-four-gun warship, *L'Elizabeth*. The *Du Teillay*, with Charles and a small band of followers, sailed from the Loire and met up with the *Elizabeth* which, in addition to arms, ammunition, and money, carried a number of French volunteers. 100 miles west of the Lizard the two vessels were sighted by HMS *Lion*, of fifty-eight guns. The *Lion* bore down and engaged the *Elizabeth*. During a five-hour battle the two ships pounded each other into wrecks. Charles urged Walsh to intervene but Walsh refused and threatened to have him carried below if he persisted. His first duty was to protect the Prince and it was doubtful if the guns of the *Du Teillay* could have given her larger sister ship much help. The *Elizabeth*, her captain mortally wounded, limped back to Brest leaving the *Du Teillay* to continue alone. It was an object lesson in the importance of British sea power and though the naval side of the 1745 campaign is often forgotten, and cannot be discussed in detail here, it nevertheless had a major influence over events on land.

Having lost the support of the *Elizabeth* with her much-needed arms and volunteers, Charles was more than ever on his own. This is emphasized by the motley group of followers that accompanied him, the most prominent of whom have gone down in tradition as the 'Seven Men of Moidart'. They included Sir Thomas Sheridan, in his seventies, Charles' tutor for many a weary year who came out of a sense of duty, because Charles trusted him, and possibly because he was used to being dragged around after the Prince. Equally old and infirm was the Marquis of Tullibardine, the forfeited elder brother of the Duke of Atholl. Aeneas MacDonald was a banker in France, with useful West Highland connections, who was really just hitching a ride with the expedition. The only other follower who played a significant role in the events to come was John O'Sullivan, an Irish officer in the French service, bluff and heavily built, an incompetent mediocrity with a convincing line of blarney which made his limited military experience and capabilities seem more impressive than they really were.

THE RAISING OF THE STANDARD

The little expedition made its first landfall at Eriskay in the Outer Hebrides between Barra and South Uist. The place where he landed is still known in Gaelic as Cladach a'Phrionnsa, the Prince's shore. The small island was rocky and infertile and a rough hut was the only accommodation available for the Prince. It was, indeed, the home of a tacksman, one of the more well-to-do inhabitants, but its primitive construction, the thick peat smoke inside which choked Charles, and the simple meal of hastily-caught fish was a good introduction to the backwardness and poverty of the area whose inhabitants were to provide the support he needed. He left no record of his first impressions of the kingdom that he had never seen before but it was a not untypical Hebridean summer day — wet and windy. Nor were his first meetings with local chiefs any more encouraging. The day after he arrived, Alexander MacDonald of Boisdale came to see him. He refused assistance, would not try to persuade his brother, the chief of Clanranald, to support the Prince, and urged him to return to France immediately. Even worse, he reported that MacDonald of Sleat and Macleod of Macleod, who had indicated their willingness to support a properly organized rising, had no intention of joining such a risky venture. A less determined, or less pig-headed man might have given up there and then!

Instead they sailed across to the mainland. On July 25th the *Du Teillay* anchored in Loch nan Uamh, a sea loch forming part of the Sound of Arisaig south of Skye and north of the long rocky peninsula of Ardnamurchan. Over the next few days various clan leaders arrived to see the Prince and to try and dissuade him from starting a rising. Charles would not be told though and gradually support began to appear — first the son of

MacDonald of Clanranald and then other MacDonald leaders including the chiefs of Keppoch and Glencoe, as well as a messenger from MacDonald of Glengarry.

The Prince was particularly keen to win over Donald Cameron of Lochiel, who was acting as chief of Clan Cameron for his exiled father. Lochiel was the most important chief in Lochaber. He could bring in several hundred men and his influence was widespread. Although Lochiel, when he first met the Prince, had major reservations and advised him to return to France, the Prince was a skilled persuader. His reputed retort that Lochiel could stay at home and read about the fate of his Prince in the newspapers stung the chief into active support. The Prince sent out messages to more distant clan leaders appointing a rendezvous at Glenfinnan in a few days time. Once the *Du Teillay* had been unloaded she was sent back to France with Antoine Walsh and Charles was committed to staying and fighting.

The Jacobites' first success came even before the standard had been raised. As a result of rumours that the Prince had landed, Captain John Scott and two companies of men from the Royal Scots were sent from Fort Augustus along the military road down the Great Glen to reinforce the garrison at Fort William. Nine miles from Fort William, Wade's road crossed the gorge of the River Spean at High Bridge. When they reached the bridge they discovered that the far end was held by a party of armed Highlanders under MacDonald of Tirandrish, a local chief. MacDonald had only a handful of men but by firing a few shots and having his pipers play he tricked Scott into believing that he had a much larger force. Scott decided against trying to cross the bridge and ordered a retreat. The Highlanders chased them along the steep shore of Loch Lochy and the sound of their stray shots echoing among the rocks attracted other Highlanders who joined the pursuit. After unsuccessfully trying to form his men into a defensive square and beat off their attackers, the Hanoverian troops surrendered; Scott was wounded and four or five of his men killed. The prisoners — some eighty men — were taken to Glenfinnan to be put on display. The skirmish was a foretaste of how successful the Highlanders could be against inexperienced troops unnerved by their distinctive way of fighting.

Meanwhile the Prince moved from Borrodale on the shore of Loch nan Uamh to join his supporters at Kinlochmoidart further to the south. From there he was rowed up Loch Shiel, a long, narrow stretch of water with rocky hills on either side, to Glenfinnan at its head. On August 19th the Prince raised his standard there. He had barely 200 followers and he was desperately hoping that the clan leaders would keep their promises. Then Lochiel arrived with 700 Camerons and other contingents of MacDonalds began to come in. Glengarry brought some 400 men, Keppoch around 250, and Clanranald 200.

The Prince was still in conventional clothes, not yet donning Highland dress as he was to do for much of the campaign, but tall, young, and enthusiastic he must have made a striking figure. The standard was raised and James Francis Stuart was proclaimed king. By the end of the day Charles had well under 2,000 men but the appearance of the Camerons had been the crucial factor which determined that the rising did not peter out. Partly by accident, partly by design, Charles' enterprise had been launched at an especially favourable time. George II was abroad in Hanover and Britain had been stripped of regular troops for the campaign against the French in Flanders. Scotland was poorly defended and even England, as Field Marshal Wade was to remark, was 'all for the first comer'.

Today Glenfinnan has a National Trust for Scotland visitor centre housing an exhibition which portrays the 1745 rebellion in misleadingly rosy, romantic, and chauvinistic terms. Nearby, and more memorable, is a monument erected in 1815 by Alexander MacDonald of Glenaladale to those who took part in the rising. It consists of a tall column set within a circular

30 The monument at Glenfinnan, looking down Loch Shiel.

enclosure. The tower has a narrow internal staircase leading to a tiny balcony, and at the top the figure of a Highlander. The classic view of the monument, seen from the hillside above, with the lone figure framed by the long glittering ribbon of Loch Shiel is beloved of tourist brochures but whether seen against the sunset, on a sunny day as part of the panorama of island, loch, and mountain, or showing only dimly through the mist, it remains poignant and evocative.

COPE'S DILEMMA

The government's Commander-in-chief in Scotland was Lieutenant-General Sir John Cope, an unimaginative but conscientious soldier. His appointment had been controversial and he was painfully aware that he had many enemies waiting to say 'I told you so' if he made any mistakes. His forces amounted to under 4,000 men. This included the veterans and pensioners who formed the garrisons of the castles at Edinburgh, Stirling, and Dumbarton, the garrisons of the forts, and some newly-raised Highland troops whose loyalty was suspect. He had only about 2,000 regular troops with which to check the incipient rising and most of these had never been in action.

Nevertheless, these forces were thought to be adequate enough. After all, the Young Pretender had landed without any military support, and few major chiefs had declared for him. The rising was not treated very seriously at first; Wightman had checked the rising of 1719 at Glen Shiel with a small force and it was hoped that Cope could do the same. In this optimistic frame of mind the authorities in Scotland framed Cope's orders. He was told to march to the Great Glen and nip the rebellion in the bud. On the way he could augment his army from the clans that were loyal to the government.

Although he initially agreed, Cope became increasingly worried about leaving the Lowlands defenceless. Perhaps concentrating his forces at Stirling, like Argyll in 1715, would be a better bet? The government officials in Edinburgh insisted that his original orders should stand. Accordingly, leaving his two dragoon regiments behind to guard the Lowlands, on August 20th he set out from Stirling towards Crieff and Wade's military road through the Sma' Glen to the Tay bridge, intending to make for Fort Augustus by the Corrieyairack road. He took 1,000 extra muskets and ammunition for issue to men raised by landowners like the Duke of Atholl. His qualms about the advisability of the expedition were probably increased when the loyal Highlanders failed to materialize. In disgust he sent most of the arms back to Stirling. Various minor acts of sabotage such as the theft of horses and ripping of grain sacks occurred on the march and added to the air of foreboding which hung over the little army.

From Aberfeldy he pushed on to Dalnacardoch, below the pass of Drumochter, where the military road from Crieff joined the one from

Dunkeld. Here an officer who had been captured at High Bridge and released on parole met them. The Jacobite army at Glenfinnan had numbered 3,000 he claimed, twice its actual size, and the rebels were planning to stop his march to Fort Augustus by blocking the military road at the summit of the Corrieyairack Pass. The prospect of trying to force a way up the road with its zig-zag traverses lined with Highland sharpshooters would have daunted a bolder man than Cope. On the windswept moors north of Dalwhinnie he held an anxious conference with his officers. They agreed that to try and cross the pass under these circumstances was madness but they could not stay put for want of provisions. A retreat down the Tay valley would only encourage more clans to declare for the Pretender. They decided to follow the original orders as far as possible and continue northwards to Inverness from where they could advance down the Great Glen. Cope pushed his men on by a series of forced marches which can hardly have helped the already sagging morale of his troops.

Unfortunately Cope's plan presupposed that the Jacobites would wait for him. When the Prince and his advisers heard that Cope had backed off from a confrontation they considered pursuing him but soon realized that the way to the Lowlands was wide open, an opportunity not to be missed. They crossed the Corrieyairack and followed the military road south without any opposition, gathering reinforcements, until they reached Perth. Meanwhile Cope, realizing he had been outmanoeuvred, marched his men from Inverness to Aberdeen where troopships were being sent from Leith to meet him. It was now a race to see who could reach Edinburgh first. Scotland was there for the taking; even the traditional support of the Whig Campbells in their Argyllshire stronghold had been removed. Ironically, estate management under 'Red John', who had stopped the Jacobites at Sheriffmuir, had modernized the running of the huge Argyll estates in a way that had destroyed Clan Campbell as a military force.

At Perth a number of important recruits joined the Jacobite army. One was young Lord James Drummond, titular 3rd Duke of Perth in the phantom Jacobite peerage which continued to bestow increasingly unlikely titles upon its supporters. Perth was a 'foolish horse-racing boy' to one contemporary who clearly underestimated him. He was an ardent Jacobite who, if he lacked experience, certainly possessed courage. His health had been poor since a childhood accident but this did not deter him from joining the rising though the harsh life of campaigning was to be the death of him.

The most significant man to join the Prince was Lord George Murray, a brother of the Duke of Atholl. Born in 1694, Murray was in his early fifties, still impressively fit and active. After a commission in the government army he had fought on the Jacobite side in the 1715 rising and had been wounded at Glen Shiel. Following this he lived abroad, serving in the Sardinian army, before being allowed to return to Scotland in 1725. During the intervening years he had made his peace with the government and his appearance at the Jacobite camp was a surprise to both sides. Many historians consider that he joined the rising due to deeply-held Jacobite convictions rather than with any real hope of its ultimate success. Others, more cynically, suggest that he had ambitions for military glory and that Cope had turned down his offer of support.

Although he was to prove a staunch Jacobite his loyalty and integrity were distrusted by other Jacobite leaders. He does not seem to have been greatly impressed by Charles and the two men were not on the best of terms almost from the start. Because he had not been an active Jacobite plotter in the years leading up to the rising, the Prince was never completely certain of Murray's loyalties. The friction between these two men was to have a major influence on the course of the rebellion. In part this was due to the Prince's mistrust of Lord George but in addition Murray was not always easy to get on with: haughty, condescending, outspoken, opinionated, and apt to be prickly, he did not suffer fools gladly. Unfortunately he considered that many of the Prince's advisers fell into this category, particularly O'Sullivan who, unfortunately, had the Prince's ear. Perth and Murray were both appointed lieutenant-generals in command of the army but Murray had little time for his colleague.

Among a host of inexperienced and bungling amateurs Murray stood out as the most capable military commander the Jacobites ever had. Had he served the Hanoverians he might have been one of the great commanders of the British army. A skilled tactician who consistently out-thought his opponents he used the mobility and unconventional tactics of the Highlanders to maximum effect. He understood their strengths and weaknesses and was prepared to lead them from the front, sword in hand, when necessary. They in turn respected and admired him. A man who seized opportunities and made contingency plans to deal with difficulties before they arose, he also paid close attention to detail. He organized an irregular and motley army to a high level of efficiency. Although deep in his heart he seems to have been convinced that the rising was doomed to failure, his military genius was to bring it close to success. Yet, paradoxically, it was his voice more than any other which halted the Jacobite advance into England at a time when a further bold stroke might have succeeded. Even after the retreat from England had he been given a free hand with the army in the later stages of the campaign it might have taken a very different course.

THE CAPTURE OF EDINBURGH

On September 13th the Jacobite army crossed the Forth at the Fords of Frew. The bridge at Stirling had been partly demolished to impede their crossing and, in any case, they did not want to come within range of the guns of Stirling Castle. The dragoon regiment which Cope had stationed there fell back as the Highlanders advanced, until it reached Corstorphine, close to

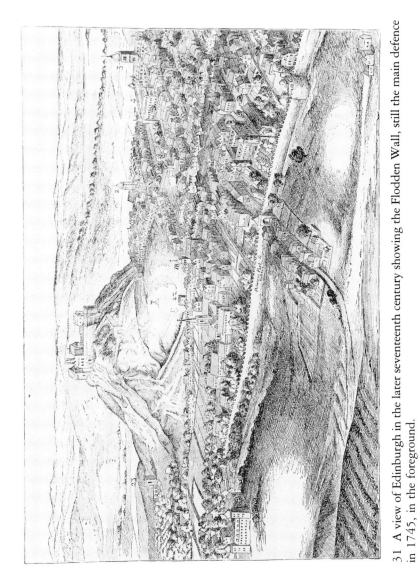

31 A view of Edinburgh in the later seventeenth century showing the Flodden Wall, still the main defence in 1745, in the foreground.

Edinburgh. There the horsemen were joined by the other dragoon regiment. The Lord Provost of Edinburgh had tried to organize the inhabitants to defend the city but he met with little encouragement. Edinburgh was still surrounded by the Flodden Wall, but this only enclosed the royal burgh itself. The Canongate, down the lower part of the Royal Mile, including the Palace of Holyrood, lay outside the wall, as did several other suburbs. Moreover the wall offered little real protection. In some places it was twenty feet high with bastions for artillery but in others it was half that height, no more of an obstacle than a high garden wall. It seemed unlikely that it could be held against a determined attack, although cannon had been brought from vessels at Leith and mounted on the ramparts. To make matters worse the attitude of the population was ambiguous and there were many Jacobites within the city.

32 One of the towers on the Flodden Wall, complete with gun loops, above the Grassmarket.

Edinburgh's town guard had been supplemented by several hundred volunteers but their enthusiasm was short-lived while the civic authorities provided little leadership. When it was proposed that they march out and join the dragoons to attack the Jacobites — a completely mad idea — the volunteers were mustered with much shouting and clashing of weapons. However, as they marched from the High Street down the Bow and through the Grassmarket towards the West Port the bulk of them had second thoughts. They hurriedly disappeared down convenient closes so that by the time their commander reached the city gate he found himself left with only a handful of friends. Provost Stewart was later accused of having Jacobite sympathies and subsequently spent fourteen months in the Tower of London before being tried for neglect of duty but it is difficult to see how he could have organized a more effective defence. Edinburgh Castle was in a better

33 The Flodden Wall and Edinburgh Castle today.

state for the small garrison of invalids and pensioners had been supplemented by some regular troops and the octogenarian General Guest who commanded it had stocked it with adequate supplies of arms and provisions.

As the Highland army approached Edinburgh, Brigadier Fowke arrived from England to take command of the dragoons and some Dutch infantry who were expected at Leith. Riding to Corstorphine to review the horsemen, he was not impressed. Men and horses were in a poor state and the officers did not inspire confidence. Colonel Gardiner, commanding one of the regiments, had been quite a rake in his youth but a religious conversion had made him a gloomy and fatalistic man who, moreover, had not fully recovered from a recent severe illness. His presentiments of coming disaster cannot have helped morale. Fowke reported his views to Guest who thought that the dragoons could do little on their own and suggested they fall back ready to join Cope when he landed. This was agreed and the horsemen set off for Leith.

Soon after this their rearguard caught sight of their first rebels. A handful of Jacobite horsemen came forward and a few pistol shots were fired. According to a story which has probably grown in the telling this caused the rearguard to gallop off hastily. They infected the main body of dragoons with their panic and the result was a headlong retreat along the Lang Dykes, where Princes Street now stands, in full view of the citizens of Edinburgh who they were supposedly protecting. The city authorities must have felt that they were being abandoned to their fate. The dragoons retreated from Leith along the coast to Musselburgh and then Prestonpans where a false alarm in the night set them off again in confusion to Dunbar, leaving a trail of abandoned equipment behind them. Their behaviour did not augur well for any coming conflict.

The Jacobite army swung round to the south of Edinburgh, out of reach of the Castle's guns, and camped near Slateford. The Prince sent a message to the city demanding its immediate surrender. Although Cope's transport vessels had been sighted in the Forth it seemed unlikely that he could land in time to save Edinburgh so the authorities wisely opened negotiations. Their first deputation was dismissed curtly when it failed to agree to an unconditional surrender, as was the second when its members pleaded for more time. To end these delaying tactics the Prince decided to try and take Edinburgh by force. A party of clansmen under Lochiel and Keppoch were given some gunpowder and sent off to try and blow up one of the city's gates.

In the event they did not have to do this. They crept up to the Netherbow Port, the heavy, towered gateway which blocked the Royal Mile at the head of the Canongate. The gateway was demolished later in the eighteenth century but its site is marked by metal plates in the roadway just below John Knox's House. The deputation had been brought back from Slateford in a coach whose driver had dropped them at a tavern in the city: they evidently needed something to revive them! In the early hours of the morning the coach rattled down the empty High Street as the driver went back to the Netherbow

34 The Netherbow Port, whose storming by Lochiel and his Camerons led to the capture of Edinburgh.

Port to take the horses and coach to their stables in the Canongate. The commander of the guard quibbled about opening the gates so late at night but eventually agreed. As the coach was going through, the hidden clansmen seized their opportunity and rushed in, overpowering the guards. They marched up the High Street to the long, low guard house which stood in the centre of the roadway above the Tron church and disarmed the members of the city guard who were on duty. The sentries on the ramparts and at the other gates were quietly told to go home and were replaced by Highlanders. The inhabitants woke up to find their city under occupation. In only twenty-eight days from the raising of the standard at Glenfinnan the Prince had captured the capital of Scotland: it was a remarkable achievement.

147

A few hours later the Prince, wearing Highland dress, entered the city and crowds of supporters turned out to welcome him as he rode to Holyrood Palace. James was proclaimed king at the mercat cross beside St Giles Church in the High Street while Murray of Broughton's pretty wife handed out white cockades to enthusiastic Jacobites. While he was at Holyrood, news of Cope's arrival at Dunbar reached the Prince. The following day he moved the army to Duddingston, a village under the crags on the south side of Arthur's Seat.

Despite having been engulfed by suburban expansion Duddingston has retained its village atmosphere, focusing on the ancient parish church which stands on a rock above the reed-fringed loch. The house in which Charles lodged at the east end of the village street can still be seen and is marked by a plaque.

PRESTONPANS

Cope reached Dunbar only a few hours after the capture of Edinburgh. He was met by the edgy and tired dragoons, and by various civilian volunteers who had escaped from the city. Cope was determined to bring the Jacobites to battle as soon as possible despite the fact that the morale of his men was very low. His raw, untried infantry had endured a long, fruitless march followed by an uncomfortable three-day voyage. They faced, so they believed, an army much larger than their own, though in fact the opposing forces were closely matched with between 2,000 and 2,500 men apiece. In addition, stories of the Highlanders' barbaric fighting methods had doubtless lost nothing in the telling. After their long, panicky retreat the dragoons were exhausted and completely unreliable. Colonel Gardiner himself admitted that, when it came to the crunch, he didn't think there were ten men in his regiment who would follow him in a charge.

On September 19th Cope moved out from Dunbar. He stopped for the night just west of Haddington and the next day continued along the main road towards Tranent. Having no indication of the whereabouts of the Jacobites he dropped down to lower ground nearer the coast where the country was more open. The area around Tranent was broken up by coal pits, cart roads, and sets of enclosures which would have made it difficult to use his cavalry or artillery. Not that there was much chance of his artillery being well served. He had only scratch gun crews including seamen borrowed from the warships which had escorted his transports. The sailors were more of a liability than an asset as they were drunk for most of the time.

Cope had intended to camp near Musselburgh but when his scouts reached the town they found the Jacobite army marching towards them and rode back quickly to warn the general. He halted his men to the east of the village of Preston on a stretch of open land from which the corn had just been harvested. At its western end his position was protected by high stone walls enclosing the 'policies' or parks around Preston House and Bankton, Colonel Gardiner's own estate. To the north were the little coal mining, salt-making, and fishing towns of Prestonpans and Cockenzie. To the south the ground rose towards the low ridge on which Tranent stood. However, at the foot of the hill was an extensive marsh crossed by drainage ditches, the largest of which was a real obstacle. Here Cope had a battlefield which gave his full scope for using his dragoons and artillery and which was difficult of access on three sides. Only to the east was the ground open.

When Jacobite patrols located Cope at Preston they thought that he would climb up through Tranent to gain the commanding heights of Falside Hill, a ridge which overlooked Musselburgh and the road to Edinburgh. The ridge had been used in this way by the invading English army before the battle of Pinkie in 1547. Lord George Murray was determined that he would reach this strong position first. Without consulting Prince Charles he swung the Jacobite vanguard off the coast road and uphill at a fast pace until they reached the summit. From Falside Hill they followed the high ground round to Tranent. Below them on the plain they could see their adversaries. But how were they to get at them? Cope has been criticized for lacking determination and for fighting a defensive battle. However, he believed that the Jacobites greatly outnumbered his own force and given this he was right to be cautious. He had chosen a position which was overlooked by the Jacobite army but where holding the high ground gave them no advantage. A reconnaissance revealed to Murray the impossibility of attacking from the west. The marsh which lay between Cope's army and Tranent was crossed at only two points by a colliery tramway and a cart road but these could easily be blocked.

At first the Prince thought that Cope might try to slip past and reach Edinburgh but it soon became clear that he had no intention of moving. Some of Lochiel's men had been posted around the old parish church of Tranent at the top of the slope overlooking Cope's army. They registered their presence by firing at one of the Edinburgh volunteers who rode up to reconnoitre the position. Cope then brought up two of his cannon and opened fire on them, forcing them to withdraw.

Lord George Murray decided the only way to get at Cope was from the east and he proposed a night march to allow the army to descend to the plain and attack from this direction. It was only after this was agreed on that Robert Anderson, the son of a local laird, came forward to say that he knew a more direct route through the marshes. The Jacobites moved out in darkness to cross the marsh and make a dawn attack. Cope, understandably jumpy, had posted a large number of sentries and some of them heard the Jacobite army on the move. Cope realized what was happening and quickly swung his army round from its position facing south towards Tranent, parallel to the marsh, to one facing east. He hurriedly drew up his men with the dragoons on each

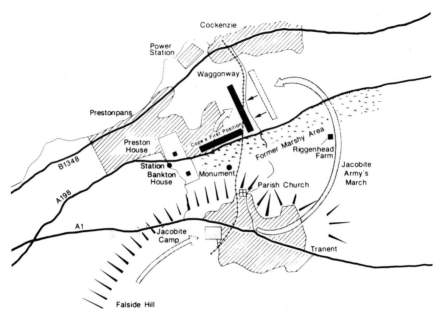

Map 9 The Battle of Prestonpans.

flank of his infantry battalions which were three-deep in the regular manner. Because there was not enough time to move them to the centre of his new line the cannon and mortars were grouped on the right of his infantry with a separate body of foot soldiers to guard the gunners. Cope rode along the front of his line encouraging his men by telling them that they would easily beat the rebels if they stayed calm and kept up a steady fire, but one wonders how confident he really was.

Crossing the marsh was accomplished almost without incident although Charles, jumping the widest of the drainage ditches, slipped and emerged wet and muddy. After passing through the marsh the Duke of Perth, leading the first part of the army, moved too far to the north in trying to ensure that he left enough space for the rearguard to form up. As a result the left and right wings of the army were separated by a wide gap. The extended line, still hidden by darkness and early morning mist, was nevertheless audible and gave Cope an exaggerated impression of the size of the army opposing him which confirmed his earlier beliefs.

The Jacobites attacked at sunrise. At first Cope mistook their front line, seen through the early morning mist, for a row of bushes a couple of hundred yards away but he soon realized his error! The Highlanders closed the gap with a wild rush which unnerved their opponents. The Duke of Perth seems to have kept his men in some kind of order but on the left the charging clansmen coalesced into dense clumps of men around their leaders. Cope's makeshift gunners blanched when they saw the Highlanders racing towards them, then turned and ran. Their two officers stood their ground and managed to fire most of the cannon and mortars. This caused the charging Highlanders to check momentarily but without gun crews there was no chance of reloading. The 100-strong artillery guard meanwhile began to edge backwards. Gardiner's dragoons, stationed behind the artillery, were ordered forward to attack the clansmen but after a few musket shots from the Highlanders they halted. Those at the rear began to turn and, riding down the artillery guard, gallop to the rear. The dragoons on the left also panicked and started to pull back out of range. So quick was the Highlanders' charge that they were able to capture Cope's artillery, turn it round, and use it on the fleeing troops though, not being trained gunners, the Highlanders were poor marksmen!

Deserted by the cavalry, the infantry were left to bear the brunt of the attack. Unnerved by the speed of the wild Highland charge, their thin line began to waver. They fired a single ragged volley at too great a distance to have any real effect. After firing at the run the Highlanders dropped their muskets and came on with their broadswords. As at Killiecrankie, the government line disintegrated in a matter of moments, broken into frag- ments by dense clumps of howling swordsmen. Despite frantic efforts by Cope and his officers to rally the infantry a total rout ensued. Many of the fleeing soldiers were trapped against the high walls around the grounds of Preston House and were cut down by broadswords, Lochaber axes, or scythe blades mounted on poles. Others were killed as they tried to force their way through the narrow gap between the walls of the Preston and Bankton estates, a gap already filled with panic-stricken dragoons and their plunging horses which had not been trained to stay calm under fire. Colonel Gardiner, abandoned by his dragoons, was mortally wounded in sight of his home while trying to rally some of the infantry. He was carried to the manse at Tranent where he died and was buried at the west end of the parish church. Some 300 of Cope's men were killed and about 500 — virtually all the surviving infantry — were captured while the Jacobites claimed to have lost only around 30 men. A handful of men escaped westwards to the safety of Edinburgh Castle. Hanoverian casualties would undoubtedly have been higher if the Prince, Perth, and Murray had not worked hard to restrain their men in the moment of victory.

Cope formed up a body of terrified dragoons near Preston village and, realizing that nothing would persuade them to attack, he led them off southwards by a road which today runs from Prestonpans station to the west end of Tranent and is still called 'Johnnie Cope's Road'. He then retreated across the hills to Coldstream and Berwick. Although the old tale that he was accused of being the first general in history to bring the news of his own defeat is untrue, Cope must have been embarrassed enough, for the whole of Scotland, with the exception of the castles of Edinburgh, Stirling, and Dumbarton, and the Highland forts, was now in Jacobite hands. It was inevitable that following such a disaster Cope should be the scapegoat and he was duly court-martialled. He has gone down in popular history as an incompetent idiot but this is unfair. He was no Marlborough it is true but it is hard to see how even a far more gifted commander could have made anything of the inexperienced troops and mediocre officers on whom he had to depend.

35 The simple monument on the site of the Battle of Prestonpans.

Today the ground over which the battle was fought is still open in part but the landscape has changed dramatically. The best view of the battlefield is from the old parish church at Tranent whose churchyard, with its ornately carved tombstones, stands to the north of the town centre at the edge of the high ground from which the Jacobites overlooked Cope's army. Immediately to the west is the deep gully of the Heugh down which ran the colliery waggonway which crossed the battlefield. The line of the waggonway has been landscaped into an attractive walk. The low ground in front of the church is criss-crossed by electricity pylons and a new by-pass and is dominated by the huge bulk of Cockenzie power station. The marshy ground which protected Cope's original front line has mostly been drained but traces of the main drainage ditch can still be seen beside the A198. A simple memorial to the battle, unadorned apart from the inscription '1745', stands by the roadside east of Preston village, close to where Cope's artillery was positioned. It is sandwiched between the road and the railway while electric power lines hum overhead. From the roadside close to the monument you can look up at the high ground around Tranent church on which the Jacobite army was originally positioned.

Only a few fragments of Preston House remain but the most evocative site associated with the battle is Colonel Gardiner's house at Bankton. It stands forgotten behind a farmyard immediately to the south of Prestonpans station.

36 Bankton House, home of Colonel Gardiner the Hanoverian dragoon commander who was killed within sight of it.

It is a roofless shell, sadly, because it once was an attractive house. Dating from the early eighteenth century it is one of the first small mansions in East Lothian to have a symmetrical facade with curving Dutch-style gables and a sunken basement. From the house an overgrown avenue of tree runs towards the railway and at its far end stands a monument to Colonel Gardiner, erected in the nineteenth century.

INTERLUDE IN EDINBURGH

The following day the Prince returned to Edinburgh where the prisoners from the battle were paraded in triumph. Charles established his court at Holyrood while most of his officers were billeted in the town and the men continued to camp in the King's Park. Legend has waxed lyrical about the glittering balls held at Holyrood during the next few weeks but several sources from the time suggest that Charles' court was rather dull and sombre. Although the ladies loved him, Charles does not appear to have been comfortable in female company, appearing distant and remote to his female admirers. He was a man's man, happier in the hunting field than in the salon. Meanwhile he had a country to rule and a campaign to mount. He established a provisional government for Scotland and sent messengers to France with glowing accounts of his victory and pleas for assistance. Despite the stranglehold which the Royal Navy was maintaining round British shores sporadic French aid began to arrive in the form of money, equipment, and men. A French envoy, the Marquis d'Eguilles also came to act as unofficial ambassador to the new regime.

Meanwhile Charles continued to build up his army for an invasion of England. Despite the enthusiasm of its Jacobite ladies, Edinburgh did not provide many recruits, though John Roy Stewart raised a small regiment from the poorer sections of the population. The redoubtable old Gordon of Glenbucket, veteran of Killiecrankie and Sheriffmuir, bent with age and riding on a shambling pony, arrived with 400 men from the north east while the Earl of Airlie sent his son Lord Ogilvy with 600 men from the Angus glens. Lord Pitsligo, like Glenbucket a veteran of 1715, collected together enough minor gentry to form a small cavalry troop and some other clan leaders, including MacPherson of Cluny, also came south to join the Prince. However, no major magnates had yet committed themselves. Jacobite support north of the Border was still very narrowly based, drawn mainly from the Lochaber clans, Atholl, and the north east. There was little effective support, and much passive opposition, throughout southern Scotland. Meanwhile Louis XV began to assemble an invasion force in northern France, under the direction of Antoine Walsh, and he promised to send more troops direct to Scotland.

In the meantime Edinburgh Castle provided the Jacobites with a problem. For a few days after Prestonpans the rebel forces occupying Edinburgh and the

37 Edinburgh Castle from the east at the end of the seventeenth century showing the defensive outworks from which the garrison exchanged fire with the Jacobites in 1745.

garrison of the castle paid little attention to each other. Hanoverian sympathizers sent supplies to the castle, hoisted up by ropes from the base of the cliffs. The aged General Guest, unable to walk, was wheeled round the battlements to check on the defences and the Highlanders avoided coming within musket shot of the walls. On September 25th, however, a false alarm was caused by some goats scrambling on the crags below the ramparts. The garrison's artillery opened fire on the city, damaging several houses around the west end of the Grassmarket. As a result the Prince ordered the castle to be more closely blockaded. Lochiel undertook the siege with his Camerons who

38 Cannonball House at the top of Castlehill, Edinburgh. The cannonball lodged in the stonework between the two windows, slightly right of centre, is popularly believed to have been fired from the castle during the bombardment of the city.

were billeted in Parliament House, close to the top of the High Street. They began to dig a trench across Castlehill, where the Esplanade now stands, but were forced to suspend operations due to heavy fire from the Half Moon battery and musketry from the outworks.

Guest reacted to this escalation of hostilities by an indiscriminate bombardment of the city which lasted for the greater part of a day and damaged many houses on Castlehill and at the upper end of the Lawnmarket.

If you are visiting Edinburgh Castle take a look at the wall of the house which faces it at the top of Castlehill. The building is known today as Cannonball House and you can see an iron cannonball embedded high in the masonry. According to tradition it was fired by one of the castle's guns during this bombardment. Alternatively you may prefer the more prosaic explanation that it marks the maximum height to which water could be raised in an early water-supply scheme! Or perhaps it was merely inserted in the wall at a later date as a result of the whim of the owner?

The bombardment killed and injured a number of people and that night the garrison made a sortie and set fire to several houses close to the castle. As a result of representations by the citizens the Prince ordered the blockade to be withdrawn and peace returned to Edinburgh.

9

1745: ADVANCE AND RETREAT

THE MARCH INTO ENGLAND

At the end of October the Jacobite leaders agreed to invade England. The decision was far from unanimous; indeed it was only carried by one vote. Few clan chiefs were enthusiastic about marching south of the Border; they could remember what had happened at Preston in 1715! Significantly, Lord George Murray was among those who opposed the idea. Some of the Prince's supporters, with more enthusiasm than sense, had urged an invasion of England immediately after Prestonpans when the Jacobite army had actually decreased from its original small size as many Highlanders left for home with their booty. The six-week stay in Edinburgh had been essential for a proper army to be assembled but the delay had given the government time to recover. Regiments were being hurriedly recalled from Flanders so that there was now no chance of taking the Whigs by surprise. Murray and many others favoured remaining in Scotland and building up a strong army with French support. Many Scottish Jacobites wanted Charles to declare the Union of 1707 dissolved and to make Scotland an independent country once more but Charles' attention was focused on regaining the throne of England. He claimed eloquently that English Jacobites would rise in large numbers if they moved south; he had many promises of support from them. Moreover, once they were in England the French would help by mounting a major invasion. If the chiefs remembered Preston and were reluctant to venture into England then he recalled how the Scottish campaigns of 1715 and 1719 had fizzled out through being confined to the Highlands and their margins by lack of decisive action.

Was the decision a wise one? It was a tremendous gamble but, as we shall see, it almost paid off. Nevertheless, it was undertaken on two dubious premises. The first was that English Jacobites would turn out in strength and the second that the French would land in force. The Prince misled his followers on both counts. He pretended that he was in touch with prominent English Jacobites who were waiting for his arrival. In fact he had done little to rally potential support south of the Border. As in 1715, the optimists,

39 The palace of Holyroodhouse where Prince Charles held his court before the invasion of England.

particularly Charles, had an unrealistic view of the amount of active support for their cause in England. Although the French were planning an invasion, the number of times that such ventures had failed in the past should have made even optimists wary of counting on foreign support. As the Prince had acted on his own initiative in sailing to Scotland, he was not in close touch with the French government and under such circumstances the problems of co-ordinating an attack on London from Scotland and France were great. On moral grounds it is impossible to defend the way in which Charles deliberately misled his supporters but one can understand it on the grounds of expediency. The Prince saw clearly that unless a determined attempt on England was made his whole enterprise would fail.

Once the decision to march south had been taken the next question was: by which route? The main consideration was how to deal with the army that Field-marshal Wade had gathered at Newcastle. Still euphoric about the walk-over victory at Prestonpans the Prince wanted to invade Northumberland and bring Wade to battle. The other leaders were more cautious. Had they known how bad a state Wade's men were in, and how timid and senile the seventy-two-year-old Field-marshal had become, they might have thought differently. The lack of intelligence concerning the movements and state of the Hanoverian forces was to let the Jacobites down continually.

Without details of the strength of Wade's forces, however, the council favoured Lord George Murray's proposal for invading via Carlisle. If they entered Northumberland their communications would be threatened by the garrison at Berwick. Berwick would be a tough nut to crack without heavy guns because its defences were formidable. Its thick, bastioned walls had been specially built for mounting cannon and for soaking up the fire of siege artillery. Carlisle, the corresponding fortress town on the western Borders, was an easier target with weaker defences and no regular garrison. There was also the point that if they challenged Wade directly he might withdraw behind the walls of Newcastle from where it would be difficult to dislodge him. A march into Lancashire, that notoriously pro-Jacobite county, might produce substantial recruits while if they went by Carlisle they might draw Wade out from Newcastle and catch him somewhere in the Tyne valley.

So it was agreed. But to confuse the Hanoverians and prevent Wade from hurrying troops to protect Carlisle, it was decided to make a feint towards north-eastern England. The Jacobite army left in two main divisions. Murray, with the main body, headed directly for Carlisle via Annandale but the Prince marched into the eastern Borders through Kelso and Jedburgh to make Wade think that they were about to descend on Northumberland. The stratagem worked admirably and the different components of the army met outside Carlisle.

The Jacobite army which entered England comprised only about 5,500 men. More were being raised in Scotland and reinforcements from France were expected but there was no time to wait for them. It was a small enough force with which to try and topple a kingdom but, as events were to show, the government and its military commanders continually underestimated the Jacobites' military ability. Although it is often thought of as a clan army, an impression reinforced by the adoption of Highland dress by many of the non-clan regiments, Charles' force contained a substantial proportion of Lowland levies from Perthshire, Angus, and the Episcopalian north east, that bastion of Lowland Jacobite support, as well as John Roy Stewart's Edinburgh volunteers. As there were also a number of Irishmen and Scots in the French service, and French officers with the army, the little force had quite an international character.

In earlier Jacobite armies each clan had formed its own fighting unit regardless of size. Under the influence of Lord George Murray and the Duke of Perth the army of 1745 had been organized into regiments and companies similar to regular armies. Although this process often seemed makeshift, with smaller clans grouped together, it was remarkably effective. It produced an army which was well disciplined and highly mobile compared with its opponents. For much of the march through England the Jacobites paid for the supplies they required from public money which they seized. The ordinary soldiers were sometimes billeted at the expense of householders but the officers generally paid for their lodgings, sometimes lavishly. Up to 500 men had deserted on the march to the Border but thereafter desertions were few as stragglers were likely to be arrested by the local authorities. The discipline and good behaviour of these savage-looking troops impressed many people who encountered them, especially as Whig propaganda had led them to believe that the Highlanders' principal recreation was spitting babies on their swords and then eating them! Many staunch Whigs had cause to reflect that the behaviour of the regular Hanoverian troops was far worse than these 'barbarous' invaders.

THE SIEGE OF CARLISLE

Lieutenant-Colonel Durand, acting governor of Carlisle Castle, was in a difficult position. The defences of the city were in a poor state. The walls were crumbling and the parapets had been removed. Although he had ordered cannon from ships at Whitehaven to be brought to Carlisle to increase the defenders' firepower he cannot have been confident of their degree of commitment. Even worse, he was at odds with the civic authorities who in turn were at loggerheads with each other. When he proposed blocking up the Scottish and Irish gates and demolishing some cottages which were too close to the walls the magistrates refused to co-operate. As a result only a limited number of volunteers could be raised to defend the town.

During the afternoon of November 9th the advance guard of the Jacobites appeared on the bluffs on the far side of the River Eden at Stanwix. Today the view of the river from the castle is partly obscured by trees. It was market day and the city's gates were open to let the crowds straggle homewards. The gunners in the castle couldn't open fire for fear of hitting the civilians so the Jacobites were able to reconnoitre the castle at their leisure while Durand watched them from the tower of the cathedral. The Jacobites sent in a local countryman with a message for the mayor: he was to provide quarters for 13,000 infantry and 3,000 horsemen or the town would be reduced to ashes. By greatly inflating the size of their army they further lowered the defenders' morale. When the market crowds had dispersed, the castle's guns opened fire on the Jacobite horsemen, forcing them to retire out of range.

Carlisle in 1745 was a small town with a population of under 4,000, almost all living within the walls. For centuries it had been the major bastion against the Scots on the western Border. Its three gates, English, Scottish, and Irish, were still closed at night when a gun was fired from the castle. A contemporary view of the town shows its skyline, viewed across the Eden from Stanwix as the Jacobites first saw it, dominated by the cathedral tower and the massive bulk of the medieval keep. The defences had last been properly overhauled in Henry VIII's day. Today Carlisle, for so long an

40 Carlisle in 1745 as the Jacobites first saw it from Stanwix, across the Eden. The skyline is dominated by the castle and the cathedral.

important market town, is rapidly developing as a regional shopping centre and is capitalizing on its heritage. The castle has been split off from the rest of the town by a wide ring road but the streets around the cathedral are still comparatively quiet. If you follow the historic trail around the town you can see a number of buildings which existed in 1745. Most of the walls have since been demolished but a section, complete with sally port, survives on the west side of the old town near the station. The old town hall, in attractive rust-coloured stucco, dates from 1717 and faces the market cross where, following the capture of the city, James III was proclaimed King by the Jacobites.

The following day, with the arrival of the main army, the siege began. Under cover of thick fog, parties of Highlanders surrounded the town. The Prince sent another message demanding the surrender of the town and castle and when no answer was forthcoming the Duke of Perth directed his men to start digging trenches and throwing up breastworks, some of them within musket-shot of the walls. Meanwhile, the Prince, who was staying at Blackwell to the south of Carlisle, received a message that Wade was ready to move out from Newcastle. Over-estimating the speed at which Wade's army could move, the Jacobites decided to march eastwards to Brampton in order to intercept Wade. The siege was temporarily abandoned and only a small force was left to watch Carlisle.

Modern Brampton is an attractive little town whose main street and market place are by-passed by the heavy traffic on the Carlisle–Newcastle road. The

41 The keep and walls of Carlisle Castle today.

42 The house in Brampton where Prince Charles stayed while waiting for Wade's army to move westwards.

seventeenth-century house in which the Prince stayed, now a shoe shop, stands in High Cross Street, a short distance north of the market place, and is marked by a plaque. The Half Moon Inn where many of the officers were billeted also survives in the main street though it is now Half Moon Wholefoods instead of a hostelry.

43 Detail of the plaque on Prince Charles' House at Brampton.

Lord Elcho's horsemen rode a mile or two further east to Naworth Castle, the seat of the Earl of Carlisle, an imposing fourteenth-century fortress set in attractive parklands below the main road to Newcastle. The following day they surveyed potential battlefields east of Brampton while an advance party pushed on to Haltwhistle to get news of Wade. There had been heavy snowfalls east of Brampton in the valley of the South Tyne and as this would delay Wade the Jacobites debated whether to wait for him at Brampton or return and besiege Carlisle. Given that the weather did not favour a fast march by Wade, Lord George Murray suggested that they could do both. Accordingly the Prince stayed at Brampton with most of the Highlanders while Murray went back to Carlisle with the Lowland regiments. Murray was in overall charge of the siege, Perth of digging the entrenchments and constructing batteries.

The move to intercept Wade had been premature for he did not leave Newcastle until November 16th. His men were in a bad state; many were ill from dysentery. Moreover, they were unaccustomed to fighting in winter. In a civilized campaign, like the one many of them had left in Flanders, both sides retired to winter quarters. Instead of comfortable billets they were sleeping in tents in bitterly cold conditions, on a makeshift campsite which was flooded for part of the time. Their commander had grown so niggardly and penny-pinching that he grudged them anything more than iron rations. Ill-equipped to fight in winter, Wade's men were also half starved. The remnants of Cope's dragoons had come under Wade's command and their grim stories of the dreaded, invincible Highlanders did not improve morale.

44 The Half Moon Inn at Brampton where the Jacobites officers were quartered.

45 Naworth Castle, east of Brampton, occupied briefly by the Jacobites as a forward post while waiting for Wade's army.

It took Wade's soldiers two awful days to flounder through deep snow from Newcastle to Hexham, a mere fourteen miles. At their overnight stop the ground was frozen too hard to pitch their tents and several of the soldiers died from exposure sleeping in the open. They were short of food and in the freezing conditions their commander had not seen fit to provide adequate fuel for fires or straw for bedding. Behind them they left a trail of men who had dropped out from sickness or exhaustion. At last they reached Hexham where even the officers were almost ready to mutiny. Scouts, sent as far as Haltwhistle, learned that Carlisle had surrendered; they had come too late. After a day's rest Wade decided to return eastwards; the efforts of his men had been in vain and they straggled back to Newcastle having accomplished nothing.

It was just as well for Wade that he had been so slow, and that he had not made a more determined effort to reach Carlisle. The likely outcome of a battle in the snow somewhere between Haltwhistle and Brampton would have been an even more disastrous repeat of Prestonpans. In retrospect, the Jacobites made a strategic error in not taking the opportunity to eliminate one of the armies sent against them. Wade's force was to present no real threat to the Jacobites throughout their English campaign. However, not for the last time, the Prince and his advisers over-estimated their opponents. Wade's largely phantom presence, ever poised to intercept them or to cut off their retreat, figured prominently in all their subsequent decision making.

Back at Carlisle, operations had been progressing successfully. The Jacobites had dug in around the town and extended their trenches towards the walls, at times under heavy cannon fire. Trees were cut down and scaling ladders fashioned in preparation for an assault on the walls. The Duke of Perth encouraged his men by helping in the trenches, trying to overcome the Highlanders' traditional distaste for manual work by wielding pick and shovel himself. The 14th of November brought heavy snow and frost and conditions in the trenches were hard for the besiegers. Perth was only able to keep their morale up by staying on guard with them. It is a remarkable comment on the adaptability of the Jacobite rank-and-file that they were able to carry out siege operations at a time of year when regular troops would not normally have considered fighting.

As the trenches were pushed closer to the castle walls the resolution of the defenders crumbled. The prospect of an all-out assault with hand-to-hand fighting against such determined attackers was not encouraging, especially as Wade had sent a message saying that he could give them no help. The townspeople effectively mutinied and told Durand that they were unwilling to fight. Durand insisted that he would continue to defend the castle even if the city fell. He spiked the cannon mounted on the town's ramparts and brought all available provisions into the castle. However, the Duke of Perth insisted that the terms of surrender included both town and fortress. Unless the castle surrendered the town would be burnt. Clearly Durand believed him and, facing a revolt from the volunteers who had joined him in the castle, he gave up.

The siege had largely been planned by Lord George Murray and he was offended when the Prince appointed the Duke of Perth and Broughton to conduct surrender negotiations. Relations between Murray and the Prince had been strained from the first but now the ill-feeling between them erupted openly. Murray precipitated matters by threatening to resign as Lieutenant-general and serve the Prince in the ranks as an ordinary volunteer. Presumably his intention was to force a vote of confidence and his ploy succeeded. Charles accepted his resignation at first but there was a chorus of protest from his supporters who knew Lord George's value. Perth generously stood down as Lieutenant-general while Broughton resigned from the council and Murray stayed on. The split between the Prince and his most able general had, however, started to widen and was ultimately to have catastrophic consequences.

On November 18th Prince Charles entered Carlisle in triumph. He lodged at Highmoor's House, the home of an attorney on the west side of English Street near the city centre. The castle provided a useful supply of arms and ammunition and he was now ready for the march south. Murray was reluctant to venture further into England as there was no sign of any rising of

46 The market cross and town hall, Carlisle.

English Jacobites or of a French landing. However, the Prince claimed to have letters from English supporters promising to join if they entered Lancashire and he suggested that French aid depended on their mounting a proper campaign south of the Border rather than a mere hit-and-run raid. They agreed to continue the advance.

THE MARCH THROUGH ENGLAND

On November 20th the Jacobites left Carlisle and headed south. Wade was on his way back to Newcastle and there were no other forces to oppose them north of the Midlands. The speed of the Jacobite advance, despite being encumbered with artillery and a baggage train, took the Hanoverian commanders by surprise. On some days, led by the Prince who marched on foot with his men, the army covered up to thirty miles. Although it was midwinter, with road conditions frequently bad, they had the advantage that from Carlisle to Derby there were sizeable towns at suitable intervals to provide accommodation and provisions. Their target, consistently, was London but they managed to keep the Hanoverian commanders guessing as to their intentions. A move across the Pennines into Yorkshire, or a diversion into Wales to link up with potential supporters there, were popular suggestions.

They marched by Penrith to Kendal over difficult moorland roads. Lord George Murray with the Atholl Brigade and the Lowland regiments formed the vanguard while the Prince followed, usually a day's march behind, with the Highland regiments. From Kendal the going was easier to Lancaster. The town was more prosperous than it had been in 1715; the trans-Atlantic trade was starting to bring some wealth to Lancaster and this was reflected in many new buildings. The town's magistrates contemplated defending the castle but, wisely, thought better of it. As in 1715 few recruits to the Jacobite ranks were forthcoming but the Prince had high hopes for Preston and south Lancashire. Preston was favourably inclined towards the Jacobites, as it had been in 1715. However, the aftermath of the battle with its pillaging and executions was still remembered vividly and there was markedly less open support than thirty years before. Some local Catholic landowners like Francis Towneley of Towneley Hall and James Tyldesley, whose fathers had supported the rebellion in 1715, joined the Prince but there was no surge of mass enthusiasm. However, the warmth of the welcome at Preston contrasted with the apathy of other northern towns they had visited and seemed to augur well for Manchester.

Manchester, the largest and most important town in the north west, was not an old-established borough like Preston. Like Topsy it had 'just growed', on the strength of its textile industries. Despite its size its administration was little more complex than that of an ordinary rural parish. Two constables were appointed to oversee the town, and their efforts to obstruct the rebels by non-co-operation provided some comic relief. The population of the town was more accommodating, however, and Manchester did produce some volunteers. This added to the general euphoria but a substantial proportion of the 300 or so men who were formed into the small 'Manchester Regiment' commanded by Francis Towneley were paupers or unemployed men, some of whom would have enlisted in whichever army, Jacobite or government, had arrived first. At a meeting of Jacobite leaders several, including O'Sullivan and Lord Elcho, proposed a retreat as there was clearly no significant support for them in England. Ever-optimistic, the Prince claimed that this was because the French had not yet landed; they must push on. Lord George Murray suggested a compromise; they should continue into Derbyshire before making a final decision. This would give more time for English supporters to declare themselves or for the French to do something useful. They agreed to continue southwards.

Meanwhile, what had the government been doing to stop them? George II had returned from Hanover at the end of August. Even before Prestonpans he had begun to recall troops from Flanders and Ireland. Until Cope's defeat the rebellion had been treated fairly lightly but following the disaster panic measures were taken. The Duke of Cumberland, commanding the King's armies in Flanders, had been ordered to send home ten battalions under the command of Sir John Ligonier. These arrived at around the same time as news of Prestonpans. Cumberland was then ordered back to England with the entire army. Some 30,000 men were now available to crush the rising. If it seemed like using a sledgehammer to crack a nut it should be remembered that there was also a risk of a simultaneous French invasion.

The government troops were divided into two main armies. One with Wade had been sent to the north east. The other, under Ligonier, was designed to block the route to London from the west coast through the Midlands in case the Jacobites slipped past Wade. Other regiments were being raised locally by landowners and civic authorities. Some of them were to play a useful part in the campaign. The same could not be said for the county militia. The development of a standing army from the late seventeenth century had meant that the training of the militia, a kind of local home defence force which had existed from Tudor times, had been neglected. Even worse, there were serious doubts over the legality of raising and funding the militia on anything other than a temporary basis. Save in a few instances where they performed useful auxiliary work for the army they were more of a liability than an asset.

Ligonier was given rather vague orders to defend a line running from Chester to Nottingham to stop the Jacobites moving either towards Wales or London. If he had time to get far enough north he was to hold the line of the Mersey. Ligonier was delayed at Lichfield by illness and the Duke of Cumberland was appointed to take over his command. As the Jacobites reached Manchester the southern Hanoverian army was still consolidating at Lichfield. Wade, in the meantime, had been ordered south to intercept the Jacobites but his progress was pitifully slow.

William Augustus, Duke of Cumberland, a younger son of George II, was known to his troops as 'The Martial Boy' and, after Culloden, more widely as 'The Butcher'. He was only twenty-four, a few months younger than Prince Charles. Tall and heavily built (he later became obese) his youth contrasted with the age of the other Hanoverian generals, many of whom were veterans of Marlborough's wars. Having decided on a military career his position had secured him meteoric promotion. The previous year's campaign in the Low Countries formed his principal experience of warfare. At Fontenoy, facing the renowned Marshal Saxe, he had led his men into a murderous fire which caused heavy casualties. However, he made an orderly withdrawal, preventing a defeat from turning into a rout, and his soldiers respected him for his coolness and bravery. Although he hardly comes over as a likeable character his men thought well of him and he seems to have been concerned for their welfare. He was hardly a military genius; his tactics at Fontenoy had been simply to lead his men into the toughest spot possible and then keep them there. However, he lacked neither courage nor determination and was to prove a formidable opponent.

Cumberland was uncertain which direction the Prince would take. The Jacobites' habit of sending small parties to towns and villages away from their line of march to collect money, seize weapons, and try to drum up recruits was effective in spreading misleading rumours as to their probable future moves. From Manchester parties rode out to Rochdale and Oldham, convincing many people that the main army was about to head into Yorkshire. On December 1st the Jacobites started to leave Manchester, heading south for Macclesfield. Cumberland's scouts drew off as they approached but he moved up from Lichfield to Stafford, waiting to see in which direction they would go next. If he advanced too far north and got on the wrong side of the ridge known as the Bow Hills, these might stop him from intercepting the Jacobites if they headed for Derby. Lord George Murray, faced with the problem of side-stepping Cumberland's army, suggested that a feint to the west would mislead the Hanoverians into thinking that they were heading for Wales. Accordingly part of the army moved towards Congleton while the Prince with the rest waited in Macclesfield to see if the bluff would succeed.

Murray reached Congleton late in the afternoon of December 2nd, nearly catching the Duke of Kingston, in command of his privately-raised regiment of light horse. The cavalrymen abandoned Congleton in haste while Murray sat down to eat Kingston's supper! He sent a smaller party to Newcastle under Lyme where they narrowly missed catching another body of dragoons. The Jacobite bluff worked admirably. Cumberland, expecting a quick battle, moved westwards to Stone to intercept his opponents, and drew his army up to meet an attack which never materialized. Gradually it dawned on him that he had been out-thought and out-manoeuvred. Murray returned eastwards to rejoin the Prince south of Leek with the road to Derby now open. The army marched by Leek and Ashbourne, reaching Derby on December 4th.

THE FATEFUL DECISION

Derby was a sizeable market town with around 6,000 inhabitants. The travel-worn condition of the army and its outlandish dress did not apparently impress the population. The Prince took up quarters at Exeter House in Full Street while his patrols pushed forward to Swarkestone Bridge six miles further on the road to London. Only 120 miles separated the Jacobites from the capital and morale in the army was high. There were no significant forces between them and London. Cumberland had returned to Stafford and his troops were in no condition, after their recent marching and counter marching, to go any further without a brief rest. The Duke made plans to intercept the Prince at Northampton, but there was no certainty that he could move fast enough to do this. Wade, meanwhile, was still dragging his heels far to the north although he sent his cavalry on ahead to try and link up with Cumberland. In London there were the beginnings of a panic for the capital was protected only by a scratch force of 4,000 troops and a larger number of volunteers. Rumours were flying round the capital that George II had ordered his yacht to be made ready to leave in a hurry while stories that the French were landing added to the confusion.

However, feelings among the Jacobite officers were mixed when they met in the long first-floor drawing room at Exeter House for a full council. At

171

Manchester Lord George Murray had agreed to defer the decision about whether they should continue towards London until they reached Derbyshire but he wanted to see positive support from the English Jacobites and there were no indications of this. He proposed a retreat and most of the other leaders agreed. The chiefs had become more and more uneasy as the distance from Scotland increased and there were good tactical reasons for pulling back when the prize seemed almost within their grasp.

Their numbers had not been increased significantly since they crossed the Border and there were, supposedly, three armies in the field against them: those commanded by Wade and Cumberland, and a third one reported to be somewhere north of London. This last army was a complete fiction. One of Cumberland's agents, a man named Dudley Bradstreet, had been sent to Derby to delay the Jacobites by any means he could. He pretended to have Jacobite sympathies and gained the ear of the Duke of Perth. His invention of a phantom army, gathering somewhere beyond Northampton and barring the road to London, was inspired. It would be simplistic to claim that the decision made at Derby by the Jacobites was taken entirely on the strength of Bradstreet's report but it helped to tip the scales in favour of retreat.

Murray considered that they stood a good chance of defeating Cumberland but inevitably there would be casualties and the Jacobite army would be unfit to fight or march for some days. This might allow Bradstreet's non-existent army or even Wade to catch up with them. The outcome of a second fight so soon after was far less certain. Even if they won a second victory or slipped past and reached London, would the travel-worn and battle-stained little army impress anyone, or be sufficient to hold the city? There would still be Wade's army, unfought, at their backs. Moreover, should they be defeated the only outcome would be annihilation; nobody would get back to Scotland through hundreds of miles of hostile country. The French aid that had arrived, such as it was, had come to Scotland: better to return there to regroup, build up a larger army, and fight another campaign.

The Prince was still optimistic and he urged that their cause could only succeed if they pressed on towards London. They could easily by-pass Cumberland, and seize the capital. This would cause the collapse of effective government and would encourage the English Jacobites to rise *en masse*, and the French to land. But where were these English Jacobites, he was asked. Challenged to produce the letters of support he had claimed to have from them, he was forced to confess, to everyone's consternation, that they did not exist, that he had not been closely in touch with supporters south of the Border. The Duke of Perth then introduced Dudley Bradstreet who repeated his story about the army to the south commanded, he claimed, by Ligonier or Hawley and nearly 9,000 strong. As the Prince realized, Bradstreet achieved as much by this as Cumberland's entire army had done. With only O'Sullivan and one or two other allies among the Jacobite leaders the Prince, who had forfeited credibility with most of his followers, was forced to concede defeat and agree to a retreat.

Of the many 'what ifs' in the history of the Jacobite movement this is the greatest and the most intriguing. Did they take the right decision at Derby and what would have happened had they pushed on southwards? Essentially the clash was between Lord George Murray's sound tactical sense and the Prince's broader, more risky but also more visionary strategic grasp. In many ways they were both right. By any conventional military yardstick, the Jacobite army at Derby was in a dangerous situation from which retreat was the only sensible course. However, Murray can be accused of over-estimating his opponents. Throughout the invasion the Jacobites had out-marched and out-thought the Hanoverian commanders and their armies. To have penetrated so far into basically hostile territory defended by forces which outnumbered them heavily, without having to fight a single battle was a major achievement. Their luck had held so far and it might have continued to hold.

This seems to have been the Prince's attitude and he may well have been right. As history has proved so often, a rebellion on the defensive is a rebellion lost and the Prince realized this. The entire campaign up to that point had succeeded by bold, unconventional moves made against superior but unprepared and slow-reacting forces. The only way the Prince could succeed was to continue to trust to his luck but this was asking too much of his supporters. The Prince was a gambler but they were not: many had joined him reluctantly, out of conviction and duty rather than in a firm belief of success. Lord George Murray was one of these. Perhaps his differences with the Prince coloured his views. A sensible man, he lacked the Prince's boundless optimism, but the whole campaign had been conceived on the basis of optimism rather than sense and perhaps on this basis it might have succeeded.

Had the Jacobites pressed onwards there is little doubt that they could have out-manoeuvred Cumberland. The forces guarding the city would probably have melted away at their approach allowing them to take over London. What would have happened then is a matter for speculation. Perhaps the Prince's English supporters would have declared themselves openly in large numbers. Some of them are reported to have been actually setting out to join him when news of the retreat reached them and they prudently returned home. Perhaps the French would have landed in his support although it is debatable whether many Englishmen would have rallied to a Stuart prince backed by a foreign army. Perhaps the Old Pretender would have been restored and the whole course of British history altered. Perhaps not.

THE LONG RETREAT

The decision to retreat had been taken. Many people, probably including the Prince, knew that this was the beginning of the end for the rising. But the Jacobite army now had to extricate itself from a dangerous position. To give them a head start, Murray sent small parties south from Derby as though scouting the route to London while the rest doubled back towards Ashbourne. This gave him a day's lead over Cumberland and reduced the chances of Wade crossing the Pennines and cutting them off from Scotland.

Cumberland must have been puzzled but relieved to hear of the retreat. He soon realized that because of the speed with which the Jacobites were moving he stood no chance of catching them with his infantry, particularly as the weather had turned bad. Instead, he detached all his cavalry and mounted a thousand infantry on horses donated by local landowners and the city of Birmingham to form a mobile pursuit force. He also ordered Wade to send General Oglethorpe and all his dragoons from Yorkshire to try and intercept the Jacobites.

When the ordinary Jacobite soldiers realized that they were retreating morale plummeted. As they returned northwards through Ashbourne, Leek, and Macclesfield to Manchester they became more authoritarian in their dealings with the local population whose attitudes had also hardened. People who had welcomed the army on its southward march now, prudently, stayed silent. The faces which the soldiers saw in the towns and villages through which they passed were sullen and resentful. Local Whigs were bolder and more active; any soldier who straggled even a short way from the main force was likely to be seized and imprisoned. Few stragglers were as fortunate as the one who, according to tradition, ended up at an inn at Lydiate, north of Liverpool, and was sheltered by the landlord and his daughter. The inn, dating from the fourteenth century, thatched and preserving its original cruck timbers, is known today as the Scotch Piper, one of the few pub names in northern England which commemorates the Jacobites. An advance party sent into Manchester with the optimistic task of trying to enlist new recruits was met by a hostile crowd which chased them through the town into St Anne's Square. A party of local militia opened fire on Lord Elcho's horsemen as they entered Stockport, killing one of them.

The weather had turned bitterly cold with snow but the retreat continued. Again the discipline of the Jacobite army and its speed were surprising. On foot, the army was travelling as fast as Cumberland's pursuing cavalry. Oglethorpe was doing his best to cross the Pennines in time to catch them but the weather slowed him down. He followed the route over Blackstone Edge from Huddersfield to Rochdale in severe conditions. The M62 takes a similar route only a couple of miles to the south today and even with modern snow-clearing equipment the journey can be difficult or even impossible in winter. Daniel Defoe, making the crossing a few years before, found it grim and was relieved to drop down from the black bulk of the Aiggin Stone which marks the summit of the road to the civilized fields and farms on lower ground.

At Preston the Jacobites halted for a day and some officers suggested that they should make a stand. The precedent of 1715 was an unappealing one

47 The Scotch Piper Inn at Lydiate, north of Liverpool, reputedly named after a straggler from the Jacobite army.

though. Their pursuers were catching up; the first of Oglethorpe's dragoons, having covered a hundred miles in three days through bitter weather, reached Preston shortly after the Jacobite rearguard vacated the town. Pushing on northwards the dragoons came in sight of the Jacobite rearguard at Ellel, just south of Lancaster. There was a brief exchange of fire between them and Elcho's horsemen, helped by some of the MacPhersons, which left four of Oglethorpe's men dead and checked the pursuit. Cumberland thought that the Jacobites were in full flight but in fact morale was recovering from its low point at the start of the retreat. The Prince wanted to turn and fight at Lancaster: he had Lochiel and Lord George Murray select a potential battlefield two miles south of the town. It was finally agreed that they should continue north to Kendal. As they left Lancaster on the road north Oglethorpe's men moved in from the south. The dragoons pursued the Jacobites a short way beyond the town then turned round and headed southwards.

With the Prince on his way back to Scotland, the government in London had become increasingly concerned about a French invasion. On December 12th a rumour of a French landing at Hastings caused the government to send urgent messages northwards. The capital was almost defenceless and Cumberland, to his chagrin, was recalled to meet this new threat. For the moment the pursuit was checked. Even after the retreat from Derby the French build-up continued but — a familiar story by now — the Royal Navy had established a stranglehold on the northern French ports. A number of French vessels were captured by British men-of-war and privateers as they were moved up and down the coast and eventually the French gave up and scrapped the operation. A less ambitious enterprise mounted more swiftly might well have got a French force ashore in England in time to help the Prince.

At Preston the Jacobites decided to send the Duke of Perth ahead to Scotland with an escort of 120 horsemen to bring south the reinforcements that were being assembled. What seemed to be a straightforward journey turned into a dangerous mission as the hostility of the local population grew. When Perth, who was ill and travelling in a carriage, reached Kendal and rode up Finkle Street to the town centre a mob attacked his party with cudgels and stones. The Jacobite horsemen opened fire and killed four of them but some were pulled from their horses and captured. They moved into Stramongate and turned, prepared to charge the mob, but one of their officers was wounded by a sniper and they decided to quit the town and continue north. As they came to Penrith they could see that the beacon on the low hill above the town was burning and that the local people were out in force to stop them. They thought better of trying to push on through country whose hedges and walls might conceal parties of militia and returned to Shap. The following day they tried once more to reach Scotland but found that the militia were guarding the bridges and defending the villages. They were chased in a wide circuit through the Eden Valley and eventually gave up and retired south to rejoin the main army.

REARGUARD ACTION

The next three days were, for Lord George Murray, the worst of the entire English campaign. With Cumberland's horsemen pressing ever closer on his heels he had to get the Jacobite rearguard from Kendal to Penrith, over thirty miles by one of the most difficult routes in England, particularly in midwinter. Even worse, although he had originally agreed to command the rearguard on the understanding that he should not be lumbered with the baggage and artillery, this was precisely what was about to happen to him.

Today the difficulty of the task facing Murray and the Glengarry MacDonalds who formed the rearguard for this section of the march is not immediately clear. By motorway or train one can cover the journey that took them three days in half an hour. However, the bleak windswept moors around Shap can still daunt the modern traveller in winter when the motorway, which climbs to over 1,000 feet, is blocked by driving snow. The railway and M6 both bypass Kendal and take a more easterly route to

48 The house in Kendal occupied by Prince Charles.

Penrith, through the magnificent Lune Gorge. In 1745 the main road north ran from Kendal to Shap by a more difficult route further to the west. This involved negotiating a succession of valleys and ridges running south eastwards from the high fells of the Lake District. The modern A6 follows the general course of this road. However, it differs in detail because it was re-aligned in 1822 for most of the distance between Kendal and Shap to make the gradients easier. The original road was improved by a turnpike trust in the 1750s as a result of the difficulties experienced by both armies in 1745. You can still walk the line of this turnpike almost continuously from a point about four miles north of Kendal to Shap (see Map 10). Although most of it is metalled it is a quiet country road through impressive scenery and the gradients are those of the unimproved road of 1745. The bridges on it are

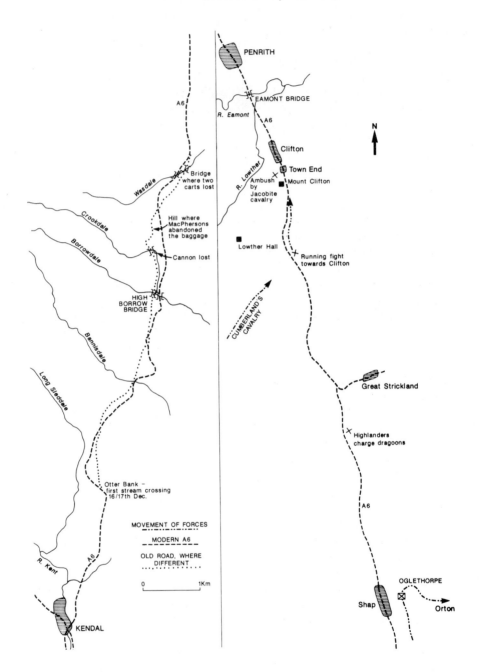

Map 10 The Jacobite retreat from Kendal to Penrith.

better than the rough narrow ones over which Murray struggled to get the army's baggage carts but are still simple and narrow.

Murray's departure from Kendal was delayed by O'Sullivan's incompetence. He had only belatedly realized that the army would be unlikely to reach Penrith in one day and that the village of Shap, the only feasible stopping place for the first night, would not have enough provisions. His orders to ensure that the men left with two days' rations were almost too late; some officers did not receive them until they were actually on the march. They then had to send their men back to Kendal to collect additional food. Murray stood in the pouring rain for much of the morning supervising the provisioning, an activity which did not improve his temper or the cold which he was developing.

As a result the rearguard were late in leaving Kendal. Burdened with the baggage waggons, they made slow progress and were halted only four miles or so north of the town. The location was possibly at the bottom of Otter Bank where the old road first diverges from the modern A6 (Map 10). Here the road crossed a swollen stream and on the far side made an immediate sharp turn and steep climb. Because of the lack of turning space for the horses the vehicles had to be manhandled across the stream. Murray and the other officers struggled up to their waists in water, helping to push the waggons, while the rain continued relentlessly. It was dark by the time they got all the waggons across; the Glengarry men and their commanders spent a damp night at a nearby farm and its outbuildings – possibly the modern hamlet of Garth Row. That night an advance party of Cumberland's dragoons reached Kendal and discovered that the Jacobite rearguard was barely four miles away. The Duke thought that he should be able to cut off and destroy at least part of the Jacobite army. He prepared to move on to Kendal himself and sent Oglethorpe's dragoons north from Lancaster in pursuit.

The main Jacobite army spent an uncomfortable night at Shap, a village which was too small to provide proper accommodation for such a force. Shap was a minor market centre on the bleak limestone plateau at the head of the Eden Valley. It was merely a cluster of stone farmsteads with two or three inns and a curious small market hall which still stands. Charles, staying in the principal inn, nowadays a private house at the north end of the village, was overcharged for his meagre accommodation! The next day they marched on, downhill through increasingly easy country, to Penrith.

Further south Lord George Murray's troubles were only just beginning. The rearguard set off at daybreak, having commandeered as many small carts as they could find from neighbouring farms. They transferred as much baggage as possible on to these from the heavy, cumbersome waggons. Only a few miles further on they encountered another difficulty. They came to a stream in full flood where the bridge was too narrow for even the local carts. Beyond was the longest, steepest climb on the entire road to Penrith. They

179

had been stopped in the valley of Borrowdale either by the main stream at High Borrow Bridge or, more probably, at Hause Foot Bridge over a tributary, the Crookdale Beck. Immediately beyond this latter bridge the old road climbs in a sharp dog leg to over 1,450 feet, higher even than the A6. It is no coincidence that this is virtually the only stretch of the old turnpike which has been totally abandoned by modern traffic!

The ascent was littered with abandoned carts containing ammunition for the artillery. Cluny and his MacPhersons had been in charge of these. The job of getting the carts over the stream had been a grim one and they had been forced to abandon one of the guns which had fallen in. They had bivouacked for the night beside the bridge in the driving rain. Getting the carts up the long, steep ascent the following morning had been too much for them.

To understand the difficulties which Murray and the Jacobite rearguard experienced in crossing these streams it should be remembered that the normal method of transport in Cumbria then was still packhorses. Carts and especially four-wheeled waggons were rarely used for long-distance transport and the streams on the road to Shap were mainly crossed by roughly-built, narrow packhorse bridges. Laboriously the Glengarry men got their carts over the stream. A messenger then arrived from the Prince with orders that none of the cannonballs which Cluny had abandoned should be left behind. Murray's party did not have the horses to haul the abandoned carts up the

49 High Borrow Bridge north of Kendal, one of the river crossings which gave Lord George Murray and the rearguard so much trouble on the retreat to Shap.

steep incline but he hit on the idea of offering the MacDonalds sixpence per head if they would each carry a cannonball to Shap tied up in their plaids!

A couple of miles further on, probably crossing the Wasdale Beck, on another narrow bridge without parapets, two of the carts fell into the stream and had to be abandoned. Fortunately this was the last difficult stream crossing and the ground beyond was easier. Nevertheless, it was after nightfall when Murray and the weary MacDonalds arrived at Shap, a village stripped bare of provisions by the main army. Charles had left John Roy Stewart and his men in the village as additional support but the departing army had also abandoned some of the artillery, giving the hard-pressed rearguard even more work.

All day, as they had struggled with the carts, Murray had been looking southwards, expecting to see the first of Cumberland's dragoons. Although their ride north from Kendal, through showers of rain, sleet, and snow, had not been pleasant, Oglethorpe's horsemen had made faster going than the Jacobite infantry and reached Shap soon after the Highlanders. Oglethorpe halted on the gently rising ground east of the village and considered the position. Cumberland had ordered him to attack if he believed that the Jacobites numbered 500 or less but local people had sent messages estimating the rebel force as high as 1,000 and Oglethorpe knew that the Jacobite rearguard had been reinforced. He had only 600 men and he was reluctant to order them to attack, dismounted, in the dark and rain, through the

50 The market hall at Shap.

enclosures around the village. They were tired, their powder was wet, and to send them against a possibly larger force in a good defensive position would have been madness. To bivouac on the open fellside without food for the men or fodder for the horses was out of the question on such a foul night so Oglethorpe decided to seek shelter in the nearest sizeable village. This proved to be Orton, over six miles south east of Shap, and in the dark, among the rough limestone outcrops, the journey was a difficult one.

CLIFTON MOOR

Murray and the rearguard were on the move before dawn. They had collected extra carts from Shap and its vicinity but though the road was far easier than the one south of Shap the carts were over-loaded and they now had most of the artillery to look after as well so that progress was slow. Murray posted scouts to the flanks and rear to give warning of approaching horsemen and sent a messenger to the Prince at Penrith asking for reinforcements, especially cavalry. Five miles or so on from Shap the Jacobites began to climb a hill near the hamlet of Thrimby when a body of horsemen appeared ahead of them on the summit. They were a party of cavalry sent on by Cumberland to try and cut off the rearguard. At the head of the Jacobite column were some men from the Duke of Perth's regiment who had been sent back to Shap to help with the baggage. Without waiting for orders from Murray, who was at the rear, their commander ordered them to charge. They rushed up the hill, broadswords drawn, to be joined by Glengarry's men from the rear of the column who had cut through the enclosures beside the road. Together the Highlanders stormed over the summit but the horsemen did not wait to meet this fierce charge: they turned and fled. One luckless horseman who fell from his mount was cut to pieces in a moment.

They pressed on towards Penrith but had only made another mile or two when they saw a long column of horsemen moving to intercept them along a road running through the park of Lowther Hall. The cavalry failed to get ahead of the Jacobites but pursued them northwards in a running fight down the narrow road which was hemmed in by walls and hedges. There was only room for a few horsemen to charge abreast and Glengarry's men turned every so often to keep them at bay while the carts trundled on towards the village of Clifton, south of Penrith. At Clifton, with the Hanoverian dragoons close behind, but the main Jacobite army only a little further north, Murray determined to make a stand.

Cumberland had now arrived a little way behind the Jacobite rearguard. He had hoped that Oglethorpe would have got ahead of the enemy and cut them off but Oglethorpe, sick and unclear about his orders, had returned to Shap too late to do this. The Duke, furious at his subordinate's failure, was further delayed by a false report that a large force of Highlanders was in a

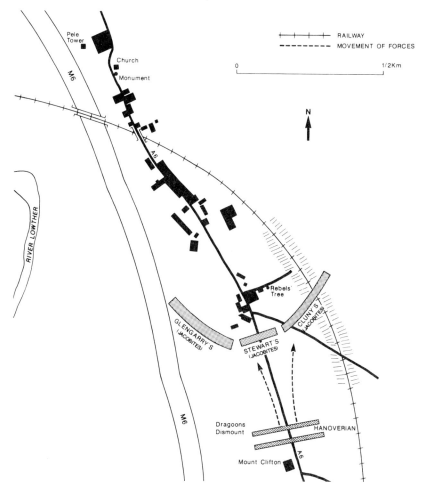

Map 11 The skirmish at Clifton.

wood near Lowther Hall and it was dusk before he arrived south of Clifton. A mixed group of government horsemen rode over the open common south of the village towards the first group of farm buildings. Here Lord Pitsligo's horsemen, who had been sent from Penrith, were waiting in ambush. A local farmer managed to slip out and warn Cumberland's men and they rode into the village ready for action. The result was a short, sharp exchange of fire between the two parties of horsemen. Pitsligo's cavalry broke off and galloped for Penrith while the government cavalry retired in the opposite direction.

The scene was now set for the last clash between major armies on English soil. South of Clifton a triangular area of open common ran gently downhill to the first houses at the end of the village. From there the village straggled up another gentle slope to the top of a low hill and dropped again to a bridge over the River Lowther. The village was surrounded by small fields and paddocks enclosed by hedges and drystone walls. In response to Murray's requests for reinforcements the Prince sent Cluny's MacPhersons and the Stewarts of Appin commanded by Ardshiel. The Atholl Brigade, with the Duke of Perth, was stationed at Lowther Bridge as a reserve. Quickly, in the gathering darkness Murray ordered his men to line the hedges and walls, forming a defensive cordon around the village. At the south end of Clifton, Murray placed the MacPhersons and the Appin Stewarts to the east of the road. John Roy Stewart's men covered the road itself, where it narrowed between the enclosures, and the Glengarry men lined the enclosures to the west.

Cumberland dismounted his dragoons on the upper part of the common, near where the farm of Mount Clifton stands today, and formed them into two lines. Murray had received a message from the Prince ordering him to retreat and not to engage the Hanoverian army. However, Murray did not think that he could retreat safely with the enemy so close. The government troops came down the gentle slope over moorland which narrowed between hedges and walls as they neared Town End at the south of Clifton. The night was dark but with glimpses of the moon between the ragged clouds. The

51 The south end of Clifton village, scene of the last clash between armies on English soil. Cluny's MacPhersons and the Appin Stewarts were lined up behind the hedges in this area.

IN MEMORY OF THE TROOPERS
OF
BLAND'S REGIMENT,
WHO LIE HERE
KILLED AT CLIFTON MOOR
1745

52 Memorial to the Hanoverian dragoons killed at Clifton Moor.

Highlanders could just make out the light crossbelts of the dragoons but their own dark tartans provided excellent camouflage.

Cumberland's men began to probe the enclosures and soon encountered the line of MacPhersons, where Murray, realizing that the action was likely to begin east of the village, had come over to join Cluny. The clansmen opened fire but the return volley was too accurate for comfort. 'What the devil is this?' exclaimed Cluny in surprise as the musket balls whistled past him. Murray then drew his sword and yelled 'Claymore!', the signal for the Highlanders to charge. They rushed forward on the dragoons, swords in hand. For a few minutes there was vicious, confused hand-to-hand fighting in the darkness among the hedges and wet ditches. Then the dragoons broke and ran. To the west of the village the action was not close enough to involve cold steel although there was a good deal of firing. Having repulsed the dragoons and gained the breathing space that he needed, Murray was satisfied and ordered a withdrawal to Penrith. The Jacobite army was already moving out towards Carlisle and after a stop to give the men who had fought at Clifton a rest and some food, Murray and the rearguard followed them. Soon after Clifton had been evacuated Cumberland sent his men into the village and took up quarters for the night in one of the houses at Town End.

The casualty figures show that Clifton was a skirmish rather than a battle. On the Hanoverian side fewer than a dozen dragoons were killed. Between twenty and thirty were wounded and several were saved by their steel caps which deflected the MacPhersons' broadswords. On the Jacobite side five men were killed. Both sides considered the scuffle a minor victory. Cumberland

53 The Rebels' Tree at Clifton where the Jacobite dead were buried, with commemorative stone.

claimed that he had dislodged the rebels from a strong position while the Jacobites maintained that they had driven off their attackers. Certainly the action checked Cumberland's pursuit and allowed Charles to march back into Scotland without further opposition.

Clifton avoided serious damage at the hands of either army in 1745, but it has fallen victim to modern transport systems. The railway line and the M6 hem it in to east and west while the A6, far wider than the road of 1745, allows heavy lorries to roar through the village. Passing on the M6, Clifton's most distinctive feature is the sixteenth-century stone pele tower, once attached to a now-vanished hall. There are few reminders of the skirmish. The modest but attractive church stands on a hill near the pele tower. In the churchyard, just to the right of the entrance, is a small modern monument to the dragoons of Bland's regiment who died in the fighting.

The dead Highlanders were buried close to where they fell. At the opposite end of the village, at Town End, a narrow lane runs back from the main road between a pub and a set of farm buildings to tunnel through the railway embankment. Just behind the farmyard, on the south side of the lane, is a large oak known as the 'Rebels' Tree' at the foot of which the clansmen are said to have been buried. The tree certainly looks old enough to have existed at the time of the battle and a small commemorative stone, set within a wooden fence, has been placed beside it. Clifton Moor has been enclosed into a series of fields but the shape of it, narrowing in towards the village, is preserved in the angle between the A6 and a minor road running south east from Town End. If you walk a short way south to Mount Clifton farm, close to where the dragoons originally formed up, you get a good panorama of the battlefield. The fields around Clifton have been enlarged since the eighteenth century so that there are fewer boundaries than there were in 1745 but the jumble of houses climbing up the far slope, particularly if viewed at dusk, gives a good impression of the difficult job that the attacking Hanoverian soldiers were faced with.

10

1746: THE RECKONING

RETURN TO SCOTLAND

Small-scale though it was, the action at Clifton checked Cumberland's pursuit and the Jacobites had enough leisure at Carlisle to hold another meeting. Lord George Murray wanted to abandon Carlisle after blowing up the castle. The suggestion that they should make a stand there was dismissed but the Prince was adamant that they should leave a garrison. This would show his English supporters that the retreat to Scotland was only temporary and that he would be back in a matter of weeks. In more immediate practical terms a garrison at Carlisle would hold up Cumberland's pursuit: he could not cross the Eden under the guns of the castle. The Prince considered that a garrison could hold out for a long time, forgetting how easily they themselves had taken the town. Cumberland had no artillery, he claimed. Lord George Murray protested that this would merely be throwing good men away. The Duke would bring heavy cannon from the ships at Whitehaven and batter the castle into submission within a matter of days. He was right: the garrison held out for only ten days after the army left.

The Prince was determined to have his way and Francis Towneley agreed to act as governor of the town while John Hamilton commanded the castle. The garrison of 300 included the luckless volunteers of the Manchester Regiment. On December 20th the army crossed the Esk at Longtown and re-entered Scotland. The river was angry and swollen. The soldiers crossed chest deep and once on the other side the pipers played reels while the men danced until they had dried off.

Cumberland reached Carlisle on December 21st and surrounded the town. The Duke established his headquarters at Blackhall in the house that the Prince had occupied. On Christmas day five dragoons who had joined the rebel army after Prestonpans and who had been captured were tried, condemned, and hanged. Towneley, who had served in the French army, put the castle into as good a state of defence as he could, strengthening the ramparts with sandbags and digging earthworks to keep the attackers at a distance. His efforts were in vain for, as Murray had predicted, Cumberland had eighteen-pounder cannon brought from Whitehaven. He referred to the castle contemptuously as an 'old hen coop' and his engineers began work on two siege batteries. The first was sited at Primrose Bank opposite the west side of the castle wall. The defenders tried to interrupt the work by firing their own cannon but their gunnery was ineffectual.

By the evening of the 27th six heavy guns were in place and the following day firing commenced under the direction of Major William Belford, a skilled artilleryman who was to play a major role in the battle of Culloden four months later. After two days of bombardment the walls of the castle had been breached and, seeing more guns arriving from Whitehaven, the garrison lost heart. On the morning of the 30th they hung a white flag out over the castle wall and agreed to an unconditional surrender. The following day Cumberland entered the town and took up residence at Highmoor's House.

The prisoners captured at Carlisle were sent to Lancaster Castle and Chester, the officers bound and pinioned on horseback, the ordinary soldiers on foot, tied together. The government concentrated its severity on the Englishmen who had volunteered for the Manchester Regiment. Towneley and a number of others were tried in London a few months later and were condemned to be hanged, drawn, and quartered. After execution, Towneley's severed head was placed on top of Temple Bar in London and those of two of his officers were set over the English gate in Carlisle, a grim reminder of the penalties for treason.

Meanwhile in Scotland two regiments of infantry from Berwick, together with the remnants of Cope's dragoons, had regained control of Edinburgh but most of the country was still in Jacobite hands. At Perth Lord Strathallan had been gathering reinforcements. Lord John Drummond, brother of the Duke of Perth and an officer in the French army, had arrived from France with about 750 men from the expatriate regiments in the French service, the Scots Royals and the Irish Brigade. Strathallan's army now matched in size the one which had entered England so that despite the loss of Edinburgh the Jacobite position in Scotland was still strong. The Prince occupied Glasgow, a notoriously Whig town, and levied a heavy fine in money, clothing, and shoes on the authorities for their cheek in raising a regiment of volunteers against him. Cumberland had been temporarily recalled to London to check the threatened invasion from France. His place had been taken by Lieutenant-general Henry Hawley, a veteran of Sheriffmuir. Foul-mouthed, vicious, brutal, and stupid he epitomized the British regular army at its worst. A harsh disciplinarian, he was detested by his men. Under him, in early January, the Hanoverian army began to build up in Edinburgh.

The Jacobites seem to have lost sight of long-term strategy and for want of a more definite objective the Prince decided to besiege Stirling Castle. Lord John Drummond had brought a proper artillery train from France including heavy siege guns but Stirling Castle was a different proposition from Carlisle. The town of Stirling, with only decrepit medieval walls, was taken with ease

54 The breached walls of Carlisle after bombardment by Cumberland's artillery.

but the castle, secure on its high rock and well-supplied with cannon, was a difficult target.

Situated on a steep-sided rocky crag, with the High Street of the medieval burgh straggling down the gentle slope from its gates, Stirling Castle closely resembles Edinburgh Castle. There may have been a prehistoric fort here but if so all traces have been removed by later development. There is nothing in the castle which you can see today which is older than late medieval times. From the fifteenth century it became a royal residence. It was James III's favourite home and it was probably he who began the building of the Great Hall whose carved woodwork is still so much admired. Mary Queen of Scots was crowned, and James VI baptized here. Although its position was strong the castle was not invulnerable. It had changed hands more than once in the fourteenth century during the Wars of Independence. In Cromwell's day General Monk besieged it and after a week's heavy bombardment the garrison surrendered. However, between 1708 and 1714 the outer defences of the castle had been strengthened. The outworks beyond the early sixteenth-century forework, were replaced by two lines of defence each protected by a massive dry ditch in front and covered by batteries of cannon. It is these that you see first today if you visit the castle and they are still impressive. General Blakeney, commanding the garrison, was seventy-four, a veteran of Marlborough's campaigns but, unlike Wade, still tough and determined.

The Prince had siege artillery but he was short of trained gunners and engineers. He was forced to rely on the dubious talents of Monsieur Mirabel de Gordon, a French officer of Scots extraction, who was supposedly a siege expert. The upper part of the town was an obvious site for a battery but, having heard of the damage inflicted on Edinburgh by the castle's guns, the townspeople naturally objected to this. Mirabel then began digging a site for a battery on the Gowan Hills, a low volcanic outcrop close under the walls of the castle to the north east. Unfortunately the resistant rock was close to the surface under only a thin layer of soil so that it was impossible to dig trenches and sandbags and other means of protection had to be carried up from other locations.

While the Jacobite army was ineffectually besieging Stirling Castle Prince Charles was enjoying the hospitality of Sir High Paterson at nearby Bannockburn. It was here that he first met Paterson's niece, Clementina Walkinshaw who, later in France, was to become his mistress and bear him a daughter. Meanwhile Hawley was preparing to move out from Edinburgh. He had about 9,000 men. Three-quarters of his twelve infantry regiments had seen action in Flanders but many were worn and tired after their long and arduous winter marches under Wade. He also had the regiment of Glasgow volunteers, a comparable force from Edinburgh, and some dragoons including those which had fled at Prestonpans. The Jacobites, with their new reinforcements, had about the same number of men but Hawley was contemptuous of their fighting ability. It was unfortunate, from the point of view of his men, that at Sheriffmuir he had served on the victorious right wing of Argyll's army which had defeated the Highlanders.

FALKIRK

On January 13th the government forces began marching westwards. Lord George Murray, stationed near Falkirk with part of the Jacobite army, made an unsuccessful attempt to lure their advance guard into a trap, then withdrew to Stirling and by the evening of the 16th the entire Hanoverian army was camped outside the small town of Falkirk. The Prince and his officers had drawn their army up near Stirling in preparation for a battle but when Hawley did not appear Murray suggested making a surprise attack on their camp at Arnothill to the west of Falkirk. South and west of the town, and Hawley's camp, the ground rose into a ridge of moorland. Murray planned to move up behind this hill, out of sight of the enemy, and climb it to gain a commanding position overlooking the Hanoverian camp. He sent Lord John Drummond with a diversionary force along the main road from Stirling to Falkirk, which ran to the north of the hill, to divert Hawley's attention while the main army headed for the crest of the moorland from the south west.

The plan worked admirably. The last thing Hawley expected was a direct attack on his camp. He hadn't bothered to send out cavalry patrols and he discounted the first reports of the sighting of Lord John Drummond and his men. Even when a party of volunteers galloped headlong into the camp shouting that the entire Jacobite army was only a short distance away he was slow to react. He had been enjoying dinner at Callender House a mile to the east of Falkirk. His reluctant host was Lady Kilmarnock whose husband was with the Jacobites. One wonders whether she had an inkling of what was going on and made sure that Hawley drank plenty of wine! At any rate, he hurried back to the camp rather dishevelled. He quickly ordered the dragoons to move out, then the infantry and artillery. They went south around the enclosures surrounding Bantaskin House and started to climb towards the moorland.

Both armies were now climbing up the same hill, the Jacobites from the west, the Hanoverians from the east. The moorland fell quite steeply towards Falkirk on the north but from its crest the slope ran down steadily eastwards towards Hawley's camp. At one point the northern half of this slope was cut by a ravine which was to play an important part in the battle. To the south the ground fell to the shallow valley of the Glen Burn whose marshy bottom limited scope for movement in this direction. Neither side saw the other until

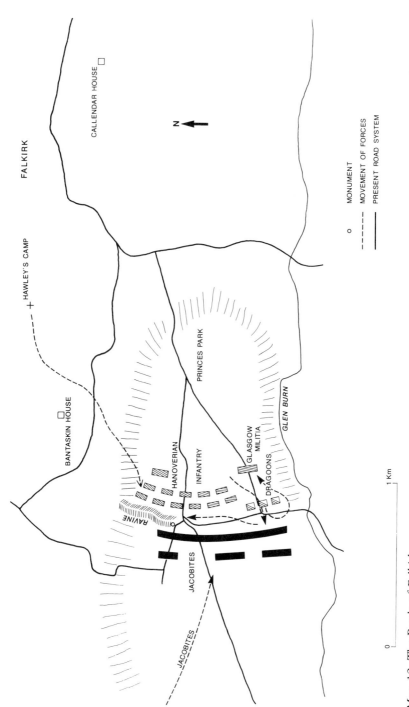

Map 12 The Battle of Falkirk.

they were both almost at the summit. The three MacDonald regiments which had been leading the Jacobite army formed into line and moved slowly forward to give the other infantry units a chance to come up with them. Murray, fighting on foot again with broadsword and targe, steadied them and urged them to hold their fire. The MacDonalds formed the right wing and as the other regiments arrived they formed up to their left until the Stewarts of Appin arrived at the left wing, on the edge of the ravine. A second line of infantry formed up behind them with a reserve in the rear made up of Lord John Drummond's diversionary force which had now joined the main body.

Hawley's dragoons got well ahead of the infantry during their climb. It was a stormy winter's day with a strong wind in their faces. As the foot-soldiers struggled up the hill a sudden heavy shower of rain drenched them and, more importantly, their cartridges so that when the battle began many of their muskets misfired. Like the Jacobite regiments they hastily formed two lines across the moorland ridge though some of the troops in the second line had not go into position when the battle began. By this time it was late afternoon and it was beginning to get dark. Hawley ordered his dragoons to attack without waiting for the infantry to come up in support. This was ill-judged; Hawley probably believed that with their supposed fear of horsemen the Highlanders would not stand a cavalry charge. Three dragoon regiments came up towards the right wing of the Jacobite army. The boggy ground of the Glen Burn prevented them from getting round the Highlanders' flank so that they could only make a direct attack. Under Lord George Murray's strenuous urging the MacDonalds waited until the horsemen were within ten yards of them. Then they fired a withering volley at close range. The dragoons recoiled in shock: at least eighty were killed immediately. A small party of them came on through the fire and tried to ride the Highlanders down. For a few moments there was a confused melee. The clansmen had no space to wield their broadswords. Some used their dirks to stab the horses, others fired pistols or pulled the riders down.

The bulk of the dragoons fled though with the Highlanders in pursuit. Some of the horsemen galloped back into the ranks of the Glasgow volunteers who, thrown into chaos, also turned and fled. Other dragoons rode off northwards between the two armies, running the gauntlet of musketry from the centre and left of the Jacobite front line. This was unfortunate for the Jacobites in some respects for, as they did not use ready-made cartridges of powder in their muskets, they had no time to reload and use their weapons against Hawley's infantry. Nothing daunted they dropped their firearms and charged downhill with their broadswords. Already badly winded by their uphill rush, with the rain in their faces, the Hanoverian infantry put up little opposition and four of their six front line regiments turned and ran. So did the second line, with the exception of Barrel's regiment. The rout was saved from turning into an utter massacre by Ligonier's, Price's, and Barrel's regiments which stood firm and provided covering fire that checked the pursuit of their fleeing comrades. These regiments had been on the right of the Hanoverian line, protected by the ravine from direct attack. They were able to fire across the gully at the Highlanders opposite and also at the clansmen who ran past them in pursuit of the troops that had fled.

The Jacobite army was now thoroughly disorganized. The Highlanders on the right wing were pursuing the dragoons, those on the left were chasing the infantry. Lord George Murray brought up the Atholl Brigade, the only troops in the second line that had kept their ranks, and moved to attack the three regiments that had stood firm. Meanwhile some of the dragoons had rallied and returned to protect the infantry which withdrew down the hill. It was almost dark now and Murray did not think that he had enough men for a pursuit. The most unfortunate Jacobite leader at Falkirk was MacDonald of Tirandrish, the victor of High Bridge. He had rushed after the fleeing government troops when most of his companions had halted. Wandering around in the gathering dark he saw a body of men that he thought were Lord John Drummond's. He only discovered that they were Barrel's regiment when he walked up to them and was lucky to be made prisoner by one of the officers: Barrel's men were all for shooting him on the spot! The battle had lasted only twenty minutes or so. The Jacobites suffered around 50 killed and 80 wounded but government losses were far higher; somewhere between 300 and 500 dead though Hawley did not admit officially to so high a figure. Again the Jacobites had caught a regular army by surprise and broken its best battalions. Had the clansmen held their ranks and been better disciplined the Hanoverian losses might have been even greater but as it was Hawley's men were retreating towards Edinburgh, having burnt their tents and abandoned their artillery.

The moorland on which the battle was fought has been enclosed into large rectangular fields which are nevertheless still rather bleak and exposed. The lower part of the slope has been built over by a housing estate and a hospital but the area where the armies first clashed is still mainly open country. As with other Jacobite battlefields there is some dispute over where the armies were actually positioned. Some maps of the battle place the conflict well down the hill to the east of where we have shown it and at least one other battlefield guide has located it a good mile and a half further west. However, there is only one place where the topography fits the contemporary descriptions really accurately.

Falkirk grew into a major industrial town in the nineteenth and twentieth centuries and you need some skill to find your way up from its centre on to the ridge where the battle took place. The initial climb out of the town is steep and you can appreciate how tiring it must have been for Hawley's infantry, in a hurry and encumbered by their heavy muskets, in the teeth of a strong wind.

A monument to the battle stands a little way off the road which runs up the crest of the ridge, beside a minor road which drops steeply into Falkirk. The

55 The rolling plateau on which the Battle of Falkirk was fought. It was much more open in 1746.

grounds around Bantaskin House have been opened to the public and from the monument a path leads into them down the east side of a small rivulet. Within a few yards the stream drops into a steep-sided gully. This is the ravine which helped to determine the course of the battle. Today it is thickly wooded but in 1746 it was probably more open. It is steep and deep enough to have provided a major obstacle to infantry and the slopes on either side are within musket shot of each other. If you retrace your steps to the monument and then back to the road which runs up the ridge, a rough path leads down through a shelter belt of mature trees towards the Glen Burn. If you walk through the trees for a short distance you will soon appreciate how the slope falls away from the road on either side; you cannot see the ravine or the monument. The significance of this small-scale topography is only brought out on the ground and is not referred to in many accounts of the battle. It makes it easier to understand why the battle was so confused for one wing of each army must have been out of sight from the other. It is not difficult to imagine how easy it would have been to lose track of events in the dusk of a wild winter's day.

After the battle Lord George Murray urged that Hawley should be pursued while his men were still disorganized. This was undoubtedly the best advice. Had it been followed the final campaign in Scotland might have been much longer. However, the Prince was obsessed with capturing Stirling Castle and

196

56 Monument on the battlefield at Falkirk.

the Jacobites returned there leaving Hawley's army in Edinburgh to lick its wounds and regroup. Back at Stirling, Mirabel de Gordon's battery of siege guns was partially completed. The three guns that had been mounted opened fire on the castle, to little effect. Return fire was more effective and soon put the Jacobite guns out of action. The siege has something of a comic opera air about it but it might have succeeded with a little more time for General Blakeney reported to Cumberland that he could only have held out for a few more days due to shortage of provisions.

After Falkirk it was clear that only Cumberland could restore morale in the government army and at the end of January he arrived in Edinburgh to take command once more. The following day he began to move his forces out of Edinburgh and take the offensive. Lord George Murray prepared a plan for meeting them but he and the chiefs were concerned that so many Highlanders

197

57 Detail of inscription on the monument.

had returned home. They told the Prince that the army was not in a fit state for another major battle and that they should retire to the Highlands, concentrate on capturing the government forts there and build up a new army in the spring. Charles protested, realizing that this would damage morale and discourage the French from sending any further aid, but in vain. The Prince blamed Murray for this betrayal and their relationship deteriorated even further. As Cumberland advanced, the Jacobites fell back. They crossed the Forth at the Fords of Frew and moved north to Perth where it was agreed that the Lowland regiments of the army should follow the coastal route to Inverness while the Highlanders went via the Tay valley and Badenoch. Abandoning most of their heavy artillery at Perth and retreating through heavy snow the two divisions of the army duly met at Inverness. The final, disastrous phase of the campaign was beginning.

198

58 Stirling Castle at the end of the seventeenth century. Stronger outworks added later made it an even tougher nut to crack in 1746.

THE FINAL CAMPAIGN

The last weeks of the Jacobite campaign had some minor successes. The three government forts in the Great Glen were besieged and while Fort William, supplied by sea and with its defences strengthened, held out the other two fell. At Fort Augustus a lucky cannon-shot from the besiegers exploded the powder magazine and the dazed garrison surrendered. At Inverness the Jacobites laid mines under the ramparts and, under threat of these, the commander of Fort George capitulated. Ruthven Barracks were also captured. When Cope had come past Ruthven on the way to Inverness he had added most of the garrison to his small army, leaving only a sergeant and twelve men to look after the post. This tiny garrison had successfully defended the barracks against an attack by 300 Jacobite clansmen who, lacking artillery, were unable to make any impression on its walls. However, when the main body of the army arrived, on their way to Inverness, the defenders wisely surrendered and the Jacobites burnt the barracks.

After rejoining the Prince at Inverness, Lord George Murray went south with 700 men into Atholl which the government had occupied with many small posts. In a plan which was a minor masterpiece, Murray attacked thirty of these outposts simultaneously and captured them all with no loss of life. Then he set about besieging the principal garrison at his ancestral home, Blair Castle. His aim was to create a diversion which might draw Cumberland away from the pursuit of the main army. Blair was the last castle in Britain to be besieged. Its defenders were in a difficult position: not expecting to be attacked they had been given little ammunition and had not laid in supplies for more than a few days. Nevertheless their commander, bad-tempered old Sir Andrew Agnew, was determined to hold out. Murray's two four-pounder cannon made little impression on the castle's thick walls. At one stage during the siege Agnew wondered why the attackers were concentrating their fire on one particular window. Going down to investigate he found that some wit had stuffed one of his old uniforms with straw and set it up with a telescope as a target! Agnew, furious, made the practical joker take the dummy down himself under heavy fire. After two weeks the garrison was almost out of food when Murray was recalled to Inverness with the news that Cumberland was on the move.

After leaving Edinburgh, Cumberland had marched slowly northwards. He had no intention of campaigning in the Highlands in midwinter and he allowed his men plenty of time to rest in Aberdeen while waiting for the weather to improve. At Inverness, as winter began to give way to spring, the Jacobite army was becoming disorganized and desperate. This was due partly to incompetent leadership. The Prince seemed to have lost all interest. He was ill for part of the time and spent much of the rest of this interlude in hunting. Murray of Broughton, the Prince's efficient secretary, also fell ill and as the officers who were in charge of supplies were particularly incompetent, the

59 Inverness, the headquarters of the Jacobites during the final weeks of the campaign.

army started to run short of food. Cumberland's men had the advantage of being supplied from the south by sea and were better fed. Reinforcements from France were still trickling in but several ships were intercepted by British men-of-war. Particularly crucial was the loss of a vessel which was bringing nearly £13,000 in gold.

In late March Cumberland began to move towards Inverness. Apart from one or two skirmishes his advance went unopposed. The Jacobites failed to dispute the difficult crossing of the Spey and Cumberland reached the small coastal burgh of Nairn without difficulty. The climax of the campaign was approaching: the Jacobites would either have to fight and win a battle in the Inverness area or disperse into the mountains for a guerilla-style campaign.

The Prince and his officers had moved out of Inverness and established their headquarters at Culloden House six miles to the east. The choice was an ironic one, for this was the home of Duncan Forbes, Lord President of the Court of Session and the Jacobites' most effective enemy in the north. In 1715 he had helped his sister-in-law to defend the house during an unsuccessful seven-weeks siege by the Jacobites and had afterwards been one of the main figures behind the recapture of Inverness for the government. At the start of the 1745 rebellion he hurried north to his estate, believing that he could be of more use to the government in the Highlands than in Edinburgh. He contacted a number of clan chiefs and urged them to support the house of

60 Culloden House, incorporating parts of the house occupied by Prince Charles and his officers immediately before the Battle of Culloden.

Hanover or at least not declare for the Pretender. His activities undoubtedly reduced support for the Prince in the Highlands. It was perhaps fitting that the last battle of the rebellion was to be fought on the doorstep of the man who had done more to hinder the Jacobite cause than any other Scotsman.

In the early eighteenth century Culloden House was a partly fortified mansion with two battlemented towers flanking a central block and surrounded by a solid stone wall. In 1772 most of the old house was demolished to make way for the present classical-style mansion although this incorporates parts of the earlier building at the base of its central block. The proportions of the new house, with its balanced facade and flanking side pavilions, make it one of the most attractive small country mansions of its period in Scotland. The Forbes family continued to live here until 1897 but Culloden House is now a fine hotel.

A NIGHT ATTACK

As Cumberland advanced the Jacobite leaders looked for a suitable site to give battle. Lord George Murray found one near Dalcross Castle where rough ground would have impeded Cumberland's cavalry and artillery while giving the Highlanders maximum advantage. However, O'Sullivan, who had the Prince's ear, did not like it. The Irishman preferred Culloden Moor, a level stretch of heathland and bog above Culloden House falling to the River Nairn on the south and the coast on the north. His rationale was that although the land was flat and open, boggy ground would protect the army. Murray thought not a single Highlander in the army would have chosen such an unsuitable site but he was overruled and on April 15th the army was drawn up in battle order on the moor to wait for Cumberland.

Morale in the Jacobite army had slumped and one dispute in particular was to have an influence on the coming battle. There had been continual disagreement throughout the campaign about who should occupy the post of honour on the right wing of the Jacobite army. The MacDonalds claimed to hold it by a hereditary right dating back to the days of Robert Bruce but the other clans disagreed and a compromise had been reached by which this position was allotted on a rota system. On this particular occasion the MacDonalds claimed that it was their turn. However, Murray wanted to place his own Atholl Brigade in this position. At Prestonpans and Falkirk they had not been in the Jacobite front line and Murray had been accused of keeping his own men out of harm. Prickly and offended he now insisted on their holding the right wing. Having overruled him concerning the choice of battlefield, the Prince gave way on this point to the MacDonalds' anger.

Cumberland did not appear that day; nor did the provisions that the army needed so badly. The supply system had completely broken down. There was food at Inverness but no one had arranged transport to bring it to Culloden. Meanwhile the army starved. Lord George Murray, having seen O'Sullivan's chosen site on Culloden Moor for himself, liked it even less. Across the River

61 Culloden Moor: the worst possible ground for a Highland charge. (Courtesy National Trust for Scotland)

Nairn there was higher, steeper, more broken ground far more suitable for the army but the Prince, who had decided to take command in person for the first time, supported his Irish adviser.

It seems to have been the Prince and O'Sullivan who, between them, concocted a plan for a night attack on Cumberland's camp at Nairn. That day, the 25th, was Cumberland's birthday and they thought that there was a good chance that the entire army might be drunk and off guard. Murray was not happy about the plan. In theory it was a bold, unconventional idea which, if it succeeded, might bring a victory more crushing than Prestonpans. In practice, Nairn was over eight miles away and night attacks were notoriously difficult to organize and co-ordinate. Nevertheless, Murray conceded, any plan was preferable to fighting on Culloden Moor.

Had the army set off early enough the scheme might have worked but departure was delayed because large numbers of men had gone off in search of food and had to be rounded up. Despite the reservations of many of his officers the Prince was determined to go ahead with the attack. Murray led the first column of the army and Lord John Drummond the second while the Prince brought up the rear with the French troops. The plan was for Murray to cross to the south side of the River Nairn to avoid the Hanoverian outposts and then re-cross it, by-passing Cumberland's camp and attacking it from the rear, while Drummond made a simultaneous direct assault. However, the night march, over rough and boggy ground, took longer than anyone expected. The French troops, with their heavier equipment, were particularly slow and the two main columns had to keep halting to wait for them. By the time the first traces of dawn were beginning to show Murray with the leading column was still two miles from his objective; two miles of open country which, with the growing light, would reveal his men long before they could reach Cumberland's men. He accepted that the attack had failed and treated with derision a message from the Prince ordering him to go forward with his column and attack on his own. The Prince, at the rear, not able to appreciate the situation, believed that Murray had deliberately undermined his plans.

CULLODEN MOOR

The army returned to Culloden in the early dawn light, starving and shattered, among the mutual recriminations of its officers, everyone blaming everyone else for the night's fiasco. Large numbers of men went off again to look for food, many as far as Inverness. Others, utterly exhausted, fell asleep. Some did not wake until roused by the thundering of Cumberland's artillery. Some were not even woken by this and slumbered on until they were cut down by Cumberland's dragoons. The Prince was furious with Murray for supposedly sabotaging the attack on Nairn and refused to consider falling back on Inverness or moving to more secure ground south of the River Nairn. However, as Cumberland had only just arrived at Nairn, they thought that he was unlikely to move out immediately without giving his men a rest, particularly on such a cold, wet morning.

There was panic then at Culloden House when messengers rode up with news that Cumberland's army was on the march in full battle order and only four miles away. He had heard about the abortive night attack and had wisely decided to catch his opponents while they were still exhausted and disorganized. Most of the Jacobite officers, like their men, had neither slept nor eaten properly, including the Prince, who had only had an hour's rest and had refused to eat while his own men were starving.

Hurriedly they started to get their men into battle positions. As there was no time to draw up a fresh plan the one devised for the previous day had to stand. Strictly speaking, it was the Camerons' turn to occupy the right wing

205

and Lord George Murray protested on their behalf. O'Sullivan would have none of it and the Atholl Brigade were placed there as on the day before with the disgruntled MacDonalds still on the left wing. The army that assembled was a shadow of the force which had faced Hawley at Falkirk. Several of its best units, including the MacPhersons, were away on detached service while a regiment of Frasers was still on its way. Large numbers had scattered from Culloden in search of food and rest and never reached the battlefield. The 4,500 — 5,000 who assembled to meet Cumberland's 9,000 were demoralized, hungry, and tired. The long winter in the Highlands had wrought havoc with the Jacobite cavalry, never a strong force, and only a handful of the horses were fit for service.

The army was drawn up almost half a mile further west than on the previous day, with no bog protecting their left flank. The moor funnelled in between two sets of stone- and turf-walled enclosures, one around Culloden House itself, the other running down to the River Nairn. The walls, O'Sullivan thought, would protect the flanks of the army. It does not seem to have occurred to him that it would be easy for the Hanoverian troops to break them down, enter the parks, and use the walls to protect them while they fired on the Jacobites. Another disadvantage of the site which was not immediately apparent was a shallow but boggy hollow in front of the army, on ground which the Highlanders would have to charge over to reach their opponents. The position of the Jacobite front line is shown on Map 13. The second line consisted of three discontinuous bodies of men covering the flanks and centre of the front line while behind them was a rag-tag of assorted small units.

Cumberland's army marched up on to the moor in three columns of infantry, the grenadier companies with their mitre caps leading each battalion. They were flanked by the cavalry on one side and the artillery on the other. Most of them were soon wet and muddy to the knee, due to the boggy ground, and they were soaked by showers of rain but there was something relentless about their slow advance which filled their adversaries with foreboding. The Marquis d'Eguilles, Louis XV's envoy, had begged the Prince not to fight. Most of the Jacobite officers, seeing the condition of their men, expected disaster but, with the Prince inflexible, they could only stand and fight for their honour with little hope of success. Even the Prince's boundless optimism was wearing thin. Two miles from the Jacobite line the Duke drew his men up in battle positions. His first and second lines each contained six battalions with a further three in reserve, and his cavalry on the flanks. The Prince had hoped that the boggy ground would prevent Cumberland from bringing up his artillery and make it difficult to deploy his horsemen. Unfortunately the ground was not wet enough. It was now early afternoon and one of his officers asked Cumberland whether the men should be allowed to eat before fighting. The Duke thought not; 'They'll fight all the better on empty bellies' he is supposed to have observed, 'remember what a dessert they got to their dinner at Falkirk!'

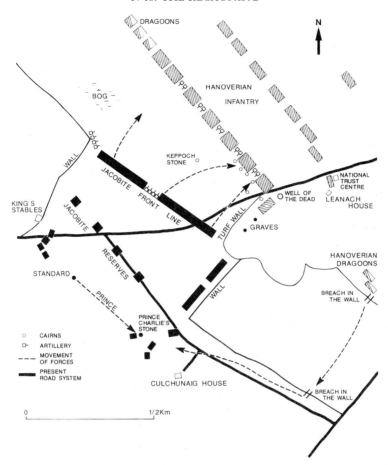

Map 13 The Battle of Culloden.

For the first time the Jacobites were facing experienced regular troops prepared for battle, on ground which favoured both cavalry and artillery. The tactics and technology of Highland warfare had not changed much since Killiecrankie but those of the British army had. These changes were to play their part in the outcome of the battle. The development of the iron ramrod and the use of paper cartridges containing measured amounts of gunpowder in place of the old powder horn allowed trained soldiers to load and fire at a much faster rate than at Killiecrankie. Three volleys a minute were possible. The use of cartridges, which the Highlanders had not adopted, made it easier to keep the powder dry in wet conditions, as on this showery April morning. Artillery had played little part in the campaign so far but now the Jacobites

207

faced guns manned by trained artillerymen. The mobility of field guns and their rate of fire had also improved since 1689. At Culloden the Hanoverian artillery, placed in five pairs in front of each of the leading regiments, was able to fire not only roundshot but case shot, cartridges containing musket balls and scrap iron which burst and spread out in a deadly swathe when the charge was fired.

Cumberland's officers had also developed a new bayonet drill designed to check the devastating impact of a Highland charge. In previous battles between Highlanders and regular troops the latter were at a disadvantage in close-quarters fighting. Facing a charging swordsman, a regular soldier would lunge at him with his bayonet. The Highlander would parry the thrust with his targe and the bayonet would be embedded in the wooden shield leaving the regular soldier defenceless against the downward stroke of the clansman's broadsword. Under the new system, in which Cumberland's troops had been carefully drilled, a soldier would thrust his bayonet at the Highlander charging his right-hand neighbour, aiming at his unprotected right side below his raised sword arm, and hoping that the man to his left would do the same for him. This simple technique gave the Hanoverian soldiers more confidence and made them realize that the Highlanders were not invincible.

With bayonets fixed Cumberland's scarlet ranks marched slowly forwards towards the waiting Jacobites. O'Sullivan, in drawing up the front line, had allowed it to bend. The MacDonalds, grumbling about their position on the left, had formed up with their flank protected by the corner of an enclosure wall which did not extend as far eastwards as those on the right flank. As a result the Atholl Brigade on the right were closer to the advancing enemy than the MacDonalds. The Duke of Perth, commanding the left wing, was unable to get the MacDonalds to move forward to even up the front line. Understandably, they were reluctant to expose themselves to Cumberland's cavalry which was now starting to move forward.

When only 500 yards of boggy moor separated the two armies, Cumberland halted his men and brought up his ten three-pounder guns. It was the Jacobite artillery which opened the battle. Their cannon were grouped in three batteries of four guns in the centre and on each wing. The guns in the centre began firing at the rear of the Hanoverian army, trying to hit Cumberland as he sat on his horse and directed his men. They came close; one ball narrowly missed the Duke and another struck down two men in front of him. However, the Jacobites still lacked trained gunners and their artillery was only manned by scratch crews. The fact that the guns were of a variety of calibres did not make for efficient teamwork and their rate of fire was slow.

Two could play at that game and Cumberland's guns now opened up, aiming at the group of horsemen that surrounded the Prince. Although he intended to command the battle in person, the Prince had positioned himself to the rear of the Jacobite second line where he could see very little of what was going on. The Hanoverian artillerymen were too accurate for comfort;

several cannonballs fell among the group of horsemen and one of the Prince's servants was killed. The Prince was persuaded to move further back and more to the right where he was better protected but even more out of touch.

Cumberland's gunners then changed their target and aimed at the dense mass of clansmen in the front line. For the first time the Highlanders were exposed to the devastating impact of accurate, fast, close-range cannon fire which tore appalling gaps in their ranks. Belford's gunners, highly trained, could fire three or four rounds a minute, as fast or faster than the infantry could load and fire their muskets. The bombardment continued for fifteen or twenty minutes, perhaps longer, while the clansmen waited with growing anger for the order to attack. The wind blew the rain into their faces while the smoke from the guns obscured their view of the enemy. Cumberland kept his troops stationary for his artillery was thinning his opponent's lines at no cost to his own men. The right-hand Jacobite battery, under Murray's direction, continued to fire the occasional shot but the Hanoverian gunners had already silenced the artillery in the centre of the Jacobite line. Major Belford's men had changed from roundshot to case shot and the dense clusters of musket balls caused even greater carnage. Conditions were probably worst on the right wing where, due to lack of space, the Atholl Brigade was drawn up six-deep, an ideal target, but the whole of the front line suffered severely.

From his poor vantage point the Prince had no idea of the scale of the slaughter that the guns were causing among the ranks of his followers. Lord George Murray, realizing that if they were not ordered to attack his men would break ranks and charge anyway, sent a message to the Prince asking for permission to advance. The Prince agreed but the returning messenger was cut down by a cannonball. Before the order finally arrived the centre and right of the Jacobite front line broke away in a desperate charge. As they ran forward the clans in the centre swerved to the right, probably to avoid a stretch of marshy ground. This caused chaos for the Atholl Brigade to the right of them, already hemmed in, were constricted even further. The result was that the charge became concentrated against only two of the Hanoverian front-line regiments instead of being more spread out. The disorganized mass of charging men was so tightly packed that many never came within reach of their enemies.

As the Jacobite centre and right charged they faced concentrated volleys of musketry from the regiments in front of them as well as the point-blank fire of the cannon. At close range the heavy-calibre soft lead musket balls, whether fired by cannon or infantry, could inflict terrible wounds. Because of the crush and lack of space the charge was slower than at Prestonpans or Falkirk and the Hanoverian infantry had enough time to reload and fire several times. The troops in the centre of the Hanoverian line raked the clansmen as they swerved towards the men on their left. On the far left Cumberland had ordered the regiment commanded by Wolfe, who was later to win fame at Quebec, forward to a position at right angles to the front line, along one of the enclosure walls. Some of the Campbell militia had also taken up positions behind the wall. From there the Campbells and the regulars poured volleys of musket fire into the charging Highlanders as they ran past. Cut down in swathes by a concentrated hail of lead it was a wonder that any of them ever reached Cumberland's front line but they pressed on, clambering over heaps of their own dead in their furious urge to get at their enemies. Those of Cumberland's men who had experienced set-piece battles in the Low Countries, even the heavy casualties of Fontenoy, had never seen regular troops come on through such devastating fire. Many of the Highlanders dropped their muskets in the confusion of the charge and the press of men was too tight for those who had kept their firearms to use them effectively, so they surged forward with their broadswords against the lines of waiting bayonets.

Barrel's and Munro's regiments took the full force of the charge and their neat ranks disintegrated into a series of desperate hand-to-hand fights. As the two front-line regiments gave way the Duke ordered Bligh's and Sempill's up from the second line to support them. They gave the Highlanders who had penetrated the front line a close-range volley of musket fire which, unfortunately, also killed a number of their own men in the regiments that had been broken. The Highlanders who got through the front line charged on to meet the second line of bayonets. The new bayonet drill was put to good use and few of the Jacobites who got this far lived to tell their story. The charging Highlanders were disorganized and almost leaderless, for casualties among their officers, who had led the front ranks, had been heavy. A high proportion had been killed or, like Lochiel who was hit in both ankles by case shot, wounded. Inevitably their charge lost momentum; they halted and then began to give ground.

Lord George Murray was one of the few leaders who had survived the storm of musket and cannon fire unscathed. His horse had been shot under him and, fighting on foot, he had lost one broadsword and broken another. Without his hat and wig, with his clothes cut in several places by bayonet thrusts, and covered in dirt, he looked a wild figure but he had not lost his presence of mind. Realizing that the Atholl Brigade and the remnants of the other regiments of the Jacobite centre and right were starting to give ground he forced his way through the crush of men towards the rear and brought up Lord Lewis Gordon's and Lord John Drummond's men to cover the retreat of the front-line troops. As a result of his prompt action the Jacobite right retired in good order, bloody but unbowed, colours flying, ready to turn again and repel their attackers if they pressed them too closely.

On the left the story was different. The Duke of Perth ordered the MacDonalds to charge when he saw the regiments on his right break forwards but they would only advance a little way. The ground ahead of them was boggy and this would have slowed their charge allowing Cumberland's battalions to pour in a devastating series of volleys before the MacDonalds even got within reach of them. Moreover, Cumberland's cavalry were hovering on their flank ready to strike. They approached to within musket shot of the Hanoverian front line, and tried to taunt the redcoats into firing first, so that they could charge while their enemies were reloading. This ploy did not work and, with their ranks still being thinned by murderous cannon fire, they saw the regiments on their right start to break up and fall back. With both flanks exposed the MacDonalds too began to retreat to the rage and shame of some of their chiefs. Keppoch and Clanranald determined that even if their men would not charge they would uphold the honour of their clans and ran forward with small groups of their friends and followers. Keppoch was killed and Clanranald badly wounded in brave but futile gestures.

As the MacDonalds fell back Cumberland's cavalry advanced and the retreat turned into a rout. The horsemen were reluctant to attack the larger bodies of Jacobite troops which still held together but as the MacDonald regiments broke apart they rode after the stragglers and cut them down in large numbers. Casualties would have been higher had it not been for the Royal Scots and the Irish Picquets from the second line who moved forward and challenged the dragoons, halting the pursuit and letting many clansmen escape. Even more bravely, one group of Jacobite gunners continued to man and fire a cannon situated near the corner of the Culloden enclosures to the left of where the MacDonalds had stood, long after the clansmen had fled. It took the concentrated fire of four of Cumberland's guns and three mortars to silence it.

On the right some 500 Hanoverian dragoons had entered the enclosures which ran down to the River Nairn, through breaches made by the Campbells, and were moving round towards the Jacobite rear. This was just the emergency that Lord George Murray had envisaged but which O'Sullivan had dismissed. Seeing this, Murray ordered Elcho's Lifeguards, a mere remnant of the original troop, and some other horsemen, to oppose them. They formed up on the opposite side of a hollowed roadway from the dragoons and held them off for a vital ten minutes — long enough to allow the right wing of the army to escape. Lord Ogilvy's two Lowland regiments, which had been second-line reserves behind the Atholl Brigade, let them past and then covered their retreat, turning several times to keep Hawley's cavalry at a distance.

The Prince made an attempt to rally his men but these efforts, like his previous actions in the battle, were totally ineffectual. Bemused and uncertain about what to do next, he allowed his close followers, including Sheridan and O'Sullivan, to lead him from the battlefield. Many of his men, on foot and exhausted, were less fortunate. Cumberland did not pursue the retreating Highlanders with his infantry. He merely marched them forward a short distance to the position occupied by the Jacobite army and rested them after their exertions. Small parties went round the battlefield dispatching the

Jacobite wounded without mercy till the redcoats looked, as one man observed, more like butchers than soldiers so splattered with blood were their white breeches and gaiters. Meanwhile the Duke's cavalry pursued the fugitives and cut down stragglers along the six miles into Inverness. The dragoons had many scores to settle and to them one Highlander was very much like another. Many local people whose only involvement in the rebellion was to have come out to watch the battle were killed, including some women and children. A number of people living near the battlefield, whose only crime was their misfortune in being there, were killed in their fields or in their homes. It was a foretaste of the brutality which was to mark the military occupation of the Highlands over the next few months.

Culloden is often portrayed as a total massacre. Jacobite casualties were certainly heavy — 1,000 or more were killed on the battlefield and as many, perhaps more, during the pursuit. Cumberland's army lost under 100 dead and 200–300 wounded. Nevertheless, a sizeable part of the Jacobite army escaped and a number of units came away intact or, like the Atholl Brigade, badly mauled but still a fighting force. Lord George Murray left Culloden with some 1,500 men. However, the spirit of the Jacobite army was totally broken. There were few men who did not realize that this was the end of the rebellion. Before the battle Murray had proposed retreating into the hills to fight a guerilla campaign but now, with all the army's supplies abandoned and no advance preparations made, it would be impossible to keep any sizeable body of men together.

CULLODEN TODAY

'Culloden' is one of the most emotive names in Scottish history along with 'Bannockburn' but while the site of Robert Bruce's famous victory has been totally altered by modern development at Culloden you can still get an impression of what it was like for the ordinary Jacobite soldier on that cold April morning with the rain lashing in his face and the smoke from Cumberland's guns blinding him. It is symptomatic of the strength of the folk-myth which surrounds the final Jacobite defeat that while the sites of victories like Killiecrankie, Prestonpans, and Falkirk are only modestly commemorated and even the dispositions of the conflicting armies are uncertain, Culloden is carefully marked out and preserved. The battlefield today is an evocative place which still has the power to grip the imagination. Until recently much of it was planted with conifers but extensive areas have been cleared restoring the site to something like its former open character. In the early nineteenth century the modern road was built through the site of the battle and the moorland was enclosed with stone dykes but the land was poor and a good deal of it has reverted to boggy heath.

The National Trust for Scotland have built a visitor centre on the battlefield, located just behind the position where Cumberland's left wing was stationed. The walls which provided cover for the Campbells and Wolfe's regiment, as well as the enclosures through which the dragoons rode to the Jacobite rear, are no longer visible. They have been replaced by larger, more regular walls. The cottage of Old Leanach, adjacent to the visitor centre, is one of the few identifiable features from the time of the battle. Although it has been altered subsequently, and heavily restored, it gives a good impression of what the better sort of rural housing in this area looked like in the mid-eighteenth century. It is thatched with heather which was more durable than straw and better suited to a wetter climate. Although it looks primitive it was a comparatively well-to-do farmhouse in its day; many of the poorer houses in this area at the time of the battle would have been built of turf rather than stone.

The area where the fiercest hand-to-hand fighting took place, Jacobite broadsword against Hanoverian bayonet, lies on either side of the road a little

62 One of the memorials to the dead at Culloden Moor. (Courtesy National Trust for Scotland)

to the west of the visitor centre and the cottage. It is marked by a prominent twenty foot high cairn just to the north of the road and smaller stones identifying the graves of members of various clans who were buried close to where they fell. Beyond the cairn is a large boulder, the Keppoch Stone, supposedly marking the place where the MacDonald chief was killed. The location of the graves of the Hanoverian dead is unknown although a stone close to Old Leanach cottage is marked 'Field of the English. They were buried here.' The use of 'English' on this stone shows how tradition and the nationalist revival have shaped the appearance of the battlefield today.

The cairn and most of the markers were only placed there in 1881. Ironically they were erected on the orders of the then laird of Culloden, a direct descendant of Duncan Forbes who did so much to thwart the Jacobites. The grave markers were placed according to local traditions; the locations of the graves of the clansmen were clearly remembered while those of the Hanoverians were not! Yet this also reflects the romantic haze with which the battle, the 1745 campaign, and the entire Jacobite movement has become surrounded, a haze which sometimes seems as impenetrable as the smoke from Cumberland's guns. The displays in the visitor centre have been criticized for their one-sided portrayal of events and it is difficult to convince many Scotsmen that the battle was not a simple contest between Scots and English which was unfairly won by the latter!

11

THE JACOBITE TWILIGHT

FIRE AND SWORD

Cumberland reached Inverness, in the wake of his dragoons, at around 4pm. The church bells were being rung in welcome, whether from patriotism or just plain prudence. Cumberland moved into the town house owned by Lady Mackintosh in Church Street. It was the best house in what the English officers considered a small and dirty town. Other officers took over the main inn opposite the tolbooth. A number of Hanoverian prisoners were released from the tolbooth to make way for the Jacobites that had been captured. There were between 500 and 600 of them including a number from the French regiments who, as prisoners of war, could claim better treatment than the remainder who were merely viewed as rebels and traitors.

Cumberland ordered parties to search all houses and cottages in the vicinity of Culloden for fugitives and he reminded the officers entrusted with this work that the Jacobite orders of the previous day had been to give no quarter. This was untrue; a copy of Lord George Murray's orders had fallen into Hanoverian hands and this addition had been inserted as a crude forgery, it is not clear by whom. Stories of atrocities committed by Cumberland's men immediately after the battle and in the days that followed have probably been exaggerated. Some probably grew in the telling and some of the most frequently repeated ones are contradicted by other evidence. Nevertheless, within weeks of Culloden Cumberland had acquired his nickname of 'Butcher'. It cannot be denied that many fugitives were summarily shot, bayoneted, or in one or two cases burnt to death in the huts where they were sheltering. The orders under which the army operated were that ordinary clansmen who had been in rebellion and who came in to surrender their arms should be allowed to return, unmolested, to their homes. Those still in arms were to be killed and the homes of those who had fled were to be burnt and their goods seized. In practice, a Highlander who approached a military post to surrender his weapons was taking a grave risk as it depended on the mood of the commanding officer as to whether or not he was treated as a rebel in arms to be shot out of hand.

A party was sent to Moy House fifteen mile south of Inverness to bring in Lady Mackintosh, the beautiful young wife of the chief of clan Mackintosh. Her husband was an officer in the Hanoverian army and she had brought out his clan for the Jacobites, to his considerable embarrassment. Moy House was plundered and all the livestock driven away. Then it was the turn of the Fraser lands which stretched from Inverness to beyond Beauly. There were systematically devastated and anything of value carried off.

These first raids were a blueprint for the actions that followed. In mid-May Cumberland moved his troops down the Great Glen to Fort Augustus. For the first time a large, well-equipped and well-organized government army had penetrated to the heart of the Highlands having defeated all serious opposition. Camping beside the ruined fort, the Hanoverian troops ravaged the territories of Jacobite clans which were within easy reach. Achnacarry, Lochiel's house, and Invergarry Castle were destroyed and countless homes of ordinary families burnt. All livestock were driven off and Fort Augustus became a huge temporary cattle market. After a poor harvest and a bad winter in a country where food supplies were always insufficient many people starved and destitute familes haunted the fringes of Cumberland's camp in the vain hope of getting a handout. The Duke was supported by naval vessels which patrolled the west coast searching for the Prince and other fugitives and landing troops on vicious reprisal raids among the islands and sea lochs. Many homes belonging to people who had played no part in the rebellion were destroyed.

This is sometimes seen as a campaign of mass genocide waged by the English. True, there was a good deal of anti-Scottish feeling among Cumberland's English officers. To many of them every Scotsman was a Jacobite and every Highlander a thief. However, some of the most brutal and hard-hearted of Cumberland's subordinates were Lowland Scots, including one Captain Scott who had defended Fort William, who earned a particularly grim reputation for indiscriminate shooting and hanging of suspects and wanton destruction of homes and property. Another Scot, Captain John Fergussone of the Navy, was every bit as ruthless and violent.

THE FUGITIVE PRINCE

Meanwhile, what had become of the Prince and the other Jacobite leader? For five months after Culloden, Charles was a fugitive, hunted through the Western Highlands and Islands by thousands of troops with a price of £30,000 — a huge sum in those days — on his head. During this time he lived rough, travelling mainly by night and sleeping in a variety of accommodation, frequently uncomfortable and wet, sometimes hungry. His courage, powers of endurance, and tough constitution seemed almost to thrive on adversity. If he had often seemed self-centred during the campaign and had callously left his supporters to fend for themselves after Culloden, his fortitude in the weeks that followed highlighted the good points in his character. Local whisky and French brandy helped to console him and may have encouraged the taste for strong drink which reduced him to a fuddled, disappointed wreck in middle age. However, during this period he created the enduring, heroic legend of 'The Prince in the heather', which has become part of popular mythology.

The reality was less romantic but nevertheless remarkable. Admittedly ordinary Highlanders were used to poor accommodation, a simple and monotonous diet, and to travelling long distances on foot over rugged mountain country or by open boat among the stormy waters of the Minch. It is the cumulative effect of Charles' hardships over an extended period which is impressive. To retrace his journey today, on foot and by boat, would be a daunting task. The modern Ordnance Survey maps of this part of the Highlands are liberally sprinkled with 'Prince Charlie's Caves' in out-of-the-way settings. Even on the mainland to follow much of his route involves walking to remote glens several miles from the nearest road either camping or sleeping in bothies, mountain shelters used by walkers and climbers. Although generally wind and watertight, Highland bothies are spartan. Even so they are more comfortable than most of the places in which the Prince stayed.

One must not forget, of course, that the western Highlands were more densely populated in the mid-eighteenth century than today. Many of the valleys in which the Prince stayed, today virtually uninhabited, are dotted with the remains of farmsteads and townships which were abandoned in the nineteenth century when their inhabitants were cleared out to make way for commercial sheep farming. Although the area was remote in 1745 it was far from being an unsettled wilderness.

It must be remembered too that hundreds of other Jacobites were on the run throughout the Highlands at this time. Cumberland's troops could devastate the glens and drive off the cattle but they were far less effective in searching for or pursuing individual fugitives. Safe in their mountain retreats some Jacobites, like MacPherson of Cluny, remained hidden for years. On the other hand the government's efforts were concentrated on finding Charles himself and it was more difficult for him to evade capture than most of his supporters.

After being led from Culloden the Prince was taken across the Water of Nairn by Wade's bridge at the ford of Faillie, south of the battlefield, and then west to Gorthlick, twenty miles away in the hills east of Loch Ness. Here he met for the first and only time the wily Lord Lovat who, intriguing with both sides, had committed himself to the Jacobite cause belatedly. Charles only halted for a couple of hours. Dismissing most of his escort and with only a small party, including Sheridan, O'Sullivan, and Lord Elcho, he pressed on through the night to Invergarry.

Lord George Murray and the Duke of Perth had gone south to Ruthven. Although there was insufficient food available to keep them together for long they were surprised to discover that Charles, far from joining them, was already heading for the west coast in the hope of escaping from Scotland by sea. Charles' last letter to the chiefs was both condescending and patronizing. None of what had happened had been his fault and he effectively dissociated himself from them and their fate. His advice that every man should seek his own safety was a mean farewell and a poor return for the trust and support he had received. It produced a bitter letter in reply from Lord George Murray who, as might have been expected, blamed everything on Charles and his advisers. In view of this it is not surprising to learn that Murray and the Prince never met again.

It was early on the morning of April 17th before the Prince and his party reached Invergarry Castle. After a few hours rest they continued down the Great Glen beside Loch Lochy then turned westwards by the northern shore of Loch Arkaig. Even today this is remote country; the road by Loch Arkaig is single-tracked and switchbacked, deteriorating into a mere track by the time it reaches the head of the loch. From there two dark glens run westwards. It was to the most southerly, Glen Pean, that the Prince was heading, to lodge at the home of one of the Cameron tacksmen. Today you can stay at a climbers' bothy not far from the site of Cameron of Glen Pean's house.

At Glen Pean the Prince had his first proper night's sleep for some time. The following day the small party abandoned their horses and continued westwards on foot. A more modern path follows their route. Glen Pean narrows towards its head between steep mountain walls but there is hardly any climbing for glaciers have scoured and lowered the pass which leads through towards Loch Morar. You reach a small crag-fringed tarn and then the path drops more steeply towards the head of Loch Morar, the deepest loch in Scotland whose bottom lies over 1,000 feet below sea level. Here Charles was only half a dozen miles from Glenfinnan where, so many months before, his hopes had been high. From Morar he made his way to Arisaig, close to where he had first landed, and stopped for nearly a week. There was no news of any French vessels which might rescue him so it was decided to take him to the Outer Hebrides where it was thought that there was a greater chance of finding a friendly ship.

In retrospect this was a bad decision. The west Highland mainland offered a much larger area in which to elude his pursuers. In the islands, smaller and quite densely settled, easily scoured by troops landed from government warships, it was much harder to evade capture. Among the islands the Prince was to move from one narrow escape to another leaving behind him a trail of helpers captured and imprisoned. The Prince sailed first to Uist with Donald Macleod, a pilot from Skye. He went in an open eight-oared boat along with O'Sullivan and Captain Felix O'Neill, another Irish officer. A storm was brewing when they left Arisaig. Donald advised Charles not to set out on the seventy-mile crossing. With characteristic obstinacy he insisted. The result was a dangerous and uncomfortable night during which Charles was violently seasick and the storm-tossed party were heartily relieved to see the grey shapes of the Outer Hebrides ahead of them at dawn the following morning.

AMONG THE ISLANDS

They landed first at Rossinish on Benbecula, the island which lies between North and South Uist. The landscape of this part of the Hebrides is an incredibly complex and broken one with hundreds of small islands and rocks fringing the coast and as many small lochs inland. There they stayed for two nights in an uninhabited hut, eating a cow which they had killed, the Prince sleeping on an old sail, while the storm raged. They sent a man several miles to the house of MacDonald of Clanranald. The chief was away but one of his sons came to see the Prince. As there were no reports of French vessels Charles decided to go to Stornoway, the only sizeable settlement in the Hebrides, to try and hire a boat to take him to Orkney from where he hoped to escape to Norway. On April 29th they set out from Benbecula and sailed thirty miles north to Scalpay, a smallish island near Tarbert on the east coast of Harris.

O'Sullivan and the Prince were to pose as father and son, a ship's master and mate from Orkney who had been wrecked on Tiree. They were trying to return to Orkney by hiring a vessel which they would load with grain for the return journey to the Western Isles. Donald Macleod was sent on to Stornoway to try and hire a ship. A few days later he sent back word that he had succeeded and the Prince, O'Sullivan, and O'Neill set out to join him. They sailed to the head of Loch Seaforth then walked overland through the low hills of north Harris and then the wasteland of lochs and peat bogs which forms the centre of Lewis. They must have lost their way on the journey; after nearly eighteen hours and thirty-eight miles they reached the little town and sheltered in a friendly house outside the settlement. By this time the Prince was in a bad way, exhausted and hungry with his clothes in rags and his shoes falling apart. Something had gone wrong with the plans. Perhaps Donald Macleod was a poor actor. The inhabitants of Stornoway seem to have become suspicious of him and divined what was going on. Scared of government reprisals, they refused to co-operate. They would not harm the Prince but neither would they shelter him or let him have a vessel and they were relieved to be rid of him.

The Prince tried to persuade the six boatmen who remained from the eight that had ferried him across the Minch to take him to Orkney. The boat was manifestly too small for such a hazardous voyage and, sensibly, they refused. The party returned to Scalpay, having to land and hide more than once on the way when patrolling warships came in sight. Charles had been lucky in crossing the Minch at a time when most government vessels had sailed off to remote St Kilda on an unfounded rumour that the Prince had taken refuge in this unlikely spot. Now they had returned and were patrolling the islands vigilantly. At one point on the voyage to Scalpay Charles' party sighted two warships. They hurriedly landed but the Prince tried to persuade the boatmen to row out to the vessels to check whether they were French. Not unreasonably they demurred, scared that if they were British vessels they might be press-ganged or arrested as rebels. Ironically the Prince was probably right in his suspicion that the ships were French. This may have been one of the many near misses that dogged his wanderings.

The *Mars* and *Bellone*, two thirty-six-gun French privateers, had been sent by Antoine Walsh with arms, ammunition, and money before news of Culloden reached France. They arrived at Loch nan Uamh at the end of April and received word of the disaster. The sloop HMS *Greyhound* and two smaller vessels, the *Baltimore* and *Terror*, got word of their arrival. Sailing into the loch early one morning they caught the larger French warships at anchor. For six hours the surrounding shores echoed to the sound of a naval battle, the spectacle being watched by hundreds of Highlanders. It is ironic that the last battle of the '45 was a sea fight but this emphasizes the importance which the Royal Navy and French aid played in the campaign. The French fired mainly at their opponents' sails and rigging so that British casualties were relatively light. But the French ships, particularly the *Mars*, took a severe pounding leaving twenty-nine men killed and eighty-five wounded, many of whom died subsequently. Both sides broke off the fight to make repairs. The British captains, considering that the French ships were too badly damaged to sail, went off to get reinforcements. The French slipped away that night having taken on board many leading Jacobites including the Duke of Perth, Lord John Drummond, Lord Elcho, and Sheridan. They had heard that the Prince was in the Outer Hebrides but the ships were too battered to search for him. The two vessels which the Prince's boatmen refused to intercept were probably the *Mars* and *Bellone* limping homeward.

From Scalpay the Prince returned to Benbecula, just avoiding another severe storm. Clanranald himself arrived a day or two later with welcome provisions. At his suggestion the party moved to a little island in Loch Skiport which he considered safer but when a man-of-war put into the loch the party moved off again and landed at Coradale in South Uist. Here they found an ideal hiding place beside a small bay from which two small, steep glens ran back into a rugged horseshoe of rocky peaks culminating in Beinn Mhor.

At Coradale, in rather better accommodation than they had enjoyed for some time, the party stayed for nearly three weeks. Charles hunted and fished and drank, seeming to enjoy the brief respite although he was troubled by dysentery. The net was starting to close in though. The authorities now knew he was somewhere in the Outer Hebrides and detachments of troops were being landed on all the islands to search for him. To try and give them the slip they returned to Benbecula for a week then retraced their steps to South Uist where they stayed for another week. Government ships were everywhere and several hundred men had been landed to scour the island. The Prince's party was too large for comfort so Charles bade farewell to O'Sullivan, Donald Macleod, and the boatmen. Taking only O'Neill and a guide he crossed the low hills to Ormaclett a dozen miles away on the low, dune-fringed west coast of the island.

OVER THE SEA TO SKYE

The scene was now set for events which have been distorted and romanticized almost beyond recognition. Three miles from Ormaclett, at Milton, lived twenty-four-year-old Flora MacDonald. Milton was her home but her father was dead and her mother had remarried. Flora's stepfather was Hugh MacDonald of Armadale in Skye who happened to command one of the companies of Highland troops searching the island for the Prince. It was O'Neill, who had met Flora before, that first approached her, trying to get information about the movements of the troops who were looking for them. Flora was a sharp girl and seems to have guessed the reason for his enquiries. There was nothing for it but to bring the Prince to her and beg for help. The Prince was an accomplished charmer and the old magic worked once more. At first Flora refused, perhaps because she did not wish to compromise her stepfather, but eventually she agreed to help and suggested that the safest course was to get Charles away to Skye. She may have devised the plan but there is more than a suspicion that it was done by some of the militia officers, perhaps even Flora's stepfather. She could get a pass to travel from her father, on the pretext of visiting her mother. The pass would be issued for herself, a man servant, and a woman, Betty Burke, who was to be recommended to her mother as a maid. Betty Burke was to be the Prince, dressed in woman's clothing.

While she was preparing the escape Charles returned to Benbecula, dodging the increasing number of troops who were scouring the islands. He also narrowly missed a French vessel which was exploring the area, unsure of his exact whereabouts. The ship managed to find O'Sullivan, worn out and hungry. Although chased by British warships the vessel managed to elude them and return to France where O'Sullivan made strenuous efforts to persuade the French to keep sending ships to the Hebrides in search of the Prince.

On June 28th Flora and her 'maid' sailed from Loch Uskevagh. Flora refused to take O'Neill in the interests of keeping the party as small as possible. After another rough crossing by night they sighted Vaternish Point in the north west of Skye. As they ran inshore a party of men shouted to them and then opened fire so they headed out across Loch Snizort to Trotternish, the northern peninsula of Skye, where the Prince was sheltered at the house of

MacDonald of Kingsburgh. Charles was a poor actor and he must have made a strange sight, tall and ungainly, in his women's clothes. His appearance certainly alarmed Kingsburgh's wife who was even more perturbed when she learnt his true identity! From Kingsburgh Charles walked over twelve miles to Portree where he and Flora parted. Their association had lasted only twelve days and, regardless of the songs which were later written, there had been no romance between them. It was O'Neill rather than Charles who fancied Flora and she had not shown much interest in him. In fact it was Kingsburgh's son that she subsequently married.

The authorities were still close on the Prince's tail. Flora was arrested on her way from Portree to her mother's house at Armadale. She was taken on board Captain Fergussone's sloop, HMS *Furnace* and, after a long period of shipboard captivity, was transferred to the Tower of London from which she was released early in 1747. After her marriage she lived at Flodigarry on the east coast of Trotternish and then at Kingsburgh where Johnson and Boswell met her during their famous Highland tour in 1773. The following year Flora emigrated to America with her husband but returned to Scotland five years later. She died in 1790 and is buried in the churchyard at Kilmuir.

Meanwhile the Prince crossed to Raasay, the long, narrow island between Skye and the mainland, but two days here convinced him that Raasay was too small for safety and he returned to northern Skye. The same night he set out for Strathaird in the south of the island which was thought to be safer country. This involved a thirty-mile walk over rough terrain but the Prince was welcomed by one of the Mackinnons of Strathaird who arranged a boat to carry him back to the mainland. On July 4th he sailed from Elgol, a township on the southern shore of Loch Scavaig, looking across the bay to the magnificent Cuillin mountains.

The following morning he reached Loch Nevis, a mainland sea loch opposite the southern tip of Skye, but parties of militia on the shore kept them on the move and they returned to Mallaig at the mouth of the loch and continued south to Morar, arriving at dawn the next day to find that Captain Fergussone had burnt the house of MacDonald of Morar. Only a blackened ruin welcomed them so they went further south to Borrodale. Again they found that Fergussone had been there before them and burnt all the settlements. Charles had to lodge in a cave instead. He then moved on to a more remote hiding place on a lochan-studded plateau north of the road from Glenfinnan to Arisaig. His pursuers were closing in again. Warships were landing men around Loch Nevis and Arisaig and he had to get out of the immediate area.

He headed for Glen Dessary at the head of Loch Arkaig and then westwards to Kinloch Hourn. On the way he discovered that his enemies were trying to trap him with a line of troops stretching from Loch Eil to Loch Hourn, sealing off a whole section of the west coast. Their camps were only half a mile apart and between these sentries were placed within hailing distance of each other. By moving silently and carefully Charles passed through their line undetected and escaped. From Loch Hourn he continued northwards to Glen Shiel. The best refuge that he could find, an overhanging boulder near Achnangart, is still pointed out. He was intending to continue northwards to Poolewe, having heard reports of a French vessel there, but finding that it had sailed he turned eastwards through Glen Affric, Strath Glass, and Glenmoriston and then southwards for Lochiel's country. He stayed in the vicinity of Loch Arkaig for ten days in the middle of August. A cave which he is said to have used lies high on the hillside above the Dark Mile, the narrow pass which joins Loch Arkaig to the Great Glen. As there was no word of any French vessel he thought that he would be safer further east in Badenoch, MacPherson of Cluny's country, so he crossed the Great Glen on August 27th, and turned southwards by Glen Spean to the bleak, barren country around Ben Alder. Here he met Lochiel, still lame from his wounds, and spent two days with him before Cluny arrived to take him to his hideout.

Ben Alder is a great square block of a mountain, still one of the most remote spots in the Central Highlands. To reach it today you have an eight-mile walk from Loch Rannoch along a stalker's path which fades out among peat hags as you approach the base of the mountain. From the north, starting at Dalwhinnie, the walk is even longer down the shore of Loch Ericht. It was among the rocks on the southern slopes of the mountain that Cluny MacPherson had established his 'cage' or lair in which he skulked for nine years before finally giving up hope of another rising and retiring to the Continent. Today walkers and climbers can follow in his footsteps and stay in the spartan accommodation of the bothy called Ben Alder Cottage which stands beside the Alder Burn near where it flows into Loch Ericht. Cluny's Cage, partly an artificial construction against the rockface, on two levels and screened by trees, was situated among the crags above the cottage but it is hard to decide exactly which cleft among the rocks was used by the fugitive chief.

After nearly two weeks with Cluny news reached Charles that two French ships had arrived off the west coast. The French had made repeated attempts to rescue him but the rapidity of his movements and their rather random character had made him impossible to find. Fortunately for Charles his pursuers now thought that he was somewhere on the east coast and were watching the ports there. With their attention temporarily diverted from Moidart the two French vessels, *L'Heureux* and *Le Prince de Conti*, remained at anchor in Loch nan Uamh for two weeks, time for news of their arrival to reach Badenoch and for Charles to hurry westwards. In the early hours of the morning of September 20th the two vessels with Charles on board the aptly named *L'Heureux*, slipped out into the open sea and reached Brittany safely a few days later.

THE AFTERMATH OF THE '45

Thoroughly scared by the near-success of the rebellion, the government systematically set about breaking the power of the Highland chiefs to ensure that the Stuarts could never raise an army in this region again. The authorities had been lenient after 1715 and they were not going to make the same mistake again. They had been badly scared by Prince Charles' advance to Derby and by the victories which his small army had achieved. It is easy, in retrospect, to consider the rebellion of 1745 as a mad gamble that was doomed to failure from the start but this was far less obvious to contemporaries. A great many people, not all of them staunchly Hanoverian, were sick of recurring Jacobite rebellions and felt that enough was enough. The advance to Derby had awakened folk memories of the Civil Wars a century earlier and, with them, the horror of full-scale war on English soil. These points help to explain why in 1746, unlike the aftermath of the 1715 rebellion, there was such a concerted effort to suppress Jacobitism. Moreover, the Jacobite cause was strongly linked with France, Scotland's old ally but increasingly in the eighteenth century Britain's great rival as a European and colonial power. The Catholic faith of the Stuarts and many of their supporters was also a matter for widespread concern. In Britain Roman Catholics were not just another religious minority; they owed allegiance to the Pope at a time when the Vatican was still a major force in European politics. Many Catholics were able to separate their religious and political allegiances but some did not, fuelling the sometimes hysterical fear of popery that had been a feature of English society since Tudor times.

In England, the feudal power of the barons had long since been broken by the Crown. After 1715 the harshest example had been made of those Englishmen, both leaders and rank and file, who had supported the Northumberland rising. This may well have been one of the reasons why there was so little active support for Prince Charles in northern England thirty years later. The Scots who had come out with Mar got off comparatively lightly. This time the harsh treatment was extended to the Scottish Jacobites, particularly the Highland clans that had been in rebellion, who felt the full wrath of a shaken government and monarch. The traditional society of the Highlands was becoming increasingly anachronistic in a country which, elsewhere, was changing with great speed. The Treaty of Union had assured the continuation of the hereditary legal powers of Scottish magnates and the military tenures by which they held their lands but these, too, were increasingly out of line with the spirit of the times. The Highland chiefs who had used these powers to bring their clans out in rebellion against the Hanoverian regime were widely considered to have forfeited any right to retain these archaic privileges. There was little regret, aside from the major landowners who received financial compensation in any case, when these heritable jurisdictions were abolished.

A disarming act was passed along with others banning the wearing of Highland dress and the use of Gaelic. Neither of the last two measures were practicable; more significant was the abolition of the heritable jurisdictions, the devolved legal powers which allowed Highland and Lowland landowners in Scotland to hold their own courts, dispense justice, and to call out their men to fight. Even so, the devastation of parts of the Highlands by the Hanoverian army did not break the spirit of the Jacobite clans. Rather the feeling that the French had let them down convinced many that there was no point in further activity. In the longer term the gradual integration of the Highlands with the rest of Britain began to turn Highland estates into sources of income rather than power. The amount of money that an estate could produce became more important than the number of fighting men it supported. The aggressive nature of the Highlanders was channelled into more useful directions, from the point of the view of the government, by conscripting growing numbers of them into the British army to fight in the wars which expanded Britain's overseas empire.

In the short term, however, the Highlanders were themselves treated as a rebellious colony, subject to the arbitrary military law which marked later British colonial expansion. The area was garrisoned long after any real threat of renewed Jacobite activity had faded. The forts which had been built following the 1715 rebellion had proved ineffectual but Fort William was repaired and continued in service as did some of the smaller posts like Bernera and Inversnaid. Even Fort Augustus, despite its vulnerable location, continued in use until after the Crimean War. Initially it was planned to rebuild Fort George at Inverness but its site was cramped and inconvenient. It was replaced by a new Fort George on a site east of Inverness near the village of Arderseir, where a promontory curved into the Moray Firth. This location was more secure than Inverness and could be easily supplied by sea. The new fortress was first planned in 1747 but finally completed only in 1769. This time the army built the strongest possible fortress using the most sophisticated technology of the day. The earlier Highland forts had been built cheaply but here no expense was spared. Fort George remains the best example in Scotland, indeed in Britain, of an eighteenth-century artillery fortification and has not been altered significantly.

Fort George, which is open to the public, is impressive in scale. The defences are concentrated on the landward side, looking towards the Highlands rather than seawards. When you approach it you come first to a huge V-shaped outwork surrounded by a ditch. This is a 'ravelin' in military terminology and was designed to keep attackers well back from the main curtain wall. It had an open back so that if it was captured the attackers were still exposed to fire from the inner defences. The scale of the fort becomes apparent when you realize that it covers twelve acres and that the area of the ravelin alone is greater than that of many larger medieval castles. Beyond the ravelin is a huge ditch, crossed by a narrow bridge leading to the main gate

63 One of the ranges of barracks at Fort George.

piercing the massive curtain wall. If you can imagine yourself as an attacker on the bridge or scrambling around in the ditch you can see how anyone who penetrated this far would be exposed to a crossfire from the bastions on either side of the gateway as well as direct fire from the wall in front. Inside the fort are barrack blocks, designed to accommodate up to 2,500 troops. The buildings, like the defences, have not changed much since they were first built and they provide an excellent example of dignified, no-nonsense Georgian architecture. Emergency barracks, designed to be proof against plunging mortar fire, were also built under the ramparts.

The fort remained in use as a barracks and depot until recent times but never fired a shot in anger. By the time it was completed the Jacobite threat had been virtually eliminated. The fort's role was later reversed and, instead of looking landwards towards a threat from within, it was redesigned to house batteries protecting the coast during the Napoleonic wars.

While Fort George was purpose-built on a grand scale the government converted a number of existing strongholds for use as outposts. Two of the most interesting are Braemar and Corgarff Castles. The former, which is open to the public, was located in a notoriously pro-Jacobite area and had seen action in previous rebellions. Corgarff stands high on a hilltop overlooking the route from Deeside to the Spey via Tomintoul. In both cases the old tower houses were surrounded by star-shaped outer walls fitted with loopholes for musket fire; the one at Corgarff stands out particularly well because of its open

226

64 Corgarff Castle, a Hanoverian outpost. The old tower house has been surrounded by a curtain wall loopholed for musketry.

site. Outposts like these were garrisoned long after their military use had become irrelevant. The troops became used as a kind of police force, for the abolition of the legal powers of the chiefs and landowners had removed local sanctions over crime. Braemar, Corgarff, and other posts were used to control cattle rustling and illicit whisky distilling and the two Deeside castles were still being garrisoned in the early 1830s.

New military roads were built too. The most notable one linked Fort George with the south, running from Blairgowrie via Spittal of Glenshee to the Dee and then over the Lecht pass, past Corgarff, to the Spey and on to the Moray Firth. By the Well of Lecht, at the summit of the pass from Deeside to the Spey, where the modern A939 is often blocked by winter snows, the soldiers erected a commemorative stone which still survives. Another new road ran from Stirling to Fort William, skirting the bleak wastes of Rannoch Moor and crossing the Devil's Staircase east of Glencoe. Other roads tied Inveraray, and the barracks at Bernera into the existing network. The post-1745 roads were similar to those built under Wade. As time went on, however, more use was made of civilian labour and eventually they were handed over to the county authorities. Many were in a poor state of repair by the later eighteenth century but with improved road-building technology in

65 Monument at Well of the Lecht erected by the troops who built the military road from the Dee to the Spey.

the early nineteenth century they were upgraded and improved. While many sections were re-aligned to reduce gradients, long stretches still form the basis of the modern road network.

THE JACOBITE TWILIGHT

Culloden was the end of effective Jacobite resistance but not of Jacobite plotting. There is evidence that Prince Charles visited London in disguise in 1750, possibly reconnoitring the ground as part of a crazy plan to stage a coup in the capital and seize the royal family. There were also wild plans for a landing in Scotland, this time with Swedish aid. Dr Archibald Cameron, Lochiel's brother, went to Scotland as the Jacobite's chief agent to try and organize resistance and perhaps also to try and recover the famed Loch Arkaig treasure. This was a consignment of French gold which had been landed from the *Mars* and *Bellone* after Culloden. Some of the money was probably used by Murray of Broughton and other Jacobite leaders but according to tradition the bulk of it was buried in Cameron country and perhaps it is there still. Archibald Cameron was betrayed by one of his own clansmen and was taken by troops from the garrison at Inversnaid. In June 1753 he was executed at Tyburn, the last Jacobite to suffer this fate.

James Francis Edward, the Old Pretender, lived until 1766. His birth helped to precipitate the Revolution that started the Jacobite movement and he outlived all effective hopes of a Stuart restoration. For Charles Edward the years after Culloden held nothing but disappointment and disillusionment. An embarrassment to France, he was ordered out of the country and returned to Italy. In 1752 Clementina Walkinshaw joined him and became his mistress, bearing him a child a year later. Theirs was a quarrelsome relationship, aggravated by the fact that they both drank heavily, but they stayed together for ten years. Charles did not marry until he was fifty-one but by this time he was too pickled to develop a successful relationship and his wife, too, left him after a few years. He died in 1788 but his brother Henry, who had become a cardinal, lived until 1807. By this time Jacobitism had turned from being a threat to the House of Hanover into an intriguing curiosity. In his last years Henry received a pension from the British government.

Many British tourists who visit the basilica of St Peters in the Vatican miss a striking monument by Canova between two of the pillars facing the left hand aisle a short distance inside the portico. Erected in 1819 and partly financed by a subscription from the Prince Regent, the future George IV, it commemorates James III, King of Great Britain and his sons Charles and Henry. It emphasizes that, from the revolution of 1688 to the aftermath of Culloden, the Jacobite movement centred on a foreign, Catholic court in exile and that the events which we have considered took place against a wider background of European power-politics which we have barely been able to outline.

The European dimension of Jacobitism is a complex and fascinating story in its own right. However, many of the most interesting events which resulted from planning and plotting abroad occurred in a more limited area between the Western Isles of Scotland and the English Midlands. If the monument in the Vatican reminds us of the foreignness of the exiled Stuarts, a range of features scattered throughout the towns and countryside of northern England and Scotland also remind us that the Stuarts were actively supported in Britain for over sixty years. It is the monuments to the endeavours of these supporters that bring us closer to understanding what Jacobitism meant to ordinary people.

At Loch nan Uamh a cairn marks the spot where Charles Edward embarked and sailed into exile. To many people it represents a romanticized vision of Jacobitism, one which never existed in reality. More prosaic but with just as much power to grip the imagination is a less well-known monument. Beside a minor road south of Brampton, a few miles from Carlisle, is a clump of woodland in which stands a pillar on the site of the Capon Tree, where the assize judges formerly used to meet. The inscription records that from the branches of the tree, on 21st October 1746, Colonel James Innes, Captain Patrick Lindsay, Ronald MacDonald, Thomas Park, Peter Taylor, and Michael Deland were hanged for adherence to the cause of the Stuarts.

66 The Capon Tree memorial to executed Jacobites near Brampton.

The names are both English and Scottish. The Jacobite story is often treated as a romantic whirl of tartans, broadswords, and Bonnie Princes. There is nothing romantic in being hanged from a tree though it was not quite as brutally horrible as being hanged, drawn, and quartered in front of a jeering crowd at Tyburn. It serves to show that the Jacobites were not the gallant swashbucklers of popular legend and Hollywood films. They were ordinary people at odds, for a variety of reasons, with the ruling regime. The reasons for supporting the Jacobite cause were varied and the people who did so came from a wide range of backgrounds. Some paid a heavy penalty for adhering to their views. We consider that it is an insult to their memory to present the story in black-and-white terms as a contest between English and Scots, oppressors and underdogs, or clumsy redcoats versus romantic tartan-clad warriors. We hope that those who take an interest in the Jacobite movement will spare the time to try and understand the complex aspirations, passions, and fears which motivated those on both sides and that they will look beyond the romantic to the mundane and to share the sense of regret and futility that one must feel that so many lives were lost and so many people suffered hardship and pain in a cause which, ultimately, achieved so little.

We have told something of the story of the Jacobites and followed their trail from Killiecrankie to Derby, Culloden, and beyond. In the process we have seen that even the sites of some of the most famous events associated with the various risings require some tracking down. There are also a great many less well-known Jacobite sites which still have great historical interest. We have presented a range of these but despite the fact that so much has been written about the Jacobites there is still plenty of scope for amateur research into many aspects of their activities, matching historical records with ancient and modern maps and the landscape itself. We hope that many of the readers of this book will wish to visit some of the places which we have described and will view them with new insight.

A NOTE ON FURTHER READING

The Jacobites have attracted a vast literature. One historian has observed that producing books about them has almost developed into a cottage industry and another that there should be a law passed to enforce some draconian penalty on anyone who writes further books in this field. Nevertheless so much of what has been written is inaccurate and partisan that is not difficult to recommend a short list of reputable books which will guide you if you want to follow the trail of the Jacobites. If you become really interested you may want to go back to some of the original sources in the form of contemporary narratives, memoirs, and correspondence. Large quantities of relevant material have been published by various historical societies but the bulk of the volumes are out of print and are only available from a limited number of reference and university libraries. Your own local library should be able to get most of them for you, at a small charge, using the inter-library loans service. We have confined ourselves as far as possible to listing books which have appeared fairly recently and should either be in print, or at least be widely available from good public libraries.

GENERAL BACKGROUND

B. Lenman, *The Jacobite Risings in Britain 1689-1746*, London 1980 is excellent in surveying the background and broader issues which we have not dealt with here. F. McLynn, *The Jacobites*, London 1985 is also a good introduction. A.J. Youngson, *The Prince and the Pretender*, London 1985 provides a salutary warning regarding the bias of much of the source material relating to the Jacobite movement. It tells the story of the 1745 rebellion twice, in two very different ways, from Jacobite and Hanoverian viewpoints.

THE FIRST JACOBITE REBELLION

Less has been written about the first Jacobite rebellion than subsequent risings. Lord Macaulay's famous *History of England* is undoubtedly the most stylish and readable account. It is heavily biased in favour of William and the

232

Whigs but his character assassinations of James II and Jacobite figures like Viscount Dundee remain literary classics. P. Hopkins, *Glencoe and the End of the Highland War*, Edinburgh 1986 is a study of events in Scotland from the Revolution of 1688 to the aftermath of Glencoe. It is tremendously detailed but rather hard going. More readable, though requiring more caution, is J. Prebble, *Glencoe*, London 1966. The Highlands in the late seventeenth and early eighteenth centuries are well discussed in B. Lenman, *The Jacobite Clans of the Great Glen*, London 1984.

THE RISINGS OF 1715 AND 1719

The rebellions of 1715 and 1719 have been relatively neglected. J. Baynes, *The Jacobite Rising of 1715*, London 1970 and C. Sinclair Stevenson, *Inglorious Rebellion: The Jacobite Risings of 1708, 1715 and 1719*, London 1971 are worth reading.

BETWEEN THE '15 AND THE '45

E. Burt, *Letters from a Gentleman in the North of Scotland*, first published in 1818 and available in recent reprinted editions, vividly describes life in the Highlands during Wade's road-building era. The military roads built by Wade and his successors are analysed in W. Taylor, *The Military Roads in Scotland*, Newton Abbot 1976. Also of interest is a recent biography of Rob Roy; W.H. Murray, *Rob Roy MacGregor: His Life and Times*, Glasgow 1983.

THE 1745 REBELLION

Literature on the 1745 rising is endless. The set piece battles of the 1745 campaign are well described in K. Tomasson and F. Buist, *Battles of the '45*, London 1978. K. Tomasson's biography of Lord George Murray, *The Jacobite General*, London 1958, is also worth reading. F.J. McLynn, *The Jacobite Army in England 1745*, Edinburgh 1983 covers this campaign in detail and J. Prebble, *Culloden*, London 1961 and later editions, provides a detailed account of the last battle. W.A. Speck, *The Butcher*, London 1981 presents a Hanoverian point of view. J.S. Gibson, *Ships of the '45. The Rescue of the Young Pretender*, London 1967, covers the neglected naval side of the campaign while F.J. McLynn, *France and the Jacobite Rising of 1745*, Edinburgh 1983 is good on the international dimension. Biographies of Charles Edward Stuart are legion. The most recent is by Rosalind Marshall, *Bonnie Prince Charlie*, Edinburgh 1988. David Daiches, *Charles Edward Stuart: The Life and Times of Bonnie Prince Charlie*, London 1973 is also readable. Conditions in the Highlands after the '45 rebellion are described in A.J. Youngson, *After the Forty Five*, Edinburgh 1973.

INDEX